POE

POE
A Biography

by

WILLIAM BITTNER

An Atlantic Monthly Press Book

LITTLE, BROWN AND COMPANY · BOSTON · TORONTO

This one, at last, is for
Alice

To the few who love me and whom I love — to those who feel rather than to those who think — to the dreamers and those who put faith in dreams as in the only realities — I offer this Book of Truths, not in its character of Truth-Teller, but for the Beauty that abounds in its Truth — constituting it true. To these I present the composition as an Art-Product alone, — let us say as a Romance; or, if I be not urging too lofty a claim, as a Poem.

What I here propound is true: — therefore it cannot die: — or if by any means it be now trodden down so that it die, it will 'rise again to the Life Everlasting.'

Nevertheless, it is as a Poem only that I wish this work to be judged after I am dead.

Eureka

PREFACE

THIS IS NOT a "fictionalized" biography but a factual one — insofar as any biography can be, for we cannot know everything about anyone's life. My foremost intention has been to interpret the facts of Poe's life and show how and why he wrote what he did. It is an attempt to present the life of Poe in light of his associates, his times, and his peculiarities, not the least of which were an extraordinary intelligence, a vivid imagination, and the capacity to work to exhaustion. Although statements of fact can be documented — and a set of appendices in the back of the book takes up the points I anticipate being challenged on — the conclusions drawn from them obviously cannot, and whatever contribution this book has to make is in those conclusions. I have tried to write a biography and not just to argue about the materials of biography — the facts of Poe's life — without any effort toward finding their meaning.

I have tried to understand Poe, and therefore I may be accused of pleading Poe's case. This is not my intention, and I have put forth conscious effort to keep from distorting things in his favor or in anyone's. What I have done consciously is to present his life from his point of view, showing his rationalizations and vacillations, his errors and flaws, as he might have been conscious of them. My "apology" is akin to his statement in the Preface to *Eureka*, which stands as the motto of this book; I believe that this biography is true — that it portrays in fact and interpretation of fact a valid picture of the life of

PREFACE

Edgar Poe — but I should like to think of it as a piece of journalism, rather than as scholarship.

My indebtedness to others is without end. In person, by letter, or through their books, I have consulted nearly all the diligent students of Poe, although I spent so many years getting ready to sit down at the typewriter that I should not wonder if some of them have forgotten me. From my own students I have gained insights more penetrating than my own. The number of libraries and librarians who helped me is so great I shudder to think of listing all of them. For the time spent in the actual writing of the book I must, even though it is unfair to all others, mention names. I am grateful to the Trustees and President of Fairleigh Dickinson University for a research grant that gave me time to think of other things than an extremely arduous teaching schedule. The New School for Social Research has been very generous in encouragement and leaves of absence. Professor Sylvère Monod of the University of Caen and Monsieur Robert Davril of the Fulbright Commission for France eased my labors there, as did Dr. Curtis Watson. To my colleagues and the library staff of the Free University of Berlin I owe the deepest thanks. And for patience, confidence, and encouragement beyond the call of duty, I bow deeply to Mr. Gunther Stuhlmann. Quotations at the heads of chapters are from *The Poems of Hart Crane*, edited by Waldo Frank (Liveright, 1933); *The Poems of Edgar Allan Poe*, edited by Killis Campbell (Ginn and Company, 1917); and from Shakespeare and Burns.

CONTENTS

POE

And when they dragged your retching flesh,
Your trembling hands that night through Balti-
     more —
That last night on the ballot rounds, did you
Shaking, did you deny the ticket, Poe?
HART CRANE, *The Bridge*

WEDNESDAY, OCTOBER 3, 1849

ELECTION TIME IN BALTIMORE. It was a minor election, for local offices, but significant to small party hangers-on all the more for the political plums that might hang low enough for them to reach. The derelicts of the city were rounded up and kept happily dazed with cheap liquor in the party "coops" until they had been sent to the polls and voted as often as possible; when so far gone they could no longer be relied on to put their X in the proper place, they were abandoned, left to find their own way back to the coop or to sleep it off wherever they might fall.

In the gray early afternoon, while a thin chill rain was falling, Joseph Walker, a compositor for the Baltimore *Sun*, was hurrying along Lombard Street past a public house called Gunner's Hall. This was the fourth ward polling place, and considering the proximity of the Whig party coop, whence often over a hundred floaters were sent groggily out to the polls, Walker was not surprised to see a man dressed in a torn black coat and ill-fitting gray trousers lying in the street, a battered palm-leaf

[3]

hat beside him. But when he noticed the handsome malacca cane clutched tightly in his hand, Walker paused.

Half conscious as he was, the man lying in the street — whom Walker recognized as Edgar Poe — managed to ask him to send for Dr. J. E. Snodgrass, who lived close by on High Street. The systematic printer maneuvered Poe into the saloon and propped him into a chair; then, finding a sheet of coarse paper, painstakingly wrote:

Baltimore City, Oct. 3, 1849

Dear Sir, —

There is a gentleman, rather the worse for wear, at Ryan's 4th ward polls, who goes under the cognomen of Edgar A. Poe, and who appears in great distress, & he says he is acquainted with you, and I assure you, he is in need of immediate assistance.

Yours, in haste,
Jos. W. Walker

To Dr. J. E. Snodgrass.

Snodgrass, who indeed had known Poe for fifteen years, hurried to Lombard Street. While he was examining the stricken man, Henry Herring, the widower of Poe's aunt, Eliza Poe, joined him, having learned, probably from Walker, what had happened. Although for many years Snodgrass had been engaged in the practice of literature rather than of medicine, he easily recognized that Poe's condition was more than a drunken stupor, and he and Herring ordered a cab. In a few minutes the limp body of the poet was being jolted along the rain-washed streets of Baltimore.

It was five o'clock when the sodden jacket, parted at the seams, was pulled from the muttering Poe in a second-floor tower room of the Washington College Hospital. He was wearing neither vest nor neckcloth, and his trousers had obviously been cut for someone of entirely different build. Poe was vaguely conscious during the undressing, but when he was lifted into bed he immediately lost consciousness. Dr. John J. Moran, the resident, examined him but decided he could do nothing until his patient became conscious again. Moran deplored having another case for his turret, "where patients were put who had been drinking freely," but his attitude was tempered by the fact that Dr. Snodgrass had brought him there. Snodgrass was a temperance man too.

Moran knew the Poe family — who in Baltimore did not, since they were substantial men of affairs? But this Poe was of the black sheep branch. His father had run off to be an actor and disappeared somewhere up North, leaving rumors of drunkenness and irresponsibility. This one was a writer, a poet, and his father's proper son, to judge by appearances. Yet Moran was a responsible physician who knew that diagnoses of "brain disease" and like generalities so common in his time — usually on death certificates — were of little use in treating a patient so obviously helpless as this one was. He was very anxious to get in touch with anyone who might know something of the history of Poe's illness.

Neither Snodgrass nor Herring had any idea what to do. They had never seen Poe dressed so badly — even when his clothes were worn, they were always neat — so he must have been away from his mother-in-law, Mrs. Clemm, for some time. No, they did not know how to get in touch with her. The last they knew, she and Poe were living in Fordham, but there was no post office in Fordham. Too, Poe moved often, unlike his solid Baltimore cousins. There was Cousin Neilson Poe; he should be informed. Neilson Poe came and went, promising to send clean linen for Edgar. He did not know how to reach Mrs. Clemm.

Moran was torn. He too soon realized that in spite of his first impression, Poe was not just in a drunken stupor. Neilson

Poe offered no evidence save that there was a "bad streak" in the family, a "weakness" that expressed itself in drunkenness and early death. Dr. Snodgrass spoke of the evidence in Poe's own writings against Longfellow and any number of respectable people, and of the rumors of drunken outbursts on the streets of New York; might this not suggest a disturbance of the brain? Or was it just the demon rum?

Through the discussions, past the time that Dr. Moran dismissed the problem from his mind and took to his bed, the limp body remained still. But at three in the morning, Poe awoke. Dr. Moran, hastily summoned, began questioning. What had happened to bring him to this state? Where had he been? Where was his wife? Who was his doctor? Where? Who? What?

It was all too complicated for the exhausted patient. *Wife, wife? There was Sis, Virginia. But Sissy was dead. She had been dying since the red death covered all their hopes, years before; she had died a thousand times, the child, and become a woman only at the last. Yet . . . Elmira . . .*

Dr. Moran concluded, from the spoken fragments of Poe's wandering thoughts, that he had a wife in Richmond. But he was wrong. Poe's mind struggled to put in order what had happened through the summer, when back in Richmond, home of his first expectations and first disappointments, he had seemed about to start over again, marrying Elmira Royster — now the widow Shelton — starting his own magazine finally, and never again being troubled over money. But just at the new beginning of his life the old would not let him go. Illness, men following him . . .

The one cogent response — that he had a wife in Richmond — from the delirious man in the hospital bed was succeeded by cries of remorse and groans of despair and pain. For three days the bare tower room echoed as the delirium became more and more violent until, on Saturday night, all the agony of the dying man burst out in a call, "Reynolds! Oh, Reynolds!" In the dizzy whirlpool of his mind he called to the mariner, the author of "Mocha Dick, or the White Whale of the Pacific," but he was then irrevocably in the Maelström. At three in the morning on Sunday, October 7, the weakness of Poe's body numbed the torment in his brain, and he lay silent. Two hours later came the last stertorous breath.

On a cold afternoon, six days after Poe had been found lying in the streets, a black-plumed hearse and one carriage passed through the streets of Baltimore to the Presbyterian Cemetery at Fayette and Green Streets. There were four mourners. Of the Poe family only Neilson Poe and Henry Herring were present. Dr. Snodgrass was there, probably already planning his lectures for temperance societies on the sordid death of Edgar Poe. If so he was premature; the story would become more dramatic and Poe's "beastly intoxication" more horrible every time he would tell it. And by an irony worthy of Poe the story-teller, the fourth crepe-hatted witness had been witness also of Poe's first drinking bouts, his University of Virginia classmate Z. Collins Lee.

At the same time that the four mourners were shivering beside the grave while the Reverend William T. D. Clemm was conducting the burial service, readers of the New York *Journal of Commerce* found, among the editorials, a warm and solemn obituary of the poet, one that concluded:

It will not be denied, even by his enemies, that Mr. Poe was a man of great ability, — and all other recollections of him will be lost now, and buried with him in the grave. We hope he has found rest, for he needed it.

But a correspondent for the New York *Tribune* who signed himself "Ludwig" was busily insuring that Poe's reputation would get none of that rest.

Edgar Allan Poe is dead. He died in Baltimore the day before yesterday. This announcement will startle many, but few will be grieved by it. The poet was known, personally or by reputation, in all this country; he had readers in England, and in several of the states of Continental Europe; but he had few or no friends; and the regrets for his death will be suggested principally by the consideration that in him literary art has lost one of its most brilliant but erratic stars.

"Ludwig" went on and on, showing great intimacy with Poe's life and career but selecting details that would present both in the most unfavorable way. And well might he know Poe intimately, for "Ludwig" was Rufus W. Griswold, the trusted friend who just a few weeks before had said that he was "flattered" to be chosen as Poe's literary executor.

N. P. Willis, Henry B. Hirst, Lambert Wilmer, even Longfellow rushed to Poe's defense. Yet in spite of refutations by Poe's friends and even by some who were not so friendly to him in person, the reputation Griswold foisted on the dead writer was circulated and grew. Griswold lied as only one who has kept a grudge for years would do. He denied that he had known that Poe was to make him his literary executor, but said that he had first heard of it from Mrs. Clemm, after Poe's death. He dropped letters and other papers from the Brooklyn Ferry. And he published portions of Poe's correspondence with emendations and forged additions, always showing the dead man as unreliable and dishonest, cringing and malicious; and occasionally he forged a passage to show how kind and forbearing he had been to Poe. Soon others took up the image of Poe created by Griswold and embellished it further with madness and drug addiction, immorality and a sickly romantic gloom.

Baudelaire, who in France had enthusiastically translated Poe's writings, was furious at Griswold's *"immortelle infamie"*; then, in his own biography of the American, re-created Poe in *his* own image. Since then, the mythical Poe has been synthesized from both Baudelaire and Griswold, and this morbid, erratic figure has been psychoanalyzed, diagnosed, and dissected. With the aid of Poe's psychological stories, critics have proclaimed him necrophilic, dipsomanic, paranoid, impotent, neurotic, oversexed, a habitual taker of drugs, until all that is left in the public eye is an unstable creature sitting gloomily in a dim room, the raven over the door, the bottle on the table, the opium in the pipe, scribbling mad verses — a simple composite of the characters in his stories.

But there are images and voices from the forty years of Poe's life to deny the jaundiced and the romanticized versions alike. And the sick man, suffering more and more frequent attacks of a chronic disease for the last year and a half of his life, was able to cling only to remnants of what he had been when he created detective fiction, defined the short story, put the spirit of modern literary journalism into a whole series of otherwise insipid and crude magazines. He was the man who, stumbling through the streets of Baltimore, bereft of his money, his clothing, and eventually of his last chance for life, clung faithfully to the handsome malacca cane he had borrowed from Dr. John Carver on the eve of his last, nightmare journey and had not had time to return.

It began in a dingy and cold theatrical rooming house. . . .

RICHMOND, DECEMBER, 1811

NO ONE IN THE ROOMING HOUSE adjacent to the Washington
Tavern was speaking of the "sunny South." In Placide's company of actors, who had taken the whole house when the
season opened in August, it had ceased being a joke. And for
the twenty-five-year-old actress in her chill bedroom, her infant
daughter Rosalie whimpering beside her, it was the tragic end
of all her hopes. Just a month before, her room had been a
social center. As one ranking member of Richmond's plantation society, Samuel Mordecai, wrote his sister Rachel:

A singular fashion prevails here this season — it is — charity.
Mrs. Poe, who you know is a very handsome woman, happens to be
very sick, and (having quarreled and parted with her husband)
is destitute. The most fashionable place of resort, now is — her
chamber — And the skill of cooks and nurses is exerted to procure
her delicacies.

But with the cold weather, most of the fashionable ladies had
disappeared.

She had been well enough to appear on the stage only three

times before her seasonal benefit performance on October 9, and had played only once since; and when she did not act, she was not paid. Toward the end of November a special benefit was given for her in her absence, a notice in the *Enquirer* announcing:

To the Humane Heart
On this night, *Mrs. Poe*, lingering on the bed of disease and surrounded by her children, asks your assistance and *asks it perhaps for the last time.* The Generosity of a Richmond Audience can need no other appeal. For particulars, see the Bills of the day.

Like her children's, Elizabeth Arnold Poe's earliest memories had been of temporary rooms, a mother radiantly dressed in the evening but sleeping late the morning after a performance, and a father who was only a dim memory constructed from her mother's talk. But hers were memories of England, tours of the shire towns, the gloriously swift mail coaches gliding over smooth roads, nights in cheerful English inns, and finally smoky London. She was nine when her mother saw more opportunity in America than at Covent Garden and they sailed for Boston. Almost at once her stage career began. At the age of fourteen she played Ophelia in *Hamlet*, at fifteen she married a fellow actor, Charles Hopkins, and at eighteen she was a widow.

Thus she served her apprenticeship. Now she was ready for a permanent repertory company, instead of the touring companies with which she struggled up and down the seaboard from Philadelphia to Charleston. Moreover, there was a handsome man of twenty-one who had joined her husband's company the year before, a beginner who had been on the professional stage only a few months. He was making rapid progress, and once he learned better control of his voice could be as effective a professional partner as he was attractive as a romantic partner. She married David Poe in 1806, and the couple opened in Boston, playing the leading roles in *Speed the Plough*, by Thomas Morton.

For three years the Poes were the leading players of Boston. Critics were not always kind to David Poe, and they occasionally considered Elizabeth Poe's talents less appropriate to tragedy than to comedy, but her star, at least, was ascendant, and his was not far behind. After the birth of her first child, William Henry, in 1807, Mrs. Poe made a sketch of Boston Harbor which she later inscribed, *For my little son Edgar, who should ever love Boston, the place of his birth, and where his mother found her best, and most sympathetic friends.*

But it was after the birth of Edgar that the friendliness of Boston audiences and the sympathy of Boston critics began to run out. The Poes had been living as permanent guests in a pleasant rooming house recently built on an as yet unnamed street south of the Common. Small families of city-dwellers generally preferred rooming houses in the days before the vast Irish migration supplied servant girls to the North. Young William Henry had been left with his Poe grandparents in Baltimore, and the pregnant Mrs. Poe opened the season playing Cordelia in *King Lear*. David played Edmund, the Iago-like bastard of Gloucester. This was not Mrs. Poe's last role before her confinement, but it was her most impressive one, and it is easy to imagine that she decided if her child should be a girl, she would be named Cordelia. But it was a boy, and since he should surely not be named after a bastard, the appropriate name would be that of Edmund's legitimate brother, Edgar.

Mrs. Poe continued to appear on the stage up to two weeks before the birth of her most famous child, although her roles became continuously less conspicuous and less frequent. Still, she played Queen Dollalolla in *Tom Thumb* in her sixth month, a venture that she could have joined in only out of necessity, for only a little over a year before, David Poe had been infuriated to the point of violence when the fastidious critic of *Polyanthous* wrote that her appearance in a similar role suggested the "hermaphroditical," and had gone looking for him with a horsewhip. The bulges the critic objected to must have been much more obvious the second time.

Edgar Poe was born January 19, 1809. On February 9, Mrs. Poe was back on the stage, playing Rosamunda in *Abaellino the Great Bandit*. She had to get work as soon as possible, for they were short of money. David left Boston in an attempt to raise funds from relatives, but his pride led him to drink heavily before braving them, and he disgraced himself. By the time he returned to Boston the famous prodigy John Howard Payne had joined the company and Poe was decidedly now in second place. The more discontented he became, the worse he played; and the worse he played, the sharper the critics sniped at him. He became known as a man with a very fiery temper that was not dampened by what he drank.

David Poe, like his son, often lost his perspective through foolish pride. He was the son of a man who had served his country so well that he was popularly known as "General" Poe, even though he had only been a major at the time he was, against inconceivable odds, providing supplies for Lafayette and other Revolutionary commanders. "General" David Poe was listed in the Baltimore directories as a "gentleman" in spite of the ebbing of his fortunes; neither he nor his descendants were ever to receive the $40,000 he had advanced to the state during the Revolution, and his widow was to eke out her life, after his death, on a pension of $240 a year. Nevertheless, it was very irksome to him that his son ran away and became an actor. There must have been some reconciliation when the child William Henry was left with his grandparents, but the disapproval remained.

Boston, whose Congregationalists despised the stage and whose theater-goers loved novelty, was becoming intolerable. Yet the Poes had proved that they were able to compete with the top of their profession. The solution came, it seemed to them, when Mrs. Poe was invited to join the Price and Cooper Company at New York's famous Park Theater, and more than that, to play opposite the celebrated Cooper. Before long David was also appearing, although mainly in the afterpieces. New York provided much more difficult competition, and the critics were acrimonious. Before long David Poe was in trouble again. He was dubbed "Dan Dilly" because of his mispronunciation of the name "Dandoli" in *Abaellino,* and the critics lost no opportunity to make fun of him. They hounded him for drinking and he drank still more. One night he and a fellow actor were too drunk to go on, another play had to be substituted for the one announced, and that brought the end. Just one day less than nine months from the birth of his ill-starred son he played for the last time, and history has no further record of him.

In spite of her continuing artistic success, Elizabeth Poe could see that there was no future for her in New York. Poor business kept the theaters closed too often for an unattached actress with two children and a destitute husband to support. After July 4, 1810, she went to Richmond to join Placide's Company, back again in the Southern circuit which she and David Poe had hopefully left four years before in search of fame and fortune in the Northern cities. From August until September she charmed Richmond theater-goers; then she retired from the stage for the birth of her third child, Rosalie. But when she rejoined the company, Mrs. Beaumont, "late of the Theatre Royal, Covent Garden," had replaced her, at least for the more important Shakespearean roles, and she was given the comedienne parts she had played in the same theaters ten years before.

After Charleston came a brief season at Norfolk, and then Richmond and the final illness. As she lay in her bed with the infant Rosalie, three-year-old Edgar probably clamoring to go out and play in Capitol Square, she would have been able to see that she should have left Poe long before, perhaps never have taken up with him. But she loved her children. And two of the wealthy women of the town who still came with jellies and broth evidently came as much for the sake of the children as for her. She knew she was dying, but she knew that the children would not be friendless; they would be taken care of, at least until David's father sent for them.

On Sunday morning, December 8, 1811, Mrs. Poe died. Mrs. William MacKenzie bundled up and carried off tiny Rosalie, and Mrs. John Allan led curly-headed Edgar from the cold room on Ninth Street across the square to her home, above the store of Ellis and Allan, General Merchants. Frances Keeling Valentine Allan was a tender-hearted woman, much dominated by her hard-headed Scottish husband. Her sister Ann, who lived with them, was able to stand up to Allan a great deal better, but Ann was not particularly enthusiastic about taking in the orphan. Perhaps they would have to send the child to his grandparents; but that could not be until after Christmas, and in the meantime they were all invited to visit Mr. Bowler Cocke on his plantation at Turkey Island, up the James River near Shirley.

Although "deprived of one of its chief ornaments," the Richmond theater went on, enjoying the prosperity of the Christmas season. On the day after Christmas, Placide's Company was playing *The Bleeding Nun* to a packed house when fire broke out. In spite of heroic rescue efforts, more than seventy people, including the Governor of Virginia, burned to death. The whole nation was shocked, the United States Senate went into mourning, and pity for the orphans of the fire was dramatized through pity for the orphans of the beautiful actress. A "Players' Address to the Citizens of Richmond," included in a miscellany of pieces published about the fire, said:

In this miserable calamity we find a sentence of banishment from your hospitable city. — No more do we expect to feel that glow of pleasure which pervades a grateful heart, while it receives favours liberally bestowed. Never again shall we behold that feminine humanity which so eagerly displayed itself to soothe the victim of disease; and view with exultation, the benevolent who fostered the fatherless, and shed a ray of comfort to the departed soul of a dying mother.

That did it! On January 7, 1812, John Allan went to Hobday and Seaton and laid out eight dollars for "1 crib."

Richmond was legally a city, and the capital of Virginia, but it had less than ten thousand inhabitants, and half of them were slaves or free servants. John Allan had settled there from his native Ayrshire in 1795, at the invitation of his uncle William Galt, who had been a leading Richmond merchant since before the Revolution. In 1800, at the age of twenty, he and a fellow clerk at Galt's, Charles Ellis, invested £1000 each to found the firm of Ellis and Allan. Three years later he married the daughter of John Valentine of Princess Anne County, and the following year Chief Justice Marshall swore him in as United States citizen. Richmond seemed the home of opportunity until the Napoleonic Wars began to strangle business.

Allan became the epitome of the self-made merchant. He bought and sold tobacco, grain and flour, tea and coffee, cloth, wines and liquors (for which he had a fine taste), agricultural implements, and hardware. He would charter ships, deal in real estate, and arrange for the hiring of horses and slaves. In 1811 he had sailed to Portugal with a cargo of supplies for the British Army, then engaged in the Peninsular Campaign. The Embargo Act and declaration of war stopped any repetition of that, so an ambitious man had to keep his eyes open for any opportunity to turn a profit.

Yet Allan was no Scrooge. He and his wife visited back and forth with the plantation aristocracy as well as with the Scottish merchants of Richmond. He lived within his income, but barely, for he knew he was heir to the enormous fortune of the uncle whose protégé he was. At times he could be even playful in his correspondence. He not only paid unstintingly for the best education Richmond could provide Edgar, but gave the same advantage to an illegitimate child of his by a Mrs. Collier — making certain, however, that the two did not attend the same school at the same time. He accepted the world as it was, and made the best of it; if at first he had reservations about accepting the orphan of an actress as his foster son, they did not show for a long time.

There was a great deal in John Allan for Edgar to admire. He was witty and a regular quoter of Shakespeare. He could tell stories of Scotland and sailing ships. And his store must have been a fairyland to the boy who had known only the sights and smells of shabby boardinghouses. Mrs. Allan — Mama, he came to call her — was much less clever and not at all literary. Her letters were full of banality and her spelling a fright. But she was inherently affectionate, and she and the boy came to love each other in a way that Allan could share with neither of them.

Edgar's life was filled with delightful and exciting things he had never heard of before. There were visits to the country, and to the plantations of friends; and there he could play with the dogs, pet the cats, and listen to the caged birds with other well-dressed, happy children. One summer the Allans and Edgar traveled deep into the Shenandoahs, to Staunton. Gradually he came to forget entirely the rooming houses where he and his baby sister had been left alone for hours; and when "Pa's" niece, Rosanna Dixon, wrote to them, telling of Rosalie's christening — because she was not expected to live — the special message for Edgar that John Allan read out was "Tell Edgar, Tib [the cat] is very well, also the Bird and Dog." But Rosalie lived, now Rosalie MacKenzie Poe, and was with her foster parents in the fall when the family returned. He, like his sister, had his foster father's name added to his, and Edgar Allan Poe was known as John Allan's "adopted son," even though formal adoption — a rarity in those days — did not take place.

After a year at Clotilda Fisher's dame school, Edgar was sent to the school of William Ewing, which Allan's illegitimate son Edward Collier had been attending. Collier was sent on to another school at that time, probably one more suited to educate him to make his own way in the world, but Allan by so doing avoided the embarassing questions that might have come when schoolmates from separate households discovered they were each calling the same man "Papa." At any rate, Edgar was a happy schoolboy, excellent in his lessons and well liked. Ewing referred to him as the "august attendant" of Mrs. Allan and her sister. But he was to spend only one year in this school as well.

Peace was in sight. While Edgar was reveling in the new-found joy of reading at Ewing's school, John Quincy Adams and his delegation had been negotiating at Ghent, to end the war against England, and John Allan was making plans for moving into a peacetime economy. Foreign trade was the thing, it was clear, and Europeans were as avid for American tobacco and cotton as Americans were for European manufactured goods. Ellis and he determined, at the first confirmation of a treaty, to establish a branch in Great Britain so they could make the best bargains on both sides of the Atlantic. The news came in February, 1815.

Edgar was just old enough to enjoy a great upheaval in his life. The packing and arranging and ordering of new clothes were a wonderful adventure for him, although John Allan was haggard with the responsibility of transferring his family thousands of miles. "Mama" was loving and ineffectual as always, Miss Valentine efficient in ordering her own affairs but flustered at her sister's lack of responsibility, and John Allan was still at work on the last details as the river boat moved down from Richmond toward Norfolk. On June 22, 1815, he sent his last instructions for disposing of his slaves — Scipio was to be sold for $600 and the rest hired out for $50 a year.

The next day they were on board the sailing ship for Liverpool. "Mama" and Miss Valentine remained sick in their cabin as the ship began to roll in the open sea, but Edgar proudly walked the deck with "Pa." Allan sent a final note off the Horseshoe, where they dropped the pilot, and the voyage of more than a month began.

[19]

We think na on the lang Scots miles,
The mosses, waters, slaps, and styles,
That lies between us and our hame. . . .
ROBERT BURNS, "Tam O'Shanter"

A LONG, SEA-TOSSED MONTH after the ship left Norfolk, they
sighted Ireland, a bluish, cloudlike spot to the northeast. Then
the purple mountains of Wales came close, and the ship
skirted the coast for days. Edgar felt that the ship had taken
a dreadful amount of time to get to sea after it left its moor-
ing at Norfolk; but it seemed a much longer time that they
traveled in clear view of the land here, without his being able
to get onto it. The water narrowed into a river, and then they
drew alongside a patch of warehouses fronting a city that
seemed all crowded together, after the wide expanses and open
parks of Richmond. But it was still a long time until the ship
was warped, with angry shouts from the pilot to the crew, into
a wharf. And then Edgar learned that they would sleep in the
ship again that night, after another skimpy meal of cold food.
It had been cold food for more than half the voyage, it seemed,
in spite of Pa's arguments with the captain for firewood.

Again John Allan made his bed on the floor of their cabin;
again Edgar and slim Mama took one bunk and Miss Valentine the other. But early the next morning they passed the
gates of the dock and walked through the narrow lanes of

Liverpool to Lillyman's Hotel. There were men in strange clothing, and tousely-looking women standing in doorways; and Pa did not greet anyone. In Richmond they could not walk ten steps that Pa did not take off his hat and speak to someone, and then Edgar had to bow. Stranger yet, there was nothing but stone — the stone houses came down to the stone street — and there were no black people. Nothing seemed really friendly until they got to the hotel, where Mr. Lillyman boomed out welcome in his big voice, and called to various people upstairs and downstairs, and they could wash, and then they had a hot breakfast.

They stayed in Liverpool for more than a week, John Allan writing his innumerable business letters in the public room — one of them to the shipowners in Norfolk, complaining about the inconveniences of the voyage — and Mama and Miss Valentine occasionally yielding to Edgar's pleas to go out and see things. They watched the changing of the guard at the Old Fort; they visited the churches; but every time that Edgar heard the bells of St. Nicholas ring, announcing the arrival of a Liverpool ship, he would hurry his companion down to the old dock to see it maneuver into the pool. Yet even more excitement was promised. They were going on a land voyage now — to Scotland.

This was wholly unlike the trip a few years before to Staunton, in the Virginia mountains. Although it was a somewhat greater distance, it did not take as long, and there was always something interesting to look at, even if Pa would not let Edgar ride on the top of the coach. The smooth roads skirted neat little farms, and a town always appeared before Edgar began to be bored with open country. Old cities swallowed the coach into their narrow streets — Preston, Lancaster, Carlisle — and after that Pa said they were in Scotland. The towns were farther and farther apart and the going slower because of the hills, but in time they came to Kilmarnock, where they hired a carriage for the short trip to the village of Irvine, on the sea.

There Edgar met two new aunts, Pa's sisters Mary and Jane, and he suddenly realized that Pa had been talking like them all along, but now he burred his *r*'s even more, and broke off some of his words as if he had run out of breath. It was a short visit at Irvine, for there was no room for them to sleep, but Allan had insisted on seeing his closest kin first. Back at Kilmarnock they stayed with Allan Fowlds and his wife and children, but they traveled all over Ayrshire in the ensuing month, and everywhere there were Allan kin. The best trip was to the beautiful Galt estate on Cree Water below Loch Doon. As they drove down along the River Doon, Pa recited strange, beautiful poetry by "Rabbie" Burns, a man who had lived there once, and the burr grew in his voice. Edgar liked "Tam O'Shanter" best, and John Allan pointed out the kirk-yard where the devil held court, and the bridge where Tam's horse lost its tail. But it rained too much.

The month was soon gone, and the time coming when they should go to London. By the middle of September they had completed their farewells and set out, going first to Greenock, since Allan had some business to transact in Scotland. There, one night, Allan despaired of conducting his correspondence in the noisy public room and sat down to write in their own sitting room. But the business part of the letter he was writing his partner was soon overwhelmed by greetings from Frances and Nancy to their Richmond friends, and eventually Edgar looked up from his storybook and chimed in, "Pa, say something for me. Say I was not afraid coming across the sea."

Next day they went on to Glasgow, where Allan again stopped to attend to business, and then to Edinburgh, Newcastle, Sheffield, and down across England to London. With all the stopovers, it was October 7 by the time they arrived, tired and chilled by the perpetual rain, at a set of most uncomfortable rooms in London. Frances Allan was suffering from a bad cold, and the rest were very unhappy with their accommodations. John Allan searched for more than a week for a place where he could establish both business and family, as he had in Richmond, but eventually he compromised on a dwelling in Russell Square, Bloomsbury. He had for the time being to do without a "compting room."

In Sloane Street, Chelsea, down by the Thames, was a school kept by two sisters named Dubourg. Their brother, George Dubourg, who occasionally helped with the school bills, was a clerk, out of work at the beginning of 1816 and very grateful when he was employed by Mr. John Allan of the newly established firm of Allan and Ellis. And when he heard that his new employer had a seven-year-old boy for whom he was seeking a school — why, Master Allan should go to the school his sisters kept.

John Allan had confidence in his new clerk's judgment. He sent Edgar off with instructions that he should be provided with all the "extras." This included one guinea a quarter for a separate bed, a half guinea for washing, three shillings for mending and shoestrings, and three shillings pew rent. Instruction in writing cost fifteen shillings extra, and books for spelling, geography, history, and religion came to eight shillings sixpence.

Meanwhile, things were not completely encouraging for John Allan's business prospects. He determined soon that he must keep the branch going for at least five years to recoup the expenses of establishing it, yet he swore he would not stay in London longer "on any account." Foreign trade was severely restricted, and prices were fluctuating madly; 1817 was to be a year of depression, with wide unemployment, heavy taxes, and widespread debt. The people of London would throw stones at the carriage of the Prince Regent.

Edgar's school term ran from January to July; then there were a few weeks of vacation. The second term was from the end of July until school was dismissed for the Christmas and New Year holiday. This scheme was most convenient for parents who felt that their children should be not only out of sight and sound, but out of mind as well; but Edgar, on occasional Sundays and holidays, would be released to Mrs. Allan or her husband, and taken through Westminster, up Piccadilly, to where they would turn off High Holborn to "47 Southampton Row, Russell Square, Parish o' Bloomsbury." He had to memorize the address in case he should ever be lost.

After the second term began, Mama never called for a holiday outing. The illness she had had when they entered the city remained with her — 1816 was the dank and gloomy "year without a summer" — and the following summer John Allan took her to Gloucestershire, to Cheltenham for the waters. There she found the clear air so invigorating after smoky, foggy London that she determined to remain in the country, and John Allan indulged her. The lease was up on their house, and George Dubourg was in firm control of the trifle of business that was coming their way that slack season of a bad year.

But in September, John Allan had to get back to work. He wrote Edgar, at school, telling him to address his letters to "Mama" in the country, rather than to "Pa" as he had been, and went back to London, taking lodgings until he could find another house. Edgar too had a move to make. He had done well at the Misses Dubourg's, but now it was time for him to go to a more advanced school. So in spite of the extra expenses of keeping a wife gallivanting from Gloucestershire to Devon, and the sad state of his business (there was trouble in Richmond, too), John Allan made arrangements for Edgar to be

admitted to the better and more expensive school of the
Reverend John Bransby, M.A. (Cantab.), in the little village of
Stoke Newington, beyond London.

Edgar had spent two years and John Allan more than sixty
guineas at the Dubourg school. He was nine years old when he
went to Bransby's Manor House School. Edgar Poe — known
in England as Edgar Allan — went to Stoke Newington with
the utmost confidence. He had always liked school; he was a
favorite of the masters because he was a good scholar and an
amiable boy; the pupils in all his previous schools had liked
him even though he stood at the top of the class. As the
coach drew into the village, with its ancient buildings and great
gnarled trees, Edgar looked forward to his new life with eager
expectation.

But the school building itself had none of the Gothic atmosphere of the village. It was a plain, square house, although it
seemed huge to Edgar, with hip roofs like pyramids perched
on a cube. Around the house and its extensive grounds ran a
low brick wall surmounted by a picket fence, and in front, by
the broad door with a fanlight above it, was a small front garden planted with box hedges. Elsewhere the grounds were bare
of trees or any decoration, and gravel almost fine enough to be
called sand made it a saharan expanse. This, as Edgar was to
learn, was the playground.

School was in session when John Allan led Edgar to the
broad door of the Manor House. When it opened, and a servant ushered them in, they could hear a hum of voices from
the open door of a room to the side. Passing the open door,
Edgar caught a glimpse of boys, a few younger than he but
most his age or a few years older, sitting in rows of desks and
benches the entire length of what seemed to him the biggest
room he had ever seen. Then they were brought into a smaller
room where a sturdy, athletic-looking man was sitting at a desk.

POE

The Reverend John Bransby was then thirty-four years old —
a few years younger than John Allan, but much more forbid-
ding in appearance. He wore a clerical stock, and black clothing
of a sober cut. While Edgar studied the botanical prints on the
walls, John Allan made arrangements. Yes, he insisted on a
separate bed. If the only separate bed available was in a room
by itself, so much the better, even if it cost twice as much as
at the Dubourg school. It did.

But the other extras he cut down on. Dancing, yes, but not
music or drawing. He would guarantee the cost of shoe repair
— Edgar was hard on shoes — but not tailoring expenses. Allan
would supply all Edgar's clothing himself. In the business, you
know. Pocket money? Allan tended to be generous, but Bransby
insisted that five shillings a quarter was plenty. Very good (he
was glad he had handed the boy a few shillings while they were
on the way). And then John Allan soberly shook Bransby's
hand, and the three walked together into the hall. He did not
know what to say as they started to the door. Be a good boy?
Edgar always was a good boy. Don't forget to write to Mama?
Edgar never did forget. Allan looked at the boy, turned, and
walked out the door to the waiting carriage. Bransby touched
Edgar's elbow, moved into the enormous room, and announced
that here was a new boy.

Every chance he had to be alone, Edgar would stand in the
great twelve-paned window and study the old building across
the street. It may have dated from Queen Elizabeth's time, it
was so studded with dormers and bristling with wings, and he
would imagine its wandering passages branching off to lead to
mysterious rooms and strange alcoves. When the school pro-
cessions passed the rivet-studded gate in its high brick wall, he
could see only the roofs, but from the second floor — they
called it the "first" here — of the Manor House School he
could see the whole house and part of the grounds.

The building across the way was ideal for imagining mysterious stories. And this boy, lonely in a school crowded with noisy pupils, was driven to live, whenever he could, in his imagination. His schoolmates mimicked his accent, still American in spite of three years in England. They laughed at his lack of skill in cricket and football and taunted him for boasting about his ability in the water, since obviously the dominie would not let any of the boys go swimming in New River. Worse, the ushers used him as an example to lagging scholars, since he knew literature and history better than even the older pupils, and he pronounced French as if it were a language and not just a school exercise. And he had his own alcove with a single bed, at the standard price of four guineas a year, instead of sleeping in the dormitory.

Thus he would dream about attending a school as ancient and mysterious as the building across the way, where he would be the leader of all the boys on the playground as well as in the classroom, and play practical jokes on the poor sweats who did not have his charm and air of command. But then he would remember that he was a "poor sweat," and imagine winning out over the popular boys by sheer moral force, and following them like the voice of conscience through life, exposing their evil ways.

They would surely be evil men, especially the one who stepped on his hand — on purpose, Edgar was sure — when they were playing football in September. And what would Pa say when he saw the surgeon's bill for thirteen shillings! That nailed boot had hurt, but the jibes at Americans had hurt more. The home of criminals, low-born traitors, and atheists, they called it, and they wanted to know what his father had been transported for.

But Edgar remained, save for the vacations of midsummer and Christmas, at the Manor House School from the time he was nine until he was eleven years old. The monotony of being awakened and being sent to bed always at the same time in the same way, study, recitations overseen by Mr. Bransby from his alcove off the long schoolroom, with the assistance of a classics usher and an "English and Mathematical," made the days a gray blur. The tremendous clock at one end of the schoolroom ticked off the hours of lessons, of school perambulations, of half holidays and game times. Mr. Bransby was a dignified, stern, but always fair man of broad interests, ranging from classics to botany, and he was enthusiastic about sports. On Sundays, as the bell reverberated in the Gothic spire of the nearby church, the boys walked two by two, the classics usher in the lead, the mathematical with his eye out for stragglers in the rear, to hear the services, one in the morning and one in the evening, and both conducted by John Bransby.

By his second term, Edgar's knowledge of French was so adequate that he dropped it, and he was at ease in construing the easy Latin authors. He still remained ahead of the best in the school in history and literature. Allan continued to slip him little sums over the official "pocket money," and years later Bransby remembered that with resentment. "Edgar Allan was a quick and clever boy," he said, "and would have been a very good boy if he had not been spoilt by his parents; but they spoilt him, and allowed him an extravagant amount of pocket-money, which enabled him to get into all manner of mischief — still I liked the boy — poor fellow, his parents spoilt him!"

But with John Allan things were not going at all well. Mrs. Allan remained in the country, and business was collapsing. At the end of 1819 he had only £100 left when Edgar came home with a £70/9/6 school bill. He wrote to Richmond for funds, but things were as bad there. The firm suspended business, and Allan had to wait for even enough money to carry the family back to the United States. In May, 1820, he had scraped together the fare, so he withdrew Edgar from school and the family set to packing for the voyage. Amid the excitement of Queen Caroline's defiant triumph through London, the crowds unhitching her horses to pull the carriage themselves while George IV was charging her with high treason before the House of Lords, the Allan family scurried through the mobs and took coach for Liverpool.

Only at the last minute was the firm of Allan and Ellis in England saved from complete disaster. The tariff bill failed to pass Parliament, and because of that Allan was able to win the confidence of a number of merchants — many of them hardly better off than he — and ship goods that when auctioned in New York, according to the new commercial technique for evading American import duty, would bring a transfusion of solid money into the Richmond store. He had them put on the *Martha*, and when that ship set out from Liverpool on June 14, 1820, a newly spirited John Allan, his sickly wife, now feeling better than she had, her robust — and overweight — sister, and Edgar Allan, once again to be called Poe, were aboard.

Lo! in yon brilliant window-niche
How statue-like I see thee stand,
The agate lamp within thy hand!
Ah, Psyche, from the regions which
Are holy land!

"To Helen"

A SUMMER MONTH AT SEA. To the inexperienced six-year-old who had traveled toward England it had been an endlessness of tedium and discomfort; but to a boy going on twelve, just released from the restrictions of an English boarding school, the voyage was a succession of fascinating novelties. The captain of the *Martha* was a different kind of man from the misanthropic creature who had kept them, most of the outward voyage, confined to a dingy box of a cabin, chewing on cold food. Edgar had the run of the ship, and studied the craft of the sea from the time John Allan's goods were carefully stowed in the hold. He learned the handling of sail in every kind of weather, and listened, equally fascinated, to the nautical wisdom of the captain and the sailors' fantastic yarns until hurricanes and mutiny, sea battles and pirates merged with reality; porpoises gave promise of whales; and the *Flying Dutchman* was scudding just over the horizon.

Thirty-six days of tossing ocean intervened between the tidy docks of Liverpool and the squalor of New York. Mrs. Allan again was ill, and her husband had to call in a Dr. Horrock at least once in the week they spent in New York. But finally the family boarded the new steamboat for Norfolk, and on August 2, 1820, they were settled in the house on the corner of Franklin and Second Streets in Richmond that belonged to Allan's partner, Charles Ellis. Ellis was struck by the improvement in Mrs. Allan's "health and color," and remarked, "They are a little Englished but it will soon wear off."

Ellis himself was weary of struggling alone with a rocky business, and as soon as Allan had concluded his visiting with old friends, went off to the mountains, leaving Allan, as he put it, "the bag to hold." He had good reason to be dispirited. The prosperity that followed the war had led to overproduction and a slump in prices throughout 1819, cotton dropping from thirty-three to fourteen cents a pound in a matter of months; and tobacco, that had brought twenty to forty dollars a hundred in 1815 and 1816, was now down to four to eight dollars a hundred. Even the banks were in trouble.

Children, however, are not aware of business slumps and forebodings save when their own desires are denied, and there is no sign that John Allan let his economic troubles alter his way of living and his generosity. Thomas Ellis, the son of Allan's partner, recalled that the biggest Christmas and birthday gifts of his childhood always came from the Allans. For nearly a year the two families lived together, and Ellis later wrote, concerning Edgar: "No boy ever had a greater influence over me than he had.

"He was very beautiful, yet brave and manly for one so young. . . . He was, indeed, a leader among his playmates; but my admiration for him scarcely knew bounds. The consequence was, he led me to do many a forbidden thing, for which I was duly punished. The only whipping I ever knew Mr. Allan to give him was for carrying me into the fields and woods beyond 'Belvidere' . . . one Saturday, and keeping me there all day and until after dark, without anyone at home knowing where we were; and for shooting a lot of domestic fowls, belonging to the proprietor of 'Belvidere,' who was at that time, I think, Judge Bushrod Washington."

Even before Allan rented a cottage for his family on Fifth Street, the following summer, Edgar was enrolled in the school run by Joseph H. Clarke in rooms over a store on Broad Street. Here he continued to be a model scholar and extended his new-found role as leader of boys, although not without demurrals from some. In this "academy," and the one that succeeded it, run by William Burke, when Clarke left Richmond, Poe was mixing in society from the top of genteel Richmond's aristocracy. The Cabell, Stanard, Thomas, and Selden families were represented among his schoolmates; and John L. T. Preston later claimed that Poe's having been the son of players, and his status with the Allans, made the boys "decline his leadership; and on looking back on it since, I fancy it gave him a fierceness he would otherwise not have had."

One young buck named Selden made some remarks about his being a liar or rascal, and Edgar, hearing of it, started a fight, even though Selden was heavier than he. At first he seemed to be getting the worse of it; then he suddenly waded in and gave his detractor a thorough beating. When his friends asked why he made little resistance for so long, Edgar explained with simple logic that he was waiting for his opponent to get out of breath. Poe's transition from being an English school-boy to becoming an American one was nothing short of a triumph. He had traveled as none of his companions had, and it can be certain that he then as later was not one to spoil a good story for the sake of the truth. Moreover, his years in the Richmond Academy were those of rapid physical change and roving interests, the time between boyhood and adolescence. From an egregious leadership at school and play, he would shift in an instant to solitary walks, long hours of reading, and, like most avid readers of twelve or thirteen years, attempts at authorship himself.

The discovery of the world of books is an exciting one, long remembered by anyone who reads for pleasure; but the sudden realization that one can all by oneself find rhymes and count out meters is treated with more awe, probably because most of us rarely exercise that talent in later years on anything more ambitious than a crossword puzzle. Joseph Clarke, Poe's schoolmaster through 1821 and 1822, claimed to recall John Allan's bringing him an entire manuscript volume of verses that Edgar had written, and on one occasion Allan started a hasty calculation of his assets on a sheet of paper lying on his desk, only to find his arithmetic running into some writing from the opposite end with the heading *Poetry by Edgar A. Poe*.

Through 1822 and 1823, Edgar's thirteenth and fourteenth years, while Ellis and Allan went into receivership and John Allan retained possession of his property only on the sufferance of his creditors, Edgar went smoothly through the pangs of growing up, making and keeping friends both older and younger than he. If anyone resented his winning first prize at the end of a course in elocution, he could not help admiring Poe's famous swim of six miles against the tide on a hot June day, across the James River from Ludlam's Wharf to Warwick. One person at least, in addition to Tom Ellis, had nothing but admiration for him, and that was little Rob Stanard.

For all his participation in the activities of his contemporaries at school and play, at the end of the day Edgar would say good-by and go home alone, never visiting with any of his fellows except the son of Allan's partner. Other boys would dine and spend the night with each other, but Poe, probably sensitive to the striking contrast between Allan's cottage and the stately homes of his schoolmates, never invited them to accompany him, and therefore his pride would not permit him to accept invitations. Before long Allan had to give up even the cottage and moved into an ugly narrow house belonging to his uncle. Between the prospective leaders of Richmond society and the "players' brat" who was ward of a failing businessman there was near-equality in public places that Edgar refused to risk for casual intimacy.

Poe finally made an exception, however, for Robert Stanard, a boy younger than he and so open and gracious that he could never be suspected of snobbery. Thus Edgar came to meet Jane Stith Stanard, Rob's mother, a woman whose grace and sympathetic nature were immediately captivating. She was young enough to put the boy entirely at his ease, and the stately rooms and quiet luxury of her home set off her beauty in a way Poe had never dreamed of. He had been in wealthy homes before, but always under the tension of "minding his manners," while experiencing courtesy that was formal and cold. Mrs. Stanard soon became "Helen" to him; he thought Jane a common and harsh-sounding name, and Helen suggested "Hellene" — the glory that was Greece.

Helen became to him the mother he could barely remember — although he treasured among "his own things" her portrait in miniature, the sketch she had made of Boston Harbor, and other trinkets. He could confide in Helen, and watching her calm supervision of her household he could forget Mrs. Allan's muddling, Miss Valentine's old-maidish sniffs, and even "Pa's" worry and occasional bad temper. He loved to watch her move about in the tasks — really rituals — performed by the mistress of the house; in the evening she alone would light the lamps, beginning with the one in the window niche at the staircase landing, first a dim shape on the shadowy stairs, then, as the whale oil began to burn, revealed in the yellow light, a goddess, "The agate lamp within thy hand."

But this idyl did not last long. A growth was already beginning to eat into her brain, and in the winter of Edgar's fifteenth year her mind began to wander, first symptom of the illness that would, by springtime, bring an end to her life. Edgar saw her but once after the malady asserted itself; then she was confined to her room, and on April 28, 1824, came the terrible news that she was dead. Like his own mother, she appeared to him briefly, a vision, and then was taken from him. His grief was all the more in that he had dramatized his feelings as only an imaginative youth can do. She became an ideal, the epitomization of beauty, unattainable and forever identified with death.

But dark moods and adoration of those who are beautiful because they die young made only one side of Poe's complex personality. This was his world of the imagination, already mature; he was fifteen years old, a schoolboy with tasks and pranks and the power to make the trivial into matters of great importance and to forget them as easily. Or, tired of childish things, he could act the handsome young man, the gallant who did not make eyes at the girls because they made eyes at him. Both sides of him came into play at the moment he turned from his mournful periodic visits to Helen's grave.

By midsummer he was lieutenant in the Richmond Junior Volunteers — the "Junior Morgan Riflemen" — who were already drilling in preparation for the visit to the United States of General Lafayette the following October. Edgar's brother Henry wrote him, telling of Lafayette's visit to their grandmother's house, where he lived, during his visit to Baltimore. The triumphant party continued south, and in honor of the visit to Richmond, the Governor approved the issue of arms to the boys from the State Armory. The gallant Frenchman selected them as his bodyguard, and Lieutenant Poe strutted before the marquee on Capitol Square under which the grand reception was held. Fascinated by their glory, the boys attempted to retain the weapons, writing to the Governor and arguing with the custodian of the armory for more than a month, and when they did finally have to give them up, petitioning the Virginia State Council to get them back.

As Edgar's spirits swooped with melancholy and soared in pageantry, however, John Allan's business affairs became worse and worse. Ellis and Allan went out of business "by mutual consent," although they continued winding up their affairs for some years thereafter. Moreover, like most parents who provide their children with education for a better station in life than they have had, Allan was confused and resentful over Edgar's manner and attitudes, and Edgar, of course, could not understand why his foster father was not pleased at his social and intellectual conquests. By this time, too, Allan's amours were too flagrant not to be talked about, and although he had moved his illegitimate son Edward Collier to another school when Edgar entered the academy, by the time Edgar was fifteen he surely had heard some gossip about his foster father's affairs.

His business ruined, living in a house provided by the charity of his uncle, his only prospect inheritance on the death of that uncle, whenever it might come, Allan found Edgar "miserable, sulky & ill-tempered," he wrote to William Henry Poe; then he poured out the bitterness he felt. "The boy possesses not a Spark of affection for us not a particle of gratitude for all my care and kindliness toward him. I have given a much superior Education than ever I received myself. . . . Had I done my duty as faithfully to my God as I have to Edgar, then had Death come when he will had no terrors for me. . . ." Allan undoubtedly recalled that at Edgar's age he had emigrated to America to work in his uncle's countinghouse; in five years had raised a thousand pounds and gone into partnership with Charles Ellis, and had kept his business going through the war and in England — and here was this foppish boy, interested only in poetry and gadding about. There was as little chance of his understanding Edgar as of Edgar's understanding him, while one of them had his whole mind set on business worries and the other was as deeply concerned over the Morgan Riflemen retaining their arms.

The winter of 1824 was a difficult one, but the following spring John Allan's troubles — but not his doubts about Edgar — suddenly blew away. His uncle, William Galt, died in March, and now he was one of the richest men in Richmond. Immediately the Allans' standard of living changed. He paid $14,950 for a large and handsome house in the fashionable neighborhood of Fifth and Main Streets, with a view of the river (his previous place was valued — probably overvalued — at a fifth that price); and instead of returning to the Burke school, Edgar was privately tutored to enter the University of Virginia the following year.

Now Edgar could invite people to his home, and he did, among them his brother, who spent part of the summer of 1825 with him, perhaps bringing Edgar the indignant letter Allan had written him the previous year. If so, Edgar may simply have attributed its tone to the despair of that winter, for he could not have helped being elated that Allan had at last given over being the mere businessman and had established himself in a life appropriate to a Virginia gentleman; in other words, he had turned to the life Edgar was being prepared for; thus he could not be angry if Edgar kept on doing what he wanted to do.

Among the pleasures of the two handsome boys — Edgar with his neat dark clothes and Henry in midshipman's uniform — was calling on an attractive fifteen-year-old girl in whom Edgar had recently become interested. He and Sarah Elmira Royster had fallen in love — or at least had affected the sighing, platonic, in-love-with-love emotion that a boy of sixteen and his sweetheart engage in. He drew her portrait in pencil, played the gallant and protector — once chiding her for associating with a girl whom he had heard make a "coarse remark" — and soon they declared they were engaged. To her he was beautiful, reticent with a romantic melancholy in his tone, with strong principles and a high moral sense. He never addressed any poems to her, probably because his enthusiasm at the time was for Byron and he felt that Byronic wit — and morality — were not proper for the innocent ears of a girl of her age. That he considered her a child is certain, for when she did become the subject of his verse, he refers to their "passion" as "childish, without sin."

Thus on Poe's seventeenth birthday the world lay before him, already conquered. A young Virginia gentleman, he lived in a pleasant home, magnificently situated, with slaves to dress him in his new, fine clothes and to bring him whatever he demanded, engaged to a beautiful little girl whose character he could mold to the ideals of truth and beauty, in a few weeks to set out on the last stage of a literary education at the University of Virginia. True, "Pa" was still carrying on with women, and he was often irritable and distant, but he would surely soon stop this ungentlemanly conduct, and then there would be nothing to embarrass him and put him in bad temper. Edgar Poe had reached the high point of his youth.

The happiest day, the happiest hour
  My sear'd and blighted heart hath known,
The highest hope of pride and power,
  I feel hath flown.

> "The Happiest Day"

ON SAINT VALENTINE'S DAY, 1826, seventeen-year-old Edgar Poe registered in the schools of ancient and modern languages at the University of Virginia. The term was supposed to begin the first of the month, but this was only the second year in the history of a very liberal institution — founded by Thomas Jefferson, who supervised the construction of its buildings with a telescope from the front porch of Monticello — and the regulations were little known and loosely enforced. Therefore February was in its second week when Edgar said farewell to "Miss Nancy," and to "Ma," and accepted a final admonition and $110 from John Allan before mounting the coach for the two-day ride into the highlands of Virginia to Charlottesville.

Poe could not have helped being struck by the beauty of the University, even though construction on the Rotunda, at the head of the vast lawn, was still unfinished. This Pantheon-like domed structure faced two rows of classic pavilions sepa-rated by the two-hundred-foot breadth of lawn, each with a lecture hall downstairs and living quarters for a professor above. Linking the pavilions were ranges of one-story dormitory rooms, their doors opening on the lawn in front and in the rear on a yard for wood to feed the open fireplace that heated each. He paid the tuition fee of $60 for attendance at the lectures of Professor Long in classics and Professor Blaettermann in modern languages — the $110 did not now seem so great a sum as it had when John Allan handed it to him — but economized by choosing not to attend Professor Key's mathematical lectures. For this he needed his guardian's permission; but that could come later, he was told. He could not leave the required deposit of $114 with the financial officer for clothing and pocket money. By the time he had paid the first installment on rent for his room he had only $35 left, and it must have been a dismayed and puzzled boy who opened the door of Number 13, West Range, found it devoid of furniture, and was confronted by the bustling "hotel-keeper."

The living services of the University were managed by concessionaires, called hotel-keepers, who sold the students furniture for their rooms and provided meals and servants — to clean the rooms and do laundry and odd tasks — at a flat fee of $150 a year from each. Using his remaining money as a down payment, Edgar arranged to buy a bed for $12, the remaining room furniture for another $12, and promised as soon as possible to pay the balance of the $50 minimum deposit for meals. The hotel-keeper would provide no servant until he not only saw the $39 he was owed, but had assurance that he would be paid for the servant as well.

Thus Edgar Poe found himself in debt his very first day at Charlottesville. He hurriedly wrote to Allan, explaining his predicament, but in the meantime another hotel-keeper, George Spotswood, took pity on him, and knowing Allan's reputation as a man of substance, offered one of his servants at a fee to be paid when it was convenient. More than a year later Spotswood was still trying to collect. After a few days of anxious waiting the expected check arrived, but it was made out for only $40!

The very minimum deposit paid, plus one dollar pocket money — what had happened to the generosity of the man who, according to Poe's English schoolmaster, had "spoilt" him with too much pocket money? Edgar wrote a careful accounting of his expenses, but this was ignored.

Attending classes and preparing for recitations made more pressing concerns for the young scholar than money. He was awakened each morning at six-thirty by William Wertenbaker, the librarian and odd-job man of the University, who himself attended classes. On Mondays, Wednesdays, and Fridays Edgar was to be found, at seven o'clock, construing Greek and Latin under Professor Long in Pavilion V; on Tuesdays, Thursdays, and Saturdays he crossed the lawn to study French, Spanish, and Italian under the Teutonic guidance of Professor Blaettermann — and perhaps to catch a glimpse of Blaettermann's attractive bride, an attraction where dowdy faculty wives and Negro washerwomen were the only females normally to be seen. After an hour of hard labor with the classics or joyous improvisation with the Romance tongues, there would be a half-hour break for breakfast, and then another hour's work.

At nine-thirty the students were free to study, read, talk, go for walks in the nearby countryside or into the Ragged Mountains, or just enjoy themselves — an ideal schedule for scholars, a snare of temptations for the young Virginia gentlemen of 1826. Some brought horses, dogs, and their personal slaves to the University with them. Gambling, drinking, fights, and even duels took place; and revelry was more convenient than study, for to withdraw a book from the library one needed to turn in a written request a day in advance, and to consult reference books the students would petition competitively for tickets, only twenty of which were issued on any one day. Even inside the library, written permission from the librarian was necessary before any of the lucky twenty could pull a book down from the shelves.

Therefore, although Edgar worked diligently on his lessons, he drew no books from the library during his first five months at the University; but he did learn to drink "peach and honey" — a glass at a gulp, without relish, and rarely more than one, but that usually sufficed — to play cards for money, and to get into debt. He quickly learned that his guardian's name was good for credit with the merchants of the town, who would advance money at exorbitant interest, urging their goods on the Allan "heir" as well — on credit. Still, Edgar did not associate with the gayest blades who took advantage of Mr. Jefferson's honor system. In a year when the faculty, almost all distinguished scholars of international reputation, were so diligent in pursuing malefactors that they became known as "those damned foreign professors," fining and even expelling anyone they caught breaking the rules that almost everyone broke, he never once came under censure.

For the first three months Poe, like any freshman of any era, was confused by the new life he was leading and homesick for the amenities of Richmond. Professor Long, an ambitious young Fellow of Trinity College, Cambridge, was already anxious to get back into the higher academic circles of his native England. Edgar was one of the more than a hundred students from whom he required a hundred lines of advanced Latin or Greek each day, with frequent written tests and minute *explications de texte*. Edgar never got to know him personally. Professor Blaettermann was less cold, but was possessed of a fierce temper. Between the impersonal but seemingly endless demands of Long, who was as likely to ask geographical or historical details about a line of Homer or Virgil as he was to chop grammatical analysis fine, and the fierce outbursts of temper from Blaettermann, Poe must have felt totally lost.

Back in his room, he would kindle a fire — with wood not paid for — and console himself with reading Byron, or write one of his long and increasingly pathetic letters to Elmira. He never got one word in reply. In early spring John Allan visited briefly, scolding him for not attending the lectures on mathematics, but he was so quickly overwhelmed by the attentions of the University authorities that Edgar had no chance to discuss his financial problems. Thus he turned more and more to the companionship of his fellow students, continuing to mismanage his borrowed money. He became a poseur, striving to be the center of attention but never quite succeeding, competing with an array of talent and wealth greater than he had ever encountered before, from the scholarly ease of his Latin classmate Gessner Harrison, who would in time succeed Professor Long, to carefree aristocrats like the one who encountered Professor Tucker in the course of a spree, and unlike his fellows did not run to escape capture but boldly announced his name and place of origin and said he was "too firm to fly and far too proud to yield." The professor said he might have added, "and almost too drunk to stand."

Allan evaded the deposit required for clothes and spending money by sending Edgar the uniform for military drill that sum was partially to cover; and when Edgar wrote that it had arrived he had a great deal to report about grand-jury sessions on disturbances at the University — some hotel-keepers were indicted for gambling offences and many students took to the woods to avoid testifying — and several fights, one of which might have ended in murder if a pistol had not failed to fire. One of his classmates from the Richmond Academy was suspended for two months. Edgar signed himself "Your's affectionately," and in a postscript asked for Tacitus' *Historiae* and soap. In return he got *Gil Blas* and the Cambridge Mathematics.

Nominally the faculty managed itself in the European manner, electing a chairman from its own ranks, but the students misbehaved so badly that no professor would accept election, and they even threatened mass resignation. Finally the aging Jefferson agreed to give them more authority over the 177 young men who caused them so much trouble, and the Board of Visitors appointed George Tucker, Professor of Ethics, to the chair. On July 4 Jefferson died, and nine days later Poe made his first withdrawal from the library, three volumes of Rollin's *Histoire Ancienne*, in French, a work which would give him background for Long's course and at the same time practice in one of the languages studied under Blaettermann. One volume he kept three weeks overdue, and although he did not pay all of his fine (he was two cents short), he was one of the few offenders who paid any.

Through the hot summer Poe eventually found himself in his studies and was able to get along without excessive preparation. Afternoons he would stroll into the cool woods, frequently alone; evenings he would visit the room of one of his friends to play écarté and gulp his peach and honey; Jefferson's taste for dry French and Swiss wine never altered the students' preference for the raw marc of the region, although Poe, unlike most, never diluted or sweetened it or seemed to care for the taste of it, but tossed it off for the effect. Sometimes he would invite friends to his room, decorated with charcoal sketches on the walls and ceiling, and read them stories and poems he had written. He strove to be popular among the playboys and the serious alike, and although both took pleasure in his company, neither took him very seriously.

In addition to the informal — and frequently illegal — social life of the students, there was a formal social life of the University. Jefferson had been in practice of inviting students in turn to Sunday dinner, but he died before he reached Number 136 on the roster — Edgar Poe. The students had planned extensive celebrations for the Fourth of July, but found themselves instead on that day planning their role in Jefferson's funeral services. They wore black armbands for two months. The new chairman of the faculty, George Tucker, was of considerable interest to Poe, since he was a writer of some note and was then at work on a fantasy called A *Voyage to the Moon.* Soon another even more distinguished writer visited the lawn. William Wirt, Attorney General of the United States and author of the popular *Letters of a British Spy* and a biography of Patrick Henry, was invited to be President and Professor of Law. He came, was received by the faculty, met the students, obviously talking at some length with Poe, who remembered him later, and then decided not to enter the academic world but remain in politics.

In September came the announcement of a general examination to be held at the end of the term. From that point on, Poe, probably already nagged by his creditors, gave up revels and worked hard, using even his leisure time for intellectual activities. He read a volume of Voltaire and an anthology and drill book on French, and in Professor Blaettermann's class won great praise for a verse translation from Tasso which the crusty German had set as voluntary exercise. No one but Poe even tried. John Allan sent him a hundred dollars, but this was too little to try to divide up among his creditors, and after he had fruitlessly begged a loan from James Galt, in bravado mixed with fear he went off and ordered a new suit — a blue coat with gilt buttons and drab pantaloons — and did not even pay for that.

On Monday and Tuesday of the first week in December, the students of classics and modern languages were examined under the eyes of a committee that consisted of two ex-Presidents of the United States, Madison and Monroe; Joseph Cabell; and General John H. Cocke; and ten days later the results were announced. Poe stood in the second rank in Latin — the only student in the first was Harrison, later Professor of Classics in the University — and in the first in French. But this triumph was of short duration; some of his wild oats of the past year had begun to sprout. He was kept in Charlottesville after the end of the term to testify in a faculty investigation of gambling, and John Allan got wind of his debts and came to look into the matter himself.

On the night before Allan's arrival, Edgar encountered Wertenbaker, the librarian, and for the first time invited him to his room. It was very cold and his firewood had long since run out, so Poe smashed up a table and ignited the pieces with the help of a few candles, and they sat by the fire and talked. He told Wertenbaker that his debts ran to $2000 and that he considered them "debts of honor" that he must pay at the first opportunity. John Allan felt differently. When he arrived at Charlottesville he paid those debts he thought "ought to be paid," but not all those Edgar could be held accountable for. Certainly the "debts of honor" about which the boy was so concerned were not among those paid. Then the two drove back to Richmond, arriving on Christmas Eve.

Thus Edgar returned to his pleasant room in Allan's house. Recriminations were suspended for the Christmas festivities, but there was no doubt that he was in disgrace. The creditors whom John Allan had refused to pay began threatening Edgar with warrants, and even the servants soon realized that he was no longer to be considered one of the family. Still another blow came when Edgar called on the Roysters and was coldly informed that Elmira was not in; she was out of the city. He began to suspect that her father — perhaps she herself — had been soured on the match by hints from Allan that he was not pleased with his ward. The letters he sent her had certainly been intercepted.

Embittered, ashamed of what people might be saying about his dissipation at the University, he stayed in his room, writing and polishing his Byronic poems. The longest of them, "Tamerlane," describes the remorse of the dying conqueror who, in Poe's version, had left his childhood sweetheart to pursue his ambition and thereby had lost both her and his childhood home. He had nine other melancholy shorter poems to work on as well. By the time Edgar reached his eighteenth birthday Allan had made it clear that he would not be sent back to the University, and fierce sarcastic remarks must have resulted a few days later when, in an advertisement in the Richmond *Enquirer*, the University of Virginia itemized its fees to a total, for one year's attendance, of $233. In vain could Edgar plead that he had had only $150 until it was too late, that this sum did not include personal expenses, or that most students had more than five hundred dollars to spend. Allan could see only extravagance and willfulness — and why hadn't he taken the mathematics?

The tension between them continued until the middle of March, with Mrs. Allan's weak attempts at reconciliation counterbalanced by the coolness of Miss Valentine, who now realized that she would never marry, and in view of the sickliness of her sister wanted to stay on the right side of John Allan for the sake of security in her old age. One morning an argument broke out between Allan and the boy — Edgar, when his opinion was demanded on some subject, dared to find Allan in the wrong — and in a moment they were both shouting, the pent-up emotions finally released. All Allan's rancor against the "wastrel" poured out in an accusation that he was "eating the bread of idleness." Poe fled the house and went to the

Court House Tavern, where he was embarrassed to see Edward Crump, to whom he owed one of his "debts of honor." But Crump was gentleman enough not to mention it in the presence of the other people in the room, and Edgar left, unable to pay for a room or even a meal, but arranging to receive his mail there under the name of Henri le Rennet. His own name might bring his creditors down on him.

After missing at least one meal, he wrote Allan, resolving to "leave your house and indeavor to find some place in this wide world, where I will be treated — not as *you* have treated me." He listed his grievances, then asked Allan to send him his trunk with his clothes and books and enough money to travel North and live there for a month. He was obviously torn between pride and hunger and would have welcomed a reconciliation, adding as postscript, "It depends upon yourself if hereafter you see or hear from me." Allan replied the next day, explaining coldly that his reference to the "bread of idleness" was "to urge you to perseverance and industry in receiving the classics, in perfecting yourself in the mathematics, etc." instead of reading *Don Quixote*, *Gil Blas*, and Joe Miller. He reminded Poe what he owed him in upbringing and education, and scoffed at the idea of sending him money. Then he fastidiously copied this off onto a clean sheet of paper and filed the draft among his business papers. Edgar was now a business dossier instead of a son.

At the same time Poe was again writing Allan, begging again for his trunk and asking twelve dollars to pay his fare to Boston. He pathetically pointed out that he had no place to sleep but walked the streets at night, and that he had not eaten since the previous morning. Two ships, the *Only Son* and the *President*, were scheduled to leave in a few days for Boston, and memory of the message his mother had written on the back of her sketch of Boston Harbor turned his thoughts toward returning to his birthplace. Allan did not reply at all this time, simply endorsing the note "Pretty Letter," and with bitter humor adding an "s" to the signature in scorn of the boy's "pose" before he filed it away.

By Sunday Edgar had got money somewhere — perhaps it was sent him by Mrs. Allan — and he sailed for Boston, arriving on April 3. He did not find Elizabeth Poe's "best, and most sympathetic friends," but a cold and money-minded city. Although John Allan at this time was saying, "I'm thinking Edgar has gone to Sea to seek his own fortunes," few berths would have been available, for two days before the quarrel broke out and Edgar left home, President John Quincy Adams had proclaimed all American ports closed to British shipping from their colonies in the Western Hemisphere in retaliation to the British Order in Council that denied American vessels access to those ports; shipping was at a standstill. But ill feeling between the two nations provided Edgar with a last resort when his money was gone. Soldiers were needed to man the forts guarding American harbors. On May 26, 1827, he signed up for a five-year enlistment in the Army. But the agony of his seven weeks of poverty in Boston had not been entirely fruitless. He had become acquainted with a young printer, Calvin F. S. Thomas, who undertook to publish Poe's youthful poems.

Thus while Edgar was in training as a recruit to Battery H of the First Artillery, in Fort Independence in Boston Harbor, the forty-page pamphlet *Tamerlane and Other Poems*, "by a Bostonian," was put on sale. Few copies were sold, and the book was not reviewed, although two journals listed it among "books received," one in August and the other in October. But he was a poet, with a published volume. He did not forget that.

6

Of late, eternal Condor years
So shake the very Heaven on high
With tumult as they thunder by,
I have no time for idle cares
Through gazing on the unquiet sky.
"Romance"

HUNGER AND DESPAIR drove Edgar Poe to enlist in the United States Army; fear of debtors' prison and shame over his fall to common soldier led him to do so using the name Edgar A. Perry. He gave his age as twenty-two, although he was really eighteen, but correctly gave Boston as his birthplace. He claimed his occupation to be that of clerk, but since this was more true in the medieval than in the modern sense, he was very likely doing no more than calling attention to his education. The recruiting officer noted that the new soldier was five feet eight inches tall, with gray eyes, brown hair, and a fair complexion.

For all his shame, Edgar's reception at Boston's Fort Independence must have seemed like finding a new home. A recruit is treated with abruptness by some of his superiors and kindness by others, but with friendly camaraderie by his equals. He must have been truly grateful at being issued the vast quantity of material that comprised his uniform and equipment, no matter how badly it fit. His own best things had certainly gone to old-clothes dealers to win him more urgent necessities. And the food, crudely prepared as it was, was nothing if not plentiful. Best of all, he need have no worry of what the morrow would bring. Although promising monotony and humiliation, his future was assured, and he had had enough uncertainty for the present.

It was, however, so vastly different from the life he had known at the University of Virginia or anywhere else since he left Bransby's school that he must have looked back with great nostalgia on his leisurely days of the previous spring. Aroused by the boom of the sunrise gun and the sound of the bugle to the dim sunshine of 5:30 A.M., he would hastily wash and shave, then line up for reveille roll call with his shivering, blinking fellows until the sergeant major, who seemed brisk and loud from dawn to midnight, reported the troops to a half-awake officer, who would stroll back to his quarters while the troops policed the parade ground and set their quarters in precise order. Breakfast followed, hot and plenty, but with strange foods for the former "heir" to a Southern gentleman. Yet it was not so strange as the hasty pudding that had cut his appetite — if it had not assuaged his hunger — the month before, for Army food is always slightly Southern.

In the morning was drill, not a difficult task at all for the former lieutenant of the Richmond Junior Volunteers, and it induced an honest tiredness, not the weariness that came from desperate hours of walking the Boston streets. New to him, however, was artillery practice, although the delicate boy, with his clerk's hands, was of less use manhandling the heavy coastal defense guns and running cannonballs and heavy bags of powder than were the former laborers and roustabouts who were his fellow soldiers. He disliked the way the clouds of smoke would blow back on the gun crew, blackening his face. The noise was unpleasant and he was overly cautious of the massive piece's recoil as well as made wary by the stories he heard of peculiar accidents with these old guns; the touch-holes quickly eroded out, and the bushing put in to prevent the charge from blowing out the rear would eventually work loose and fly screaming. Although the gun was rarely elevated enough for it to hit the crew, it was always a danger.

All through the summer Edgar trained and drilled, cleaned equipment and stood inspection. He came to tolerate living in close quarters with a mass of men who were crude and used foul language; he even came to overcome his squeamish-ness and appreciate their qualities, although the sordid condi-tion in which some came back from leave days in Boston turned him from joining them in off hours. Drinking, which he had never enjoyed, he eschewed entirely. The officers were gentlemen, of course, and some were from Virginia; but they certainly would not have recognized the Allan boy in the soldier Perry, even if they were given to noticing individual soldiers. On a military post, a uniform is the best disguise of all.

Eventually the time came when practice had taught Edgar the art of soldiering; the endless tasks now were simply habit, the guns no longer seemed so menacing and dirty, the routine had been assimilated until it was as unconscious a thing as breathing or eating. The experienced soldier not only learns to do his tasks efficiently; he also learns how to avoid them. And intelligent and educated men who could keep records, do mathematics, and write a clear hand were as scarce in that army as in any peacetime military establishment. As the time drew near for the regiment to pack its equipment and take ship for Fort Moultrie, South Carolina, it was no trouble for Private Perry to find more sedentary work than drilling and working the guns. He began by assisting in the commissary, and before long he was company clerk. Promotion — a rare thing in one's first year of service — was promised him.

On November 8, 1827, Battery H embarked on the brig

Waltham, and in company with other vessels carrying the rest of the First Regiment of Artillery, set sail out of Boston Harbor, with its ring of forts, down the coast. From the brisk November air of Massachusetts to the subtropical breezes of Charleston Harbor took eleven days. The place he had come to was the North American opposite of Boston; the life he was to live there was happy and peaceful, studious and reflective. Charleston, a city of gracious aristocratic tradition, was in sight from Fort Moultrie. Adjacent to the irregular-sided brick fortification was Sullivan's Island, a long, sandy island partially grown over with myrtle, and a treasure-trove for the study of shells, insects, and birds.

In the extended leisure time that Edgar was able to take by virtue of his clerical position in this easygoing post, he met Dr. Edmund Ravenel, a specialist in natural history who lived on the island, and from him gained an enthusiasm for the curiosities of biology and a good education in classification. In Charleston he met Colonel William Drayton, not a professional soldier but a gentleman of distinction of the city, whose political ambition had just led him to turn from Federalism in hopes of riding the rising Democratic tide. He wandered the countryside around the charming city, observing the mansions with their roads colonnaded by oak trees hung in Spanish moss and the marshy environs of the fort, with its tall tulip trees; and his manners, especially since he was introduced by Drayton, could cause even the gentlefolk of Charleston to overlook his humble rank.

But Charleston was nine miles away, and transportation infrequent. Edgar spent most of his leisure time tramping the island with Ravenel, learning the classes of shells and searching for exotic insects, among which were the click beetle, with its two black, white-edged spots that suggest the eyes of a skull, and the gleaming golden *Callichroma splendidum*. He was sufficiently fascinated by the island and its legends of pirates and lost treasure to look up the records of the wreck of the *Cid Campeador* off the South Carolina coast in 1745, which were preserved in the State House. The Charleston Library Society was in the same building.

On the first of May, 1828, the soldier of little more than eleven months won his first promotion — to the rank of artificer, with increases in pay and in personal freedom. His little book, which had disappeared into oblivion the previous summer, was still able to keep him heartened about his writing, and he was already at work augmenting its contents. His greater maturity, the integration of his literary learning with the scientific attitude of Dr. Ravenel, and the dampening of his Byronism made these new efforts considerably better than the poems of the first volume. Among the half dozen shorter poems he wrote in the Army, the best was "Sonnet — To Science," which reflects an interest in Coleridge and Keats to replace the flamboyant hero of his youth. The long work "Al Aaraaf" is a loosely constructed fantasy in which the poet locates the limbo of the Moslems in the star discovered by the Swedish astronomer Tycho Brahe, which appeared and disappeared in a few days; but aside from the unsuccessful narrative, it contains passages of remarkable beauty and very original lyricism.

Through Ravenel and Drayton, Edgar's reading had become wider than ever before, and his appetite for it nearly insatiable. Before, his knowledge had been largely of the classics and history, his enthusiasms the French and Byron; Professor Blaettermann had widened his awareness to include Italian, Spanish, and a smattering of Anglo-Saxon, old Germanic, and Norse literature. Now his imagination was fired with science and his aesthetic senses soothed with more modern works, including the popular *Lalla Rookh* of Thomas Moore, which probably inspired the Moslem apparatus of "Al Aaraaf."

Before the poem was finished, however, Edgar's cloistered existence was broken into by two omens of change. Orders came down for the regiment to move to the more active post of Fortress Monroe, in Virginia; and an emissary arrived from John Allan, who, alarmed by a crisis in his wife's illness, sent to inquire after him. Edgar had probably confided his true identity to his two older friends, and the news may have trickled North that the lost Edgar was serving in the Army. A Mr. John O. Lay carried a letter from Allan to one of Edgar's officers, Lieutenant Howard, expressing hope that the boy would prosper in the Army. Howard called "Private Perry" in, and for the first time his military superiors became aware of his true identity. It made a difference. Even the colonel of the regiment interviewed him, spoke of his acquaintance with the late "General" Poe, and promised to discharge him if he and Allan should be reconciled. And Edgar, lured by the hope that he should again be a Virginia gentleman, became dissatisfied with being a soldier.

On December 1, Edgar wrote Allan a calm and dignified letter, requesting the reconciliation that would release him from service. The regiment was to sail for Virginia on the eleventh, and so he went about bidding farewell to his Charleston friends, among whom was Colonel Drayton, then happy enough to promise anyone the moon. Drayton's party had won in the recent election, and General Jackson might very well offer him a cabinet post — probably the War Department. Edgar must be an officer. Of course he must go through West Point, but with his education and military experience that should be no problem at all.

On the fifteenth the regiment arrived at Old Point Comfort, at the mouth of the James, and went into garrison at Fortress Monroe. A few days later, while his fellow soldiers were stiffening to the stricter rule of this post, where the artillery school and the Corps of Engineers were in bitter rivalry, Edgar was detailed for duty in the adjutant's office. He impatiently awaited a letter from Allan. He wrote to John MacKenzie, son of the family that had adopted Rosalie Poe, to intercede for him with his foster father, but there was still no response. On January 1, 1829, Edgar was promoted to sergeant major, the highest noncommissioned rank in the Army. He was stricken with a fever soon afterward and confined to the hospital, but by February 4 he was back on duty and wrote again, pleading with Allan to write and release him from the Army. From the comments of Drayton, and possibly from some of his officers, he got the idea that since he had already a training in the "practical" part of soldiering, and had studied at the University, his cadetship would be only a formality "which I am positive I could run thro' in 6 months."

At the end of the month reconciliation came, but not as Edgar would have wanted it. Frances Allan died on February 28, and Edgar, granted a ten-day emergency furlough, arrived in Richmond the evening after the funeral. Allan, his remorse over his wife's death before she could see her boy perhaps fortified by recourse to the whisky which he, like all good householders, bought by the barrel, forgave the prodigal and again called him son. He ordered a decent black suit for Edgar from the stock of the store, gave him fifty dollars, and planned with him ways and means of getting an appointment to the Military Academy. When Edgar left to return to his duties, Allan was not awake, so rather than disturb him the boy left without saying good-by; but immediately on arriving at his post he wrote Allan, addressing him for the first time as "My dear Pa," and signing himself "affectionately."

The regimental commander, Colonel House, was in Washington, congratulating Andrew Jackson on his election as President of the United States, but on his return he wrote to the general commanding the Eastern Department of the Army, requesting permission to discharge Edgar from the service, citing his background, his reconciliation with Allan, and the availability of a qualified substitute. There was one more formality than reconciliation to conclude for Sergeant Perry to be set free; he had to hire a substitute. Edgar knew the Army regulations and customs; the officers in charge could simply accept as substitute the next recruit offering himself and charge the departing soldier regardless of rank the minimum fee of twelve dollars. But Lieutenant Howard was on leave and Colonel House absent on business on April 15, when Special Order No. 28 ordered the discharge, and Edgar had to prevail on Sergeant Samuel Graves, a man who had been in the Army at least three years when Edgar joined, and who was married and obviously a typical old-Army man. The bounty for Sergeant "Bully" Graves was seventy-five dollars, and Poe, short as always of money, had to give him twenty-five in cash and his note of hand for the balance.

Sergeant Graves was duly re-enlisted two days later, but Edgar stayed on at the post to collect letters of recommendation from his absent officers. On the twentieth, Lieutenant Howard returned and wrote a glowing commendation, concluding, "His habits are good and intirely free from drinking." This was endorsed, to include Edgar's service after he had left Howard's company to become regimental sergeant major, by the adjutant and, since Colonel House was still absent, the post commander. With these testimonials in his pocket, he hurried to Richmond, where James T. Preston, a member of the House of Representatives, Judge John J. Barber, and Major Gibbon assured him that they would write the Secretary of War in his behalf.

There still remained the letter without which the others were worthless, that from John Allan. But John Allan was a cautious man always, and often a suspicious man. He was not only recommending a boy whom he at best thought "wilful," but his letter was to be addressed to Major John Eaton. Drayton had not been offered the position of Secretary of War, although Jackson would offer it to him two years later. Instead he had appointed his old crony Eaton, who became the butt of jokes and gossip which had already tarred the reputation of the whole Jackson administration, including that of the President himself. At the beginning of the year Eaton had married Peggy O'Neale Timberlake, widow of a Navy purser and daughter of a Washington tavern keeper, who lived and helped out at her father's tavern. Gossip even had it that her first husband had cut his own throat because of his wife's amours with Eaton. Churchill Cambreleng was reminded, on the wedding day, of Swift's comparison "about using a certain household [vessel] and then putting it on one's head."

John Allan's letter was cold and full of reservations. He assured Eaton that Edgar was no relation to him whatever, but merely one of the many in whom he took interest; and he was especially careful not only to make clear that he asked nothing himself of the unsavory cabinet officer, but that he would like "to reciprocate any kindness you can show him." To underline the feeling that he was dabbling in things he considered dirty, he concluded, "Pardon my frankness, but I address a soldier." Poe's application was filed away, not to receive any consideration for months.

— in the dawn
Of a most stormy life — was drawn
From ev'ry depth of good and ill
The mystery which binds me still —
   . . .
From the thunder, and the storm —
And the cloud that took the form
(When the rest of Heaven was blue)
Of a demon in my view.
       "Alone"

CONFIDENT THAT HIS APPLICATION to the Military Academy was smoothly being processed through the War Department, Edgar Poe's thoughts turned again to poetry. John Allan, recovering from the emotional shock of his wife's death, had no objection to getting Poe out of the house and out of town; he was already consoling himself with a Mrs. Elizabeth Wills, who would later bear him twins to be added to the "many" in whom Allan took an "active interest." There was no publisher in Richmond to whom Edgar could offer the new book that was already taking shape, nor was there any other interest for him there, in his present ambitious turn of mind. Shortly after he had entered the Army, Elmira Royster had married A. Barrett Shelton, and the places Edgar identified with her were sad reminders of a lost childhood. Allan handed him fifty dollars and saw him off for Baltimore.

Poe's first act on arriving in Baltimore early in May, 1829, was to seek out his family. He had never seen any of them before, save his brother Henry; and discovering their condition must have been a shock. His grandmother, widow of "General" Poe, was a paralytic and sickly woman in her seventies, yet her pension of $240 a year was the mainstay of the household. Living with her was her daughter, widow of William Clemm, with her two children, eleven-year-old Henry and seven-year-old Virginia, and Henry Poe. Henry had not been to sea for two years, was drinking considerably, and, to Edgar's great chagrin, soon revealed that not only had he written a story based on Edgar's tragic love for Elmira Royster, which was published in the Baltimore *North American*, but he had copied two poems out of the copy of *Tamerlane* Edgar had sent him, and had published them in the same journal over his own initials.

In spite of the poverty and illness in their crowded little house, Edgar found himself attracted to these people; his hunger for a home, for refuge and affection, could hardly be satisfied by them in their present condition, but unlike the ties with the Allans, with Mrs. Stanard, and with Elmira, these were the ties of blood relationship. Henry might be a drunkard and a poetaster, but he was Edgar's brother; and Maria Clemm, not quite forty years old, was a motherly person. Little Virginia, with her dark hair and eyes, seemed even more of a sister than Rosalie, and Edgar, responding to her natural affection, began calling her "Sissy." But Edgar, with money in his pocket, had no intention of adding to the crowded condition of their house and of sharing in their scanty table. Besides, he had business to take care of.

He knew that William Wirt, the author-lawyer whom he had met at the University, was in Baltimore. He introduced himself, and "for a first attempt at self introduction succeeded wonderfully." Wirt read "Al Aaraaf" at a sitting, and excused his inability to make much of the poem by his "ignorance of

poetry and modern taste." In addition to suggesting that Poe
go to Philadelphia to consult Robert Walsh and Joseph Hop-
kinson, with introductions from himself, he had influence
enough to have extracts from the poem printed in the Baltimore *Gazette*.

Fired with enthusiasm, Edgar went to Corbin Warwick, a
relative of John Allan, to see what he could do about getting
money to take his book to Philadelphia. At Warwick's suggestion he drew a draft for fifty dollars on Allan, and then,
calling at the post office, found a letter from Allan with a draft
for one hundred dollars enclosed. With the sly forgetfulness
with which he was capable of modifying his elephant-like
memory, Allan had written to suggest that Poe find out
whether his grandfather had been an officer in the Revolution,
since descendants of Revolutionary officers got preference for
admission to West Point, and, if successful, present documents
to that effect to the War Department. Something, the history
of which reached back to the letter he wrote Henry Poe five
years before, kept him trying to make dissension between Edgar
and the Poe family. But Edgar did not take offense at the hint
that the Poes had invented their family history, replying calmly
that his grandfather's record was so well known at Washington
that no documents were necessary.

Either out of generosity or misunderstanding Allan paid both
drafts, and in great joy the poet went to Philadelphia, took a
room at Heiskell's Indian Queen Hotel, and carried his manuscript to Walsh, editor of the *American Quarterly Review*.
Walsh, however, was just about to leave the city, so he did
little but promise to review the poem (which he never did)
and advise Poe to see a publisher. So Edgar sent his poems
to Isaac Lea, of Carey, Lea and Carey, with a cover letter that
fairly bubbles with enthusiastic joy. With it he enclosed a
criticism from Wirt commending the title poem as sure to

please modern readers, even though it would not "take" with old-fashioned readers like himself.

After a short wait, Poe called on Lea at the Chestnut Street shop of the publishing firm and was received with the non-committal courtesy that publishers are in the practice of giving unknowns with distinguished sponsors. Lea would submit the poem to his partners; and in the meantime the young man might like to attempt something for the firm's annual, the *Atlantic Souvenir*. Edgar's enthusiasm was somewhat dampened by this reception, but he kept up hope. The trip had cut excessively into his funds, however, and so he packed his bag and returned to Baltimore to await a decision. On May 27 it came, couched in the usual terms for a publication about which the partners had commercial doubts. If he would guarantee the cost of publication there would be much more chance of issuing the book at an early date. This was the customary procedure for publishing the works of American poets.

Edgar wrote immediately to Allan, beginning, "Dear Pa, I am now going to make a request different from any I have ever yet made." He emphasized the importance of being brought "*before the eye of the world*" at his age, and estimated that subsidizing the publication would cost Allan not more than one hundred dollars, hastening to add that the book might turn a profit instead. To take away the sting of previous disapproval of his versifying, he told Allan that he had "long given up *Byron* as a model."

Allan replied in fury, and Edgar hastened to withdraw his request. To this Allan did not reply at all. But by the time two weeks more had passed, Edgar was weary of being an exile in Baltimore, anxious about hearing nothing of his West Point application, and short of money. Moreover, he had offered the hospitality of his room at Beltzhoover's Hotel to his cousin, Edward Mosher Poe, who responded by going through his pockets while Edgar was asleep and stealing his last forty-six dollars. The next day Edgar accused Mosher of the theft and got ten dollars back and a letter of confession. So in his next letter, after explaining that he would not permit the poems to be published at all if his foster father disapproved, he asked for money and strongly hinted that he wanted to return to Richmond.

As always in a crisis, however, he said a little too much. To forestall accusations of extravagance, since he had gone through more than one hundred and fifty dollars in a month — money which Allan apparently had intended to take him to West Point — he finally told of the large bounty he had to pay Sergeant Graves, and opened the way for trouble later on by claiming that he had paid him the balance due, even though he had not. Moreover, perhaps to prepare the way for possible rejection from West Point, perhaps because he for a moment believed, romantically, what was probably a malicious joke made by one of the Poes, he wrote, "Since I have been in Baltimore I have learnt something concerning my descent which would have, I am afraid, no very favourable effect if known to the *War* Dept: viz: that I am the grandson of General Benedict Arnold — but this there will be no necessity of telling —"

Before visiting Baltimore, Poe knew little of his mother save that she had been an actress; he knew hardly anything at all of his father, and he was woefully misinformed about his grandfather's fortune and rank. Coming from the genealogically minded South, brought up in Richmond, and having just spent a year in the vicinity of Charleston, he would make his ancestry the major subject in his conversations with his newly found family, probably to their utter boredom. His grandmother had never approved of the bright-eyed English beauty who had lured her son to a wasted life; Maria Clemm had been eighteen years old, living in her father's house, when David and Elizabeth Arnold Poe visited Baltimore and left their infant elder son with his grandparents. She was probably the one who had to do the work, and she had no prospects of marriage herself then; she did not marry for another nine years, when she became the second wife of her cousin Harriet's widower. As Edgar pondered who his "illustrious ancestor" had been on his mother's side, the apt name for someone to supply would have been "Benedict Arnold." Perhaps the Poes really believed it.

Three weeks passed with no reply from Allan. Edgar wrote again, more calmly, simply suggesting that he would like to return to Richmond through Washington, where he expected to receive his appointment for September. This time Allan immediately replied, enclosing fifty dollars with the remark that men of genius ought not to apply to his aid — not an unkindly remark considering Allan's style of humor — chiding Edgar about making a bad bargain in hiring a substitute, and discouraging him from visiting Richmond.

Poe immediately set out in the July sun to walk to Washington. The journey took a day and a half, but he went directly to see the Secretary of War. Eaton received him with courtesy but told him that there were still ten names ahead of his on the waiting list for the Academy. The incoming plebes were already in encampment at West Point, but there was still hope of his entering that fall if more than ten resigned by then; at any rate, Poe would be appointed the following year. In the end he lamely said that he regretted Poe's useless trip to Washington. So Edgar turned around and walked back to Baltimore.

But not all the news of that July was bad news. The poems he had worked on through his Army days, revising the old as painstakingly as he created the new, were beginning to be talked about in Baltimore. Just two days after his weary journey to Washington, Edgar wrote Carey, Lea and Carey, asking for the return of his manuscript. He reminded them of Lea's suggestion that he write for the *Atlantic Souvenir*, and to get on their good side and to show he was aware of literary currencies, made disparaging remarks about John Neal, editor of the *Yankee and Boston Literary Gazette*, who had been sniping at the annual. Then, with the hypocrisy of ambition, Edgar sent this very same Neal a copy of "Fairy-Land." Neal liked it and commented on it in his September number, giving a tremendous lift to Edgar's confidence.

"Al Aaraaf" went to Hatch and Dunning, a Baltimore publisher, along with six new poems, and six from the 1827 volume, including a "Tamerlane" so completely revised that scarcely one line in twenty remained the same. When proofs were ready, Poe sent sets to a number of editors, and Neal responded again with enthusiasm. Out of gratitude Edgar dedicated "Tamerlane" to him in the new volume. Nathaniel Parker Willis poked fun at the poems in the *American Monthly Magazine*, but by the time his notice appeared in November, Edgar was past being discouraged about his poems.

At the beginning of August, however, Poe's money was again running out. There had been no news from John Allan for two weeks, and then he had rejected Edgar's proposed visit to Richmond with the words, "I am not particularly anxious to see you." For the first time since Mrs. Allan's death Edgar addressed his foster father as "Dear Sir," and although he did not ask for money, he did plead for an answer. Allan responded by sending money and implied that he would supply more if necessary. Edgar at any rate replied, optimistically estimating his expenses until the beginning of classes at West Point at thirty dollars, and even more unrealistically stating that if he was not appointed in the fall he could live on eight to ten dollars a month. Carefully correcting the wording as he wrote, he added, "I am not so anxious of obtaining money from your good nature as of preserving your good will." Then he asked for a small trunk of books and letters he had left in Richmond, "& if you think I may ask so much perhaps you will put in it for me some clothes as I am nearly without."

Early in October it was evident that Poe was not to attend West Point that year. Allan wrote chiding him again, but not with rancor enough to arouse the boy to the formal salutation in his reply. Perhaps Allan was impressed with Neal's statement in the September *Yankee* identifying "E.A.P. of Baltimore" as a poet with considerable promise. At any rate he inquired after the manuscript, reminding Edgar that he had still not seen it. When Poe's reply to the letter went unanswered for two weeks, the boy wrote again, begging for money. He had been living for the past three months on a third as much as he had spent the first month in Baltimore and Philadelphia. Such economy was possible only because he had begun boarding with his aunt, but the family needed every penny they could get to supplement his grandmother's twenty dollars a month pension. This time Allan sent eighty dollars, with strict instructions on budgeting it. Another forty dollars flowed into the household on December 10, when Edgar handled the assignment of Mrs. Clemm's slave Edwin to Henry Ridgway for a nine-year term.

But the glory of regular publication of a book of verse distracted Edgar from his material problems. He wrote an exuberant letter to Neal, asking him to review *Al Aaraaf*, and the editor printed his letter in its entirety. The book was published in December, 1829, and the not quite twenty-one-year-old poet sat in his grandmother's shabby house awaiting the reviews. The *Ladies Magazine* was lukewarm, but still compared him to Shelley. The Baltimore *Minerva* praised the revised version of "Tamerlane" but not the other poems, and utterly devastated the obscure title poem.

Respectability, won entirely by his own efforts, had finally come to Edgar Poe. His cousin Neilson, a completely self-centered and conventional man, wrote his fiancée, "Edgar Poe has published a volume of Poems one of which is dedicated to John Neal the great autocrat of critics — Neal has accordingly published Edgar as a Poet of great genius etc. — Our name will be a great one yet." Edgar was lionized in the literary fringes of Baltimore and asked to recite his poems and to write them in autograph books. And John Allan finally proffered the long-expected invitation for Edgar to visit Richmond.

INTERLUDE

> Dim vales — and shadowy floods —
> And cloudy-looking woods,
> Whose form we can't discover . . .
> "Fairy-Land"

THROUGH JANUARY, 1830, Edgar Poe lived in John Allan's house and in his good graces. But from the last of January, when Allan bought him six pairs of wool hose, until May 3, when Edgar wrote Sergeant Graves from Richmond, we do not know where he was. Perhaps he simply stayed at Allan's Main Street house, writing in his comfortable room overlooking the river and visiting his boyhood friends. Perhaps he was at "The Byrd," Allan's plantation, enjoying the coming of spring in the Virginia countryside. Perhaps this was the time he revisited Europe, traveling, as he claimed in an autobiographical memorandum eleven years later, to Russia, with the objective of joining the Greek revolution, but, losing incentive — and out of funds — in St. Petersburg, being sent home by the United States Minister, Henry Middleton. If he ever did make this journey, it must have been at this time.

Although we do not know Poe's physical whereabouts for the first months of 1830, we do know what he was doing. Having succeeded enough in "the field of my choice" at least to impress John Allan, he was inspired to the highest lyric impulse of his life and produced five or six poems, among them his ultimate masterpiece, "To Helen." Ever since the death of Jane Stith Stanard six years before, he had wanted to write a poem expressing what she had meant to him. News of her death came almost simultaneously with news of the death of his boyhood poetic hero, Lord Byron, at Missolonghi in Greece. Study of the classics under the fastidious Professor Long had created in his imagination an image of Greece as a bright land studded with gems of architecture, to which the seafaring Greeks returned in joy from voyages among peoples unenlightened with their ideals of beauty, just as he had taken refuge with his "Helen" from the realities of John Allan's business worries and the pretensions of his schoolfellows.

Thus he mingled in his verses the "Nicéan" bark that carries the weary voyager back to the land of classic beauty and the woman, her hair in hyacinth curls, poised in a window niche like the statue of a goddess. The poem was not yet perfect; over the years he was to replace a dozen words, focusing more sharply on the reality — Mrs. Stanard revealed by the light of the agate lamp — and the fancy that sums up the ancient civilizations as "the glory that was Greece / And the grandeur that was Rome."

All the poems Poe wrote and rewrote that spring display a calm and steady competence. He had confidence in himself that outweighed whatever apprehension he might have had about his future; indeed, at this peak of poetic glory he could have given hardly a moment's thought to specific plans. At the end of March formal notice of his acceptance for the following session at West Point arrived, and Allan wrote his permission for Edgar to serve as a cadet for five years, as was required by the rules. This he could have done in Poe's absence. On May 3 a letter arrived from "Bully" Graves, inquiring about the money Poe owed him. Even though this was a day in which Allan fiercely showed his temper (probably at being asked for money again) and cursed out the whole Poe family, Edgar's reply, written in a large, confident hand, was friendly to the point of breeziness, sending regards to his old acquaintances, assuring the sergeant that he would get his money, and explaining away Allan's misapprehension that the money had already been paid with the words, "Mr A is not very often sober." Whether true or not, that statement was the biggest mistake Poe made in his life.

No surer sign of Edgar Poe's high sense of his own importance can there be than the signature on his letter to Bully. He was, like many people who sense rightly or wrongly that they are going to make their mark on the world, beginning to experiment with his autograph. In place of the clerkish flowing hand he had used in the Army, he went back to the pointed capital A and the *P* that is a loop with a line through it that he had learned in England, but far more elaborate, increasing the size of the *P* while he diminished the A, much as the *Allan* it stood for meant less than the *Poe* that followed. He was to continue such experimenting, not only with his signature, but in creating a manuscript hand that closely imitated italic printing, probably with the typesetters in mind.

A poet, a Virginia gentleman, one of the corps of United States cadets, soon to be an officer, perhaps in command of his old comrades of Fortress Monroe, he could be magnanimous in writing Bully; and he would pay him, as soon as Allan put up the money, but something like that could hardly worry him. The pride was there, and soon would come the fall.

If I could dwell
Where Israfel
  Hath dwelt, and he where I,
He might not sing so wildly well
  A mortal melody,
While a bolder note than this might swell
  From my lyre within the sky.

                      "Israfel"

ALTHOUGH ALLAN PERMITTED bad temper to break out in recriminations against Edgar and all the Poes, that spring of
1830, he was no longer dealing with a naïvely proud boy but
with a young man who had learned the outward signs of humility in the Army, and who by virtue of his book of poems
and friends of his own making, like Wirt and Colonel Drayton,
was too sure of himself to be provoked into storming out of the
house as he had three years before. Thus, when the time came
for his departure for West Point, Allan sent him to the Ellis-
Allan store, where he picked out four blankets and a few
handkerchiefs, and a few days later he accompanied him to the
steamboat and provided him with funds for the journey. Edgar
sensed, but did not dare admit to himself, that this was the
end of his Virginia home. He later wrote, "When I parted
from you — at the steam-boat, I knew that I should never see
you again."

For all his selfish urge to see the last of the boy whose
interests and abilities ran so counter to his own, Allan's affec-

tions for him caused him remorse, and all afflictions, by John Allan's experience, could be relieved with money — but as cheaply as possible. Hoping that it would catch Edgar at his stopover in Baltimore, he wrote a letter enclosing twenty dollars. But it did not, and the new cadet went north to New York City, then up the Hudson to the Military Academy, arriving in time for the examinations in the last week of June. He passed them with no trouble, for they consisted only of tests in English and mathematics at the level of the Richmond Academy; and on July 1 he was sworn in and placed in the summer encampment.

Here he was drilled in the rudiments of soldiering so familiar to a former sergeant major that he did not even need to think about them. Indeed, some of the comradeship he had felt for his crude fellows in the ranks was missing here. He did not stand out in a way he could be proud of; there were Virginia gentlemen aplenty, and nearly every cadet was descended from a Revolutionary officer. His practiced ease in drill and camp was something that needed to be explained away, and so he fabricated adventures and even new journeys abroad. Halfway to his twenty-second birthday, he was much older than most of the other cadets — the age of admission was from fourteen to twenty-one — and his varied experience and education made him much more mature than even the oldest, while his temperament made them think of him as a "wild one." Furthermore, he soon discovered that the Assistant Instructor of Tactics, the officer in charge of spying out infractions of discipline and reporting them, was Lieutenant Joseph Locke, one of the hated Engineering officers from Fortress Monroe, whom he had certainly encountered there in the post adjutant's office.

From his twenty-eight dollars a month pay and subsistence allowance Edgar had to buy virtually everything that he needed — uniforms, cleaning equipment, candles, textbooks, and writing materials. So when, on June 25, he finally received Allan's letter and twenty dollars, forwarded from Baltimore by his brother Henry, it was very welcome. Allan had, however, complained at his having taken some books and an inkstand from his room, and in his reply Edgar insisted that he had taken "nothing except what I considered my own property." He emphasized the difficulty of the course, pointing out that even the son of the Governor of Virginia had failed the entrance examination, but added, "I find that I will possess many advantages & shall endeavor to improve them."

Allan did not reply, for unknown to Poe he was then at his plantation in the country, where he met a woman of thirty who had just as strong a character as he, Miss Louisa Gabriella Patterson, from a prominent New York family. He was a widower of fifty, whose virility was well testified by the bulging form of Mrs. Elizabeth Wills, who was in fact delivered of his twins the first of July. Allan was tired of a bachelor life, even alleviated by amours — which he had to make pretense of hiding from the "fat and hearty" sister of his dead wife. First fastidiously confessing his past "faults," he now proposed marriage to Miss Patterson and she accepted.

But while this was going on, Edgar was in the last phase of his encampment, bullied by the upperclassmen, nagged at by Locke, chastised by Lieutenant Kinsley, Locke's superior, and irked by discipline and regimented hours which were more severe than he had known even as a recruit in Boston. Yet his familiarity with military life probably made his lot less irksome than that of any other member of his class. On September 1, the term began in earnest. Edgar was quartered in Number 28 South Barracks, along with Thomas W. Gibson and Timothy Pickering Jones. In Gibson he found a spirit kindred to his drinking companions at the University; Jones was more studious, but sincere to the point of dullness, and a gull to the hoaxes that Edgar was beginning to enjoy perpetrating.

His days were rigidly planned out. Reveille sounded at dawn, and roll call came immediately after. In a half hour, the room and its occupants stood inspection; then they studied mathematics until seven o'clock, when they were marched to breakfast. Even at table the martinet-like discipline continued, with each squad seated at one table headed by a "carver," who was the only one who could speak — and he only to the waiter. Guard-mount followed after a half-hour's breakfast, then parade, and at eight o'clock all marched to the academy building for three hours' drill in mathematics. Roll calls were frequent. At eleven Edgar returned to his room, "free" to review his morning's study until noon, when he was to turn to French.

Dinner parade came at one o'clock, and after chewing tough beef or forcing down unspeakable soup, biscuits, and molasses, he and his fellow cadets were free even to practice music (under certain limitations) until the two-o'clock formation for marching on to French class. Four-o'clock drill was succeeded by dress parade, with a sweaty body in a clean dress uniform, and another meal of a quality which would have caused mutiny at Moultrie or Monroe. Then mathematical study followed again until tattoo and roll call at nine-thirty; inspection; and lights were put out — theoretically, at least — at ten. Sundays were a little less crowded but just as hemmed in; Saturday afternoons the library was open for two hours.

The rules were rigid. No cadet could use tobacco, alcohol, or playing cards. Games, novels, and plays were taboo anywhere on the grounds — somehow, to Poe's satisfaction, poetry had been omitted from the index. He could subscribe to one publication, with the Superintendent's approval. Everywhere off the grounds, and some places on, were off limits, except with special leave. But the more rigid the rules, the more young men are interested in breaking them, and this the Superintendent, Colonel Thayer, knew. Since 1817 he had been hard at work to raise the standards of the school and develop discipline there, and although his practice of using spies — like Locke — to discover infractions was offensive, he himself kept aloof and therefore was more highly respected than those who carried out his orders.

Outside the grounds were several off-limits hotels, where each cadet still managed to spend an average of fifty dollars a year. Since growing boys could supplement their bad rations only by visiting forbidden taverns, many of them had as soon be hanged for sheep as goats, and brought back not only food but drink. Moreover, although cadets were often caught breaking the rules, and many of them were court-martialed, very few were dismissed; among the many a few years before had been Cadet Jefferson Davis, who had gone to a hotel and been caught with the glass in his hand. He was sentenced to be dismissed, but in view of his previous good record was permitted to stay on and graduate.

In contrast with the severity of the rules, which he frequently broke but, with an old soldier's cunning, was never caught breaking, Poe found his studies comparatively easy. He stood in the upper fifth of his class in mathematics, and it is no wonder that he was with little effort third man from the top in French, for the textbook chosen by Claudius Bérard, in addition to his own grammar and *Lecteur Français*, was the first volume of one of the works John Allan had accused Edgar of wasting his time with — *Gil Blas*. Indeed, the instruction he received in both subjects was more a relief from the regimentation of the rest of his day than an irksome task. Bérard and he had love of French literature and good taste in common; Charles Davies, head of the mathematics department, was a witty and interesting lecturer, and the whole mathematics staff were among the most capable teachers of that subject in the country.

General Winfield Scott visited the Academy, and while he was there he found time to talk to Edgar, whom he had met often at Allan's house. Other visitors from Virginia brought him news of Allan's engagement to Miss Patterson, and after the marriage, which took place in New York on October 5, he waited anxiously to see if his foster father would bring his bride up the river to West Point. When Allan returned to Richmond without making the additional journey, Edgar wrote to him, his only evident coolness appearing in addressing the older man again as "Dear Sir," and in not referring to the marriage at all but only adding "Mrs A" to the group to whom he asked Allan to "give my respects." He asked for materials for his mathematical studies, "or forward to Col: Thayer the means of obtaining them; for as I have no deposit, my more necessary expenditures have run me into debt."

Allan surely heard echoes in this letter of Poe's complaints about being sent to the University of Virginia without enough funds. He bided his time, and Edgar, getting no reply, must have sunk into despair again over his dreamed-of inheritance. For some time he had had doubts about interrupting his career as poet to go to what for him was an extremely elementary school. The fond dream that he could "run thro'" West Point in six months dissolved in the shouts of upperclassmen and the spying of Locke. He began to remember that an officer without a private income was a miserable creature, hardly better off than a sergeant but with more appearances to keep up. He took to tippling regularly at the bottle of brandy always hidden in his room, and although he never appeared drunk during the day, nor was he in any more than high spirits at night, writing lampoons about the officers and organizing the smuggling of contraband, it soon became clear that some change must be made.

Allan provided the impetus. During the Christmas holidays he got hold of the letter that Edgar, in buoyant spirits, had written to "Bully" Graves, and the comment "Mr A is not very often sober" glared at him as if it were written in fire. Allan wrote that he did not want to hear from Edgar again. This letter, wiping out the future Edgar had hoped for, came as a devastating blow; he had forgotten the debt to Graves, and never imagined that the letter would ever be seen by Allan. It had the shock of a bullet wound.

In a tone more severe than his letter from the Court House Tavern nearly four years before, Edgar told over again all his grievances with Allan, and defied him. He asked only one thing — that Allan write his permission for him to resign from the Academy, for then he could collect mileage to his home when he left, a sum of $30.35. If Allan would not do that in ten days, he would neglect his duties to the point of being dismissed. Allan did not get the letter until a week had passed, too late a date to reply, and noted on the back, "I did not from its conclusion deem it necessary to reply. I make this note on the 13th & can see no good Reason to alter my opinion. I do not think the Boy has one good quality. He may do or act as he pleases, tho' I wd have saved him but on his own terms & conditions since I cannot believe a word he writes. His letter is the most barefaced one sided statement." The letter arrived on the tenth, and the thirteenth was the last of Edgar's ten days. Allan was obviously arguing with himself.

Edgar had not waited for a reply. The court-martial for offenses of the past year was already sitting, and he was afraid it would adjourn before his dismissal. Five days after writing, he began absenting himself from roll call; a week later he quit altogether and devoted his time to polishing and making fair copies of his poems. Surely a New York publisher would issue a new volume of his poems, augmented by the decidedly superior ones he had written since *Al Aaraaf*, and if a publisher had any doubts about selling the volume, he would take pledges from the cadets to subscribe to the book. They were sympathetic over his problems, and even the officers cooperated, at least to the extent of advising him to refuse to obey orders to make sure he would be released. The officer of the day called on him Sunday, January 23, 1831, so he could refuse to go to church, and the same thing happened the following Tuesday so he could refuse orders to go to class.

Poe was brought before the court-martial at its last sitting, January 28, pleading "guilty" to refusing to obey orders and "not guilty" to not having obeyed them, making it impossible for the court to show any leniency. He was found guilty on all charges and sentenced to be dismissed from the service of the United States. On February 8 the Secretary of War approved the proceedings, and Poe was scheduled to be dismissed on March 6. But he stayed at the Academy only long enough to get Colonel Thayer's permission to take subscriptions to his book. Certainly there was little reluctance on the part of those young men to subscribe to a volume by one of their number, dedicated to "The U. S. Corps of Cadets," even if it did cost seventy-five cents. Moreover, the rumor got around that the book would include Poe's lampoons on the officers. Edgar did nothing to dispel it.

On February 19 Poe left West Point, nearly penniless, with a bad cold and an infected ear, dressed in the light clothing he had worn from Virginia in May, and too proud to wear his uniform greatcoat. He hired a cheap room in Manhattan and was immediately confined to bed. In desperation he wrote to Allan for help, but no reply ever came. A letter to his brother was equally fruitless; Henry was himself ill and would not last out the year. In two weeks Edgar's health had improved, but his fortune not at all. He wrote Colonel Thayer, asking for a letter of recommendation to the Marquis de Lafayette; his intention was to travel to Paris in order to join the revolutionary Polish army. This too came to nothing. But he started writing again, and he found his publisher, Elam Bliss of 111 Broadway.

Among the works that Poe had read before the Military Academy reduced his wide intellectual curiosity to French, mathematics, and two hours a week in the library were the poems of Thomas Moore and George Sale's *Preliminary Discourse on the Koran*. In these — from the Koran itself, of course — mention is made of "the angel Israfil, who has the most melodious voice of all God's creatures." In Moore's "The Light of the Haram," Israfil sings to the lute, the hearers unable to say whether "voice or lute was most divine." Early in 1831, Pierre Béranger published *Le Réfus*, in which there is reference (in quite different context, it is true) of one whose heart is a hanging lute that, whenever one touches it, resounds. The pieces clicked together in Poe's mind, and in astonishingly little time he produced the plaintive "Israfel," to be added to the new volume.

The galleys of type being set up in the print shop of Elam Bliss made a center around which Poe's life could begin to be re-formed. This book, the best expression of his youthful lyric impulse, was organized with infinite care. All but three of the shorter poems previously printed were weeded out, and among the six new works were poems of such beauty that if he had died in his shabby New York room that spring, only twenty-two years old, he would still be known as one of America's greatest poets.

In addition, Poe included something he had never tried before, a critical essay. At the front of the volume appeared "Letter to Mr. —— ——," beginning, "Dear B ——." In this he pleaded that the best critic of poetry was a poet "on account of his intimate acquaintance with the subject," and went on to oppose the metaphysical in poetry, lambasting Wordsworth with sharp wit. "Yet let not Mr. W. despair; he has given immortality to a wagon, and the bee Sophocles has eternalized a sore toe, and dignified a tragedy with a chorus of turkeys." Coleridge, in spite of metaphysics, he finds admirable, and proves his allegiance by taking his own credo from the *Biographia Literaria*: "A poem, in my opinion, is opposed to a work of science by having, for its *immediate* object, pleasure, not truth; to romance by having for its object an *indefinite* instead of a *definite* pleasure, being a poem only so far as this object is attained; romance presenting perceptible images with definite, poetry with *in*definite sensations, to which end music is an *essential*, since the comprehension of sweet sound is our most indefinite conception. Music, when combined with a pleasurable idea, is poetry; music without the idea is simply music; the idea without the music is prose from its very definiteness." This, rather than the rules of commerce, law, or social custom, was what Edgar Poe was determined to live by.

And much of Madness, and more of Sin
And Horror the soul of the plot.
"The Conqueror Worm"

In April, 1831, *Poems* by Edgar A. Poe, Second Edition, was published. A friendly review, probably by the same Willis who had found Poe's previous volume ridiculous, appeared in the New York *Mirror* May 7, and a briefer notice was printed in the Philadelphia *Casket*. But by then Edgar had left New York, using what remained of his share of the sale to the cadets to carry him to the one refuge he knew, his grandmother's house in Baltimore. He was willing to do anything that would bring in a little money, and shortly after his arrival, hearing that his cousin Neilson had given up his position with William Gwynn, editor of the *Federal Gazette*, he wrote asking for a job. Next he got in touch with Dr. Nathan C. Brooks, who had recently opened a boys' school in a nearby town. There were no openings at either place.

Edgar had by this time formed the habit of working on his writings regularly and diligently. In his leisure moments in the Army, during his travels, and at West Point, he had written a good body of poetry and a smoothly constructed critical essay. He worked as hard as ever in his attic room in the little house on Wilkes Street — although it brought in no money or seemed likely to. Through influence of friends like the outgoing Wirt, he gained access to the Baltimore Library, and he read even more widely than he had before. The Gothic movement in literature was in its fullest and most ridiculous stage, with *Blackwood's Magazine* publishing accounts of the sensations of people in impossible predicaments, and horror and ghost stories appearing everywhere. With his appetite for omnivorous reading, Edgar consumed these along with encyclopedias and works of philosophy, science, and literature. He read everything he could get his hands on.

He was not, however, invited to the Delphian Club, the literary society that his first favorable critic, Neal, had belonged to during his stay in Baltimore, as did William Gwynn and Poe's cousin, Henry Herring. This group had felt their importance enough once to invite Byron to be a member, but the romantic Lord had other things to do. Washington Irving was willing enough, during his visit to the city, to attend a dinner they gave in his honor. Pique at being overlooked by the Delphians and amusement at the unconscious humor in the popular literature he was distracting himself with gave Poe an idea. He would write a book of criticism, poking fun at the current fashion in fiction as sharply as he had "done up" Wordsworth in the "Letter to B ———." He would create the Folio Club, a "Junto of *Dunderheadism*," whose intention was "to abolish Literature, subvert the Press, and overturn the Government of Nouns and Pronouns."

This idea crystallized when, in the June 4 issue of the Philadelphia *Saturday Courier*, he read the announcement of a contest in which one hundred dollars would be given the best short story submitted by December 1. Nearly seven months; he could write a whole book in that time! Soon the ideas were clear in his mind. The members of the club would be American imitators of more famous contemporary authors. They would meet once a month for dinner, and each would read a tale prepared for the occasion. The author whose effort was voted the best would be president for the next meeting; the one whose work was least approved must provide the dinner and wine. The tales would be parodies of popular works, the members' comments a burlesque on criticism.

Edgar set to work. He would naturally satirize the precious N. P. Willis, who had abused *Al Aaraaf*; Willis's "Editor's Table" in the *American Monthly Magazine* presented the columnist as perpetually reclining on an ottoman, eating olives, and thinking delicate thoughts. *Blackwood's Magazine* deserved to be satirized too. Moreover, Poe had found wearisome the historical novels of the time, set in the Holy Land, and with more instruction than literature in them. The worst of these was Horace Smith's *Zilla, A Tale of the Holy City*. There should also be "in imitation of the German" a horror story with ancient families and tongue-twisting names, and a story of pointless philosophical disputation, with the Devil in it.

For the "quiz on Willis" Poe wrote a short piece, larded with French, called "The Duke de l'Omelette," in which a sensitive French nobleman dies of shock at being served an ortolan without paper ruffles, and finding himself in hell, plays cards with the Devil for his soul and wins. Even the punch line, when the Duke, exiting, offers the polite compliment that if he were not de l'Omelette he would have no objection at all to being the Devil, was written in French. The story satirized Willis in its very flimsiness, but the point was made perfectly clear by the Duke's implausibly elegant manners, his enumeration of the fashionable shops where his clothes were made, the outré description of the Devil's "apartment," lighted by a ruby hung on a chain whose farther end was lost, "like Coleridge," in the clouds, by the extreme statuary, and, above all, by the opening, in which de l'Omelette is reclining languidly, as

Willis was always describing himself, on an ottoman, eating an olive "to restrain his feelings."

In the philosophical satire "A Bargain Lost," Poe invented a restaurateur, Pedro Garcia of Venice, dressed in fantastic clothing, who is completing a manuscript entitled "A complete exposition of things not to be exposed" when the Devil calls on him. They get drunk together, and the Devil confesses that he has a great deal of trouble keeping himself supplied with his favorite food — fresh souls, preferably of philosophers — and displays bills of sale in which several eminent persons, among them Voltaire, have agreed to sell their souls *"vivente corpore."* Being a philosopher, and intrigued by the gastronomic concept of fricasseed soul, Pedro offers his, only to be rebuffed by evasions such as "Am supplied at present," "Have no cash on hand"; and in his effort to fling a bottle at the Devil instead knocks down a hanging lamp which in turn prostrates him. Although the general effect was different, the presence of the Devil and some details, such as the hanging lamp, were enough like "The Duke de l'Omelette" to arouse cries of plagiarism in the Folio Club. There was even an ottoman.

The Jerusalem story was a weak joke — Jews besieged in the Temple bargaining with their besiegers for a sheep for the sacrifice and receiving instead a pig — filled out with mock erudition on the topography and customs of the Holy City and burlesques of Hebrew words and names, one of which, Abel Shittim, leads to a scatological punch line. The parody of *Blackwood's* outdid even that magazine's penchant for getting a character into a difficult situation and then philosophizing and analyzing his feelings. "A Decided Loss" is told in the first person by a man who literally loses his breath. First he memorizes two plays about Indians so he can communicate with people in grunts. After a night in a stagecoach so crowded that it dislocates all his limbs, he is taken for a corpse, but he escapes from a garret where he had been locked awaiting burial only to land in an executioner's cart, where he is mistaken for a mail robber and hanged. In the same bland, digressive style his partial dissection is described ("Having deprived me of both my ears, he discovered signs of animation"); also his being subjected to the effect of a galvanic battery, and his death, in a fit of kicking and plunging: "All this was, however, attributed to the effect of the new Galvanic Battery, which the apothecary, upon learning my situation, had brought with him, and from the moment of his entrance to that of my decease, which took place a few minutes afterwards, had never ceased to apply with the most unremitting assiduity."

Even based on a bad pun and written in an excruciatingly calm and reflective style, the story has moments of truly effective horror in it, for mingled with absurdities are details so terrifyingly real, such as a cat fight that takes place on the victim's face, that the reader is nearly ready to accept the story on its own grounds, only to be brought up short by the next absurdity. When Poe came to write his satire on the sort of German horror story that had been made famous by E. T. W. Hoffmann, this fastidiousness in detail produced an entirely different effect from the one he was seeking.

He found parody very easy in the other stories; all that was necessary was to carry the excesses of the originals just a little farther. In "Metzengerstein," however, his sense of empathy took over, and in the feud between the family of the orphaned Baron Metzengerstein and the vigorous old hunter Count Berlifitzing, he began seeing the young man as himself and John Allan as the Count. The narrative is ridiculous enough — a horse in a tapestry becomes real and is possessed by the spirit of Berlifitzing, who had died in a fire set by the young Baron. Metzengerstein becomes obsessed with the horse, and eventually he rides it to his death in the burning of his own castle, after which the smoke from the fire takes the shape of a gigantic horse. But too many of the feelings of this character were Poe's own, and he was too attracted by the similarity of the setting of the story with his own dream-world, in which he was always rich and of ancient family but possessed of a tragic flaw that caused his destruction. The joke did not come off, the story was not funny — but because of the sincerity of the author's feelings, it was more effective as horror than most examples of the type it was intended to parody.

Somewhat puzzled by his failure at satire that had resulted in something new in literature, Edgar worked on at his stories, never content with their form but always revising, and suffering his poverty with more composure than he ever had before. In the beginning of August his brother Henry died; consumption, in the manner in which it received its name, had used up the young man's body, and Poe wrote into "Metzengerstein," "I would wish all I love to perish of that gentle disease. How glorious! to depart in the hey-day of the young blood — the heart all passion — the imagination all fire — amid the remembrances of happier days — in the fall of the year, and so be buried up forever in the gorgeous, autumnal leaves."

In September a more painful illness was evident in the city. Baltimore then reached the peak of a plague of cholera, and Edgar wrote into his "A Bargain Lost," the story of Pedro Garcia, the Devil's opinion of the souls of physicians: " 'Don't mention them,' here the stranger retched violently, 'ugh! I never tried but one, that rascal — (ugh!) — Hippocrates. Smelt of asafoetida — (ugh! ugh!) — took particular pains with the villain too — caught a wretched cold washing him in the Styx — and, after all, he gave me the cholera morbus.' "

Writing "Metzengerstein" did more for Poe than convince him that he was capable of writing a moving tale. It served also as effective therapy in helping him sort out his feelings about

John Allan. Destroying Allan's image in the story — and then being destroyed by it — dissolved all his resentment, and on October 16 he wrote Allan a letter full of dignified humility, apologizing for his practice in the past of only writing when he needed money, and regretting that not only had he not heard from Allan for a long time, but that he had had no news of him either. "I have always applied to you," he wrote, "but it is only at such a time as the present when I can write to you with the consciousness of making no application for assistance, that I dare to open my heart, or speak one word of old affection." He ended by saying that he was "wretchedly poor," but that he was out of difficulty and out of debt. But he spoke too soon.

In less than three weeks an old debt came back to haunt him. It may have been the long unpaid note to Sergeant Graves; at any rate, there was a warrant out, and Edgar was in serious danger of going to debtors' prison. He held out as long as he could, then appealed to Allan for eighty dollars. When two more weeks passed with no response, Mrs. Clemm wrote Allan saying that she had managed to raise twenty dollars, but it was not enough to get Edgar out of trouble. This moved Allan to write to John Walsh, in Baltimore, instructing him to have Edgar released from prison (although he had not actually been imprisoned), and to give him twenty dollars besides; but he neglected to mail the letter. Poe wrote twice again, at two-week intervals, but it was not until January 12, 1832, that Allan sent the assistance the young man pathetically begged of him. He probably had been at his plantation for the Christmas season, and on his return he carried the letter to the post office himself. By then Edgar had probably found some way out of his difficulties, and feeling that his "Pa" had betrayed him, he cut the older man from his memory, not communicating with him again for more than a year.

Still another disappointment came at the same time. The five "Tales of the Folio Club" had been sent to the Philadelphia *Saturday Courier* before the deadline of December 1, and on the last day of the year, shortly after Poe had sent his last fruitless letter to Allan, the prize was announced. One hundred dollars had been awarded to Delia S. Bacon for a sentimental story entitled "Love's Martyr." Miss Bacon was to go on writing this sort of thing, turning out soppy novels, championing Francis Bacon as the author of Shakespeare's works, and eventually dying mad. But Poe had no prize, and the *Courier* had his stories. They published all five, beginning with "Metzengerstein," at regular intervals through the year 1832.

Yet the world went on, and Edgar swallowed his disappointment and kept on writing. William Wirt had been nominated for the Presidency of the United States the previous September on the Anti-Masonic ticket; and following the Anti-Masons' lead, the National Republicans and the Democrats adopted the use of a national nominating convention, selecting Henry Clay and the incumbent Jackson as their respective candidates. All three conventions took place in Baltimore. While the delegates shouted in their halls and got drunk in the local taverns, Edgar kept to his writing table, turning out new stories and revising the old.

Having avoided debtors' prison, with stories being published, even though there was no pay for them, Edgar began to be interested in the sort of amusements that bachelors of twenty-three usually are. He rediscovered that he was attractive to women, with his courtly manners, military posture, and romantic background. Shortage of clothing led him to wear his West Point overcoat in cold weather, and rather than making him look ridiculous, it appealed to the sentimental nature of the girls who saw him. He wrote verses in their autograph albums and engaged in flirtatious games, but without seriousness.

For more wistful romanticizing he still had two sketches he had made before 1826 of Elmira Royster, whom he was coming more and more to identify with the security and comfort of his lost Richmond home.

The truth of the matter, unrecognized by Poe, was that he had not changed but the country had. Not only were his Richmond manners more courtly than those of Baltimore, but they were out of date in Jacksonian America. Aristocracy of birth and land ownership was well on the way to being supplanted by the dominance of the businessman. There was now universal white male suffrage. And greater and greater numbers of Irish and German immigrants were flowing into the country, populating the Eastern cities as New Englanders and others of the Northern and Middle states moved West. Railroads were spreading through the land, and the opening of the Southwest was already wreaking ruin on all of his old friends of the landed gentry who were not willing to recognize that slave breeding, for sale "down the river," was their only economic salvation.

However, Poe was making male friends too, among them newspapermen like John Hewitt, and Lambert Wilmer of the Baltimore *Saturday Visiter*. He showed them his stories (Hewitt was actually mentioned in "A Decided Loss"), and in August an editorial in the *Visiter* commented favorably on them, promising "With Mr. Poe's permission we may hereafter lay one or two of the tales before our readers." Their publication in the Philadelphia paper probably prevented this, for they never appeared.

In the six new stories he was working on, Poe found much the same thing happening to his satire as had happened with "Metzengerstein." Exaggerating the excesses of his models did not make them funny, since he almost unavoidably created atmosphere that would have made anything credible. The result was greater horror than existed in the original, and since it was believable — at least while being read — the parody was not comic but was also effective as horror. Thus his attempt at a mock sea story — poking fun at Jane Porter's *Sir Edward Seaward's Narrative* or *Symzonia* by "Captain Adam Seaborn," the pseudonym of John Cleve Symmes — although full of absurdities such as a ship that grows like a living thing and a narrator who keeps a diary through storm and shipwreck and casts it adrift in a bottle when his last ship sinks, became the powerful "MS. Found in a Bottle." Poe's knowledge of the sea was profound enough for him to use an excessive amount of technical language probably intending to compound the absurdity. Instead it made the story remarkably real.

A downright cribbing from Hoffmann's *Doge und Dogaressa* gained a tension totally missing in the original through the drawing of the main character, which was obviously based on Poe's Byronic image of himself. In "Epimanes," another historical piece on the ancient Middle East, Poe created a grotesque fable of remarkable effectiveness, in spite of his painstaking efforts to mimic the ridiculousness of the "dear reader" style so beloved of Scott and other devotees of that painfully leisurely manner of narration. Only in two works, "Lionizing" and a parody of the ridiculous Irish stories of Lady Morgan, did his efforts come out simply funny, for the sheer flimsiness of incident in them gave Poe no basis to work in atmosphere.

By the following spring his Folio Club seemed to be complete, with eleven tales and eleven members invented for the club, among them himself as author of "Lionizing," the story that would be voted worst, leading him (as a character in his own fiction) to publish the lot as an exposé of the club's pretensions. They were (in Poe's manuscript) to meet at the house of Mr. Rouge-et-Noir, who wrote the story voted worst at the previous meeting. "The members generally, were most remarkable men. There was, first of all, Mr. Snap, the President, who is a very lank man with a hawk nose, and was formerly in the service of the Down-East Review. Then there was Mr. Convulvulus Gondola, a young man who had travelled a good deal. Then there was De Rerum Naturâ, Esqr., who wore a very singular pair of green spectacles. Then there was a very little man in a black coat with very black eyes. Then there was Mr. Solomon Seadrift who had every appearance of a fish. Then there was Mr. Horribile Dictu, with white eyelashes, who had graduated at Göttingen. Then there was Mr. Blackwood Blackwood who had written certain articles for foreign magazines. Then there was the host, Mr. Rouge-et-Noir, who admired Lady Morgan. Then there was a stout gentleman who admired Sir Walter Scott. Then there was Chronologos Chronology who admired Horace Smith, and had a very big nose which had been in Asia Minor."

Despair settled down again on Poe in the spring of 1833. Possibly he had heard as well that John Allan was ailing, but in any event he wrote "one more attempt to interest you in my behalf." The note was short but asked for help, stating that Edgar was without friends, without means of obtaining employment, and in deep want. When he received it, Allan read through his file of Edgar's letters, and on the fiercely belligerent letter that announced the boy's determination to quit West Point, wrote, "Suffice it to say my only regret is in Pity for his failings — his Talents are of an order that can never prove a comfort to their possessor." Thus ended the relationship between the good-hearted but stubborn and suspicious Scotish merchant and the boy he had reared to be a gentleman and then recoiled from because he had succeeded too well. Allan died the following spring, remembering even his illegitimate children in his will and long-pondered codicils, but not mentioning Edgar Allan Poe.

On April 20, the *Visiter* printed Poe's new poem, "Serenade," and two weeks later Edgar shipped off a copy of "Epimanes" to the *New England Magazine*, offering as well all the "Tales of the Folio Club" to them. They did not respond. But on June 15, the *Visiter* announced a prize contest — fifty dollars for the best tale and twenty-five for the best poem to be submitted by October 1. Edgar made clean copies of his new tales and bound them in a small quarto volume. Along with them he sent a new poem, "The Coliseum." On October 12 the prizes were announced. The judges, three men of letters of Baltimore, among them John P. Kennedy, the well-known novelist, had found "The Tales of the Folio Club" unquestionably the best submitted, and for the prize they chose "MS. Found in a Bottle," not because it was better done than the others but because of its originality and length. It filled just four columns in the *Visiter* of October 19, 1833. The poetry prize went to the editor of the *Visiter* (who had submitted his verses under an assumed name), but Edgar was told that had he not won the greater prize, the one for poetry would have gone to him. "The Coliseum" was printed in the issue of October 26, along with an advertisement of the proposed publication, by subscription, of a volume of "The Tales of the Folio Club." But that announcement was premature.

Thus on the coffin loud and long
I strike — the murmur sent
Through the gray chambers to my song
Shall be the accompaniment . . .

"A Pæan"

ALTHOUGH HE HAD COME TO KNOW the members of the *Visiter* staff, Poe had never met any of the committee who awarded him the prize, so immediately upon discovering the lines PRIZE TALE BY EDGAR A. POE in the first column of the paper, he dressed himself as neatly as he could in his now threadbare clothes and called on each of the three to introduce himself and thank them. John H. B. Latrobe was in his office in the Mechanics' Bank building when the erect and poised young man, dressed entirely in black, entered and introduced himself. His frock coat was buttoned up to his black stock, so that not a particle of white showed. Latrobe noticed that "Coat, hat, boots, and gloves had very evidently seen their best days, but so far as mending and brushing go, everything had been done, apparently, to make them presentable. On most men his clothes would have looked shabby and seedy, but there was something about this man that prevented one from criticising his garments." This judgment Latrobe arrived at after Poe's departure; while he was present his manner drew attention away from details of his shabby dress.

In his melodic, almost rhythmical voice, Poe started telling

Latrobe about a story he was then writing, about a voyage to the moon, and, growing excited, waved his hands; and at the point where the moon's gravity overcame that of the earth on the balloon, causing a "bouleversement," he clapped his hands and stamped his foot by way of emphasis. Striking as this interview was to Latrobe, Poe was himself more impressed with meeting John P. Kennedy, a prominent attorney who had, the year before, published *Swallow Barn*, and was then working on another novel, *Horse-Shoe Robinson*, that would be even more highly acclaimed. Kennedy was full of practical literary advice, and as a result they selected "The Visionary" from the Folio Club tales and sent it off to *Godey's Lady's Book*. Poe might have also traded a bit on his acquaintance with the son of the editor, Mrs. Sarah Josepha Hale, who had been at West Point with him. The story was published in the January number, and a few more dollars were added to the fifty from the prize. With rent to pay and food to buy, none was left to replace Edgar's clothes, however. So long as they held together they would have to do.

Poe entered into the year 1834 with some local fame and a great deal of hope. Rumor has it that he went to Richmond in the early spring and called at the familiar house on Fifth and Main. A strange woman — the new Mrs. Allan — answered the door, and when she told him that Allan was too ill to receive visitors, he strode past her and went upstairs to the older man's bedroom. Allan raised his cane threateningly, and without a word, Edgar turned and left. The end was near. On March 27 Allan died, and it can be certain that Poe made careful inquiries about the will, which was entered into probate May 8. Allan had made a mess of the matter, employing an incompetent to draw the document in the first place, and then adding two codicils, the last, written less than two weeks before his death, with no purpose but to state that his illegitimate twins were conceived before his marriage to his present wife, and to cancel the bequest to the one of them who had died. His wife had to renounce her executorship and let the estate be untangled by the court. In any case, Edgar got nothing, but litigation merely extended the time through which his hopes were sinking.

Nothing came of the proposed subscription by which the "Tales of the Folio Club" were to be published, so Kennedy submitted the manuscript — the same one that had been offered for the prize — to Carey and Lea, his own publisher, and Edgar continued writing stories. The one about a voyage to the moon was called "Hans Phaall, a Tale," and is a kind of double hoax, purporting to be the account of a hoax played on the people of Rotterdam by a bellows-mender named Hans Phaall. At noon a miniature balloon, piloted by a dwarf, descends on the central square of the city and a manuscript is dropped, addressed to "their Excellencies Von Underduk and Rub-a-dub, President, and Vice President of the States' College of Astronomers, in the city of Rotterdam." In it Phaall claims that recent interest in politics has ruined his business, since instead of using bellows, the citizens fan their fires with the newspapers all are now buying. Besieged by creditors, he writes, he prepared a balloon and equipment for a trip to the moon, then ascended, after lighting a fuse to four hundred pounds of gunpowder, which blew up the "duns." In exchange for pardon for that offense, he offers information on the moon and its inhabitants, of which the dwarf is intended to be a sample. But he has flown off, and so the phlegmatic Dutchmen see no way of delivering the pardon.

The body of the story is an ingenious and carefully reasoned speculation on the difficulties to be encountered in space flight, told in a remarkably realistic manner, down to the assumption that there is no "limit beyond which *no* atmosphere is to be found," and that the farther the balloon travels from the center of the earth, the less effect gravity would have on it, thus the faster it would rise. In the style of *Robinson Crusoe*, Poe invented all sorts of dangers and difficulties for his voyager — he is thrown from the balloon by the force of the explosion that canceled out his creditors, is supported by a rope entangled in his foot, and crawls back with the aid of his belt; he rises through a thundercloud; to relieve the pain of low atmospheric pressure he bleeds himself; he is bombarded with volcanic fragments (which, Poe claims, is what meteoric stones really are!); and only at the last minute is he able to check the rate of his acceleration by lightening the car. This was the longest story Poe had ever written, and it is likely that, with a little encouragement, he would have continued it with an account of life on the moon, in the manner of *Gulliver's Travels*. But instead he set out writing more Folio Club tales, probably mindful that the *Visiter* had chosen "MS. Found in a Bottle" from them not only because of its originality, but because of its length; and "Hans Phaall" was already more than four times as long.

In "Berenice" more than in any previous story, the parody is carried to absolute horror, even though the incidents are more ridiculous than anything to be found in *Blackwood's*; for the characters, although abnormal, are real, and their peculiar actions are perfectly motivated by their physical and mental condition. Egœus is a young man whose "intensity of interest" is so great that he spends hours entranced with "some frivolous device upon the margin, or in the typography of a book . . . a quaint shadow falling aslant upon the tapestry, or upon the floor." His heightened "attentiveness" is at length focused on the teeth of his cousin and bride-to-be, an epileptic. Eventually her illness strikes her down, and some time after the funeral he recovers from one of his deep studies to discover that while in his trance he had dug up the body and had extracted the teeth; but Berenice had herself been buried alive while in a deep fit, and the pain had brought her back to consciousness so that the servants, summoned by her cries, found her disfigured but still breathing by her grave.

This ludicrous story was turned into a piece of almost disgusting horror by the same means that "Metzengerstein" gained terror that is "not of Germany but of the soul —" in that it symbolized his feelings for someone close to him, not John Allan this time, but his cousin Virginia, who was beginning to occupy more and more of his thoughts. After the death of Henry Poe the Clemms had moved to a tiny house in Amity Street, and before long Mrs. Clemm's son had had enough of their grinding poverty, and left home never to return. Mrs. Clemm had her hands full cooking, mending, and taking care of her invalid mother, so that the other two members of the household were thrown more closely together. Virginia was twelve and could hardly be dismissed as a little girl any longer; She was almost at the age Elmira had been when Edgar and she were "engaged." For four years they had been living under the same roof, sharing the same experiences, as close as brother and sister, and yet not brother and sister.

Virginia was bright and cheerful and could share his joys and console his disappointments. She had always been pretty, and as she grew, the woman she was to be began to be visible in her, as, in the manner of girls at the edge of puberty, an occasional pose or gesture would create the illusion of maturity. In the story, Egœus, like the Baron Metzengerstein, has the wealth and ancient family Edgar dreamed of for himself. "Berenice and I were cousins, and we grew up together in my paternal halls — Yet differently we grew. I ill of health and buried in gloom — she agile, graceful, and overflowing with energy." A disease falls on the girl — as the shadow of tuberculosis hung over the real Virginia — while Egœus aggravated his "mono-mania" with opium. Edgar had once, on the occasion of a champagne supper with some West Point friends, come home drunk; and since there was generally some liquor in the house — it was cheap enough then — he surely knew well the heightened sense of attention that is one of the first effects of alcohol, but here he attributed it to the more exotic drug.

Analyzing his own musings, distinguishing between the kind of concentration on an object that sets up associations leading far afield and the kind of trancelike attention that gives the object "refracted and unreal importance," Edgar, through Egœus, says, "my disorder revelled in the less important but more startling changes wrought in the *physical* frame of Berenice, and in the singular and most appalling distortion of her personal identity." She appeals to him as an idea, rather than as an object of love; but Berenice loved him, and so he "spoke of marriage."

Even in Poe's efforts to create ridiculous details — Berenice grows taller as a result of her malady, and the strain turns her blond hair black — there are hints of the changes taking place in Virginia and the shift of his attention to her from the women of "hyacinth hair" of his youth. The story ceased to be ridiculous to him, and he used greatest delicacy in the last paragraphs, where a servant tells of the opened grave, then points out the muddy, bloodstained clothing of Egœus, the spade, and finally the ebony box out of which fall dental instruments "intermingled with many white and glistening substances."

Gradually Poe was becoming aware that he could create the most effective atmosphere of horror by feeling horror himself, and this he could do by writing of harm befalling those he most cherished. One of the pseudoscientific details so effective in "Hans Phaall" was having the voyager take with him a cat that has kittens in the rarefied upper atmosphere. This was to show that low air pressure was not permanently harmful but only something that one needed get used to, since the kittens did not share their mother's discomfort; but at a climax in the story he had the felines fall from the balloon. Considering Poe's great affection for cats, this was intended to be a shocking incident; nine years later, in "The Black Cat," he described the hanging of a cat as a sin beyond the mercy of God to forgive, and when the character in that story kills his wife too, and dismembers her, he is caught as a result of his bad conscience *over the cat.*

In November, Edgar wrote John Kennedy, asking if Carey and Lea could not be prevailed upon to give him an advance on the Folio Club tales, adding a cock-and-bull story about having had an annuity from John Allan that had stopped, along with his hopes for an inheritance, with Allan's death. Carey replied — just as Kennedy was leaving for nearly a month's stay at Annapolis — that the book would probably return no profit, but he offered to sell some of the tales to the publishers of annuals. These ornate volumes were anthologies of prose and poetry, lavishly illustrated with "art studies," and they paid better than the magazines. Without communicating with Poe, who was in the meantime becoming very hard up, Kennedy agreed, and on December 22 he was able to ask Poe to call on him to receive fifteen dollars from the *Atlantic Souvenir.* Thus the Clemms and Poe had a merry Christmas, even if it was not a lavish one.

During the previous August a printer in Richmond, Thomas W. White, had founded the *Southern Literary Messenger.* James E. Heath, a literary-minded politician, had agreed to serve temporarily without pay as editor. It was to this magazine that Kennedy next suggested Poe submit his work, and still careful not to submit anything that might be published elsewhere, Edgar sent "Berenice." He was not aware that the story that bought his Christmas dinner was "MS. Found in a Bottle," but thought that Miss Leslie of the *Souvenir* had chosen another. The *Messenger* not only took "Berenice" and invited further stories, but offered Poe books to review, and this raised the spirits of the family at Number 3 Amity Street still more, even though the actual income to be expected did not warrant it.

In the middle of March, 1835, Edgar saw an advertisement in the paper offering a teaching job, and he wrote Kennedy asking his support for the position. Kennedy sent a note back inviting Poe to dinner, causing excitement, consternation, and then despair. Edgar's suit had responded to its last brushing and mending. Reluctantly he abandoned the dignity with which he had borne himself previously before the novelist and wrote, "Your kind invitation to dinner today has wounded me to the quick. I cannot come — and for reasons of the most humiliating nature — my personal appearance. You may conceive my deep mortification in making this disclosure to you — but it was necessary. If you will be my friend so far as to loan me $20 I will call on you tomorrow — otherwise it will be impossible, and I must submit to my fate." Kennedy responded generously, buying him clothing, giving him food, and even providing him with the use of a horse from his stable for exercise.

Edgar did not get the teaching position — the commissioners seem to have been optimistic in offering it at all — but Kennedy did write to the proprietor of the *Messenger*, explaining, "He is at work upon a tragedy, but I have turned him to drudging upon whatever may make money," and suggesting that Poe contribute something to every number of the magazine, "and that you might find it to your advantage to give him some permanent employ." The tragedy was *Politian*, based on the so-called "Kentucky Tragedy" that had been in the papers throughout Poe's last youthful year in Richmond. Jeroboam O. Beauchamp had killed his wife's seducer, Solomon P. Sharp, the Attorney General of Kentucky; then his wife committed suicide, and he attempted it the day he was scheduled to be hanged. Any number of writers treated the case, Thomas Holley Chivers using it as the source for his *Conrad and Eudora*, as did Charles Fenno Hoffman in *Greyslaer* and William Gilmore Simms in *Beauchamp*. Poe's version was set in Italy, with some details borrowed from his "Visionary"; but it was inferior as poetry to his other work, and Kennedy was right in thinking that it would bring in no money.

The theme he had turned up in "Berenice" had so struck Poe's fancy that he turned to another variation of it in "Morella." This time the woman is a scholar and the attraction intellectual: "my soul, from our first meeting, burned with fires it has never known — but the fires were not of Eros. . . . Yet we met: and Fate bound us together at the altar: and I never spoke of love, or thought of passion." Under her instruction, he becomes obsessed with speculation on the notion of identity *"which at death is or is not lost forever,"* until she and her philosophy became one in his interest, and eventually the person faded as the idea grew. She dies, bearing a daughter with uncanny resemblance, even in learning, to the mother. When, at the age of ten, the daughter is baptized, he impulsively gives her the name Morella; at which point she responds, "I am here!" and dies. When she is buried, "I found no traces of the first in the charnel where I laid the second — Morella."

This story bears little resemblance to his relationship with Virginia, although the child "grew strangely in stature and intelligence," so that at the age of ten she was identical with her mother; although everything about that unlikely event save the girl's early age serves in the story as an answer to the narrator's speculation about the nature of identity and its meaning in terms of personal immortality. Poe would later return to fictional investigation of his feelings toward his cousin; in the meantime the story pleased White, who had considered "Berenice" "by far too horrible," even though he published it in the March issue.

"Morella" appeared in the April *Messenger* along with a scathing review of *Confessions of a Poet*. This book, published anonymously, was by Laughton Osborn, although Poe guessed it was the work of John Neal. In the manner in which he was to gain the reputation of being a literary hatchet man, Poe devastated the book, saying, "The author has very few claims to the sacred name he has thought proper to assume." This aroused the Richmond *Courier and Daily Compiler* to an article attacking Poe's criticism on the ground that he had not read the book. Edgar talked White out of replying to the article, pointing out that the only basis for such a claim was that the newspaper disagreed with his opinions, and commented, "If this is a good reason one way it is equally good another — ergo — *He* has not read the book because he disagrees with me — Neither of us having read it then, it is better to say no more about it." Incompetent as Poe was in business matters, he was already a canny journalist.

There was no question that Poe had found his market. He submitted "Lionizing" and "Hans Phaall," which were published in the May and June issues respectively. For May he also wrote three long reviews — of his friend Kennedy's *Horse-Shoe Robinson*, of *I Promessi Sposi*, and of the *Journal* of Frances Anne Butler (Fanny Kemble). In these he showed that his critical writing could be as assured and pungent in praise as it was in ridicule. He accurately placed Manzoni's novel in relation to other works of the time, and called attention to its publication "equal in matter to any two of Cooper's novels, and executed at least as well, which we receive at the moderate price of forty-two cents!" In the breezy review of the British actress's observations of life in the United States he welcomed her criticisms but boggled at her frequent mannerisms of vocabulary, then found her insufficiently "feminine" in her manner of stating opinions. The June *Messenger* carried his review of Dr. Robert M. Bird's complex historical novel *The Infidel*, in which Poe summed up the characters and incidents with dexterity rare in the most experienced of reviewers.

Heath left the magazine in April, and Edward V. Sparhawk took over the editorship temporarily. Edgar was obviously maneuvering to be offered the job next, offering technical advice — often very good advice — to White in the letters he was now writing him regularly. At the end of May, acknowledging payment of $9.94 for the twelve-and-a-fraction columns he had filled in that month's issue, he commented on the arrest of William Gwynn Jones for pilfering money from the mails; in "A Decided Loss" Edgar had recommended hanging as a punishment for mail robbers, and the arrest was even more meaningful to him since Jones had been brought up by William Gwynn (former employer of Neilson Poe) much as he had been by John Allan, except that the criminal had stayed in his benefactor's good graces.

The strain of scurrying around Baltimore working up publicity for the *Messenger* in addition to keeping up his strenuous writing schedule told on Poe by the end of May, and he became very ill. But in spite of the gloomy prognosis by Dr. Buckler, husband of one of the *Messenger* contributors, "that nothing but a sea-voyage would save me," he was fully recovered by the middle of June and hard at work on a long review of the second edition of Justice Marshall's *Washington*. White wrote him on June 18, and after criticizing the punctuation in the copy Poe was submitting, sounded him out on coming to Richmond. Edgar replied that he was "anxious to settle myself in that city," and asked White to look out for any employment he might get there, strongly hinting that he wanted to work on the *Messenger*. As further evidence of his ability, he suggested a change in the typography of the magazine, a change which White eventually accepted. Edgar was delighted at this opportunity, but it must have caused some consternation to Mrs. Clemm to see how anxious he was to go back to the place of his childhood.

Through the summer trickles of money came in from the magazine — Poe complained once that he had been underpaid for "Hans Phaall" — and new stories went out. One of them was a parody of a passage in Disraeli's *Vivian Grey*, "King Pest the First, A Tale Containing an Allegory." This is a vivid and amusing account of drunken sailors in plague-ridden London, who encounter a company of looters drinking in a deserted undertaker's shop and playing at being the court of "King Pest the First." The sailors intrude, upset a barrel of ale, and carry off the women, proving, it seems, that if one is going to drink he had better get roaring drunk. Another tale, "Shadow, A Fable," is written in the style of "Siope," and is a fanciful account of the rain of meteors and cholera plague that Poe had witnessed in Baltimore. In addition to writing new stories he continued revision of the old, and he recast "A Bargain Lost" completely, retitling it "Bon-Bon," filling it with details of French cuisine, and making it in general much more amusing. Eventually he considered the story sufficiently changed to submit to the *Messenger*, even though its prototype had appeared in the Philadelphia *Saturday Courier* two and a half years before.

On July 7 old Mrs. Poe died, seventy-nine years old; and along with the burden she had been to the family disappeared

also her pension. Now Edgar was the sole support of his aunt
and cousin, and the small sums he had been getting for writing
— twenty dollars had thus far been the most he could gain
a month — showed little sign of making up for the income they
had lost. Mrs. Clemm began to be deeply worried over the
future for her daughter and herself; and Edgar, in addition
to hinting broadly that it was time for White to put him on
the payroll, set about writing to all the prominent Poes in the
country, looking for a benefactor for her. Eventually the call
came from White, and in spite of Mrs. Clemm's trepidations,
Edgar set out proudly and happily to take his post as editor of
the *Southern Literary Messenger*.

The ring is on my hand
And the wreath is on my brow;
Satins and jewels grand
Are all at my command
And I am happy now.

"Bridal Ballad"

FOR THE SECOND TIME since childhood Poe returned triumph-
antly to Richmond. But this time he could not, as before, go
from the wharf to the stately house at Fifth and Main, nor
need he fear what John Allan's greeting would be. He took his
trunk to a boardinghouse and called on his new employer.
Thomas White was hardly the literary associate Poe could
have hoped for — he was a simple printer and cautious businessman — but he was cordial if perhaps a bit paternal in his
attitude. He did not give Edgar the title of editor but took
him a month "on trial" as his own assistant, at the salary of
ten dollars a week. Poe's contributions to the magazine would
be paid for as before. But although White considered the
young man as merely his helper and secretary, Edgar considered himself editor of the magazine.

It was a tremendous satisfaction, after eight years of struggle,
finally to be a professional literary man. The editorial offices
that he had addressed, sometimes timidly, sometimes exuber-
antly, faded in importance at the thought of his own editorial
desk. Here the manuscripts of hopeful authors would come,

and the books for review. Even though he was on the other side of the fence now, he remembered the suspense of waiting for an answer about a submitted tale, the pain he had felt when a review curtly dismissed a book of his poems while it praised at great length a piece of puffed-up nonsense by some member of the ruling clique — and he remembered with gratitude the heart-swelling joy he had felt when John Neal lauded his *Al Aaraaf*. He wrote four reviews for the September issue, finding something good to say about each of the books while keeping a sternly high standard. In his review of the *Gift* he said nothing of his own "MS. Found in a Bottle," although it rankled him that Miss Leslie, in spite of his writing her that the story had already been published elsewhere, had not used "Epimanes" or "Siope" instead. The *Messenger* had already reprinted his "Visionary" from *Godey's*, and the totally revised "Bon-Bon," so he inserted three stories, one also extensively revised from the *Courier*, and, out of deference to White's attractive daughter, a poem beginning, "Eliza! — let thy generous heart / From its present pathway part not!" It was a very useful poem, with applicability to Eliza White, Eliza Herring, and Virginia Eliza Clemm.

It was a social triumph, too, to be back in Richmond. There were many old friends to see, and Southern hospitality flowed freely for the "wastrel" who had surprised his friends as well as his foes by breaking into prominence in the world of letters. Indeed, it flowed more freely for the man than it had when he was a boy, since now simple courtesy required that he be offered a toddy on his arrival, when he came calling, and a cordial before leaving. If the ladies invited him for tea, someone would certainly see to it that he had something "a little stronger" at some interlude in the ceremony, and after dinner the gentlemen would remain around the table sampling the host's brandy after the female exit to the drawing room. Edgar soon began finding himself groggy and depressed in the mornings, with no clear idea of how he had got to bed.

Moreover, there were constant letters from Mrs. Clemm to worry him, complaining about insecurity and ill health. He wrote his cousin William Poe, a well-to-do citizen of Augusta, Georgia, soliciting help for her and Virginia. With ten dollars a week coming in, plus occasional sums for contributions, and four dollars going out for his weekly board, he had more money to spare than he had had for years, but it did not seem to last. He saw Elmira Royster on the street — now Mrs. Shelton — and not long after that, he discovered he could get through the morning less painfully by starting the day with a pick-me-up.

He began planning to bring the Clemms to Richmond, but toward the end of August, Mrs. Clemm wrote that Neilson Poe had offered to take Virginia and herself into his home, and the thought of his "Sissy" in the hands of that sanctimonious man was excruciating to him. He wrote his aunt in a frenzy, pleading his great love for Virginia, and overestimating his income. Supporting them would reduce his present salary to virtually nothing, but even though they would hamper the social life he was enjoying — enjoying all but during the mornings after — he missed the home life that was as necessary for him as financial security. "Ask Virginia," he wrote. "Leave it to her."

This worry hung over him for two more weeks, and on September 11 he wrote Kennedy a strange letter, half in gratitude for the job the novelist had secured for him, half a cry of despair. He defined his feelings as a "depression of spirits," and asked for consolation. Then he calmed down and added a postscript conveying White's request that Kennedy submit something for the magazine, and on the back of the page, in still more confident tones, he discussed some of his own liter-

ary achievements, commenting on the *Gift's* reprinting the
Visiter prize tale, announcing that White would print the
"Tales of the Folio Club," and calling attention to an article
that resembled "Hans Phaall" that had appeared in the New
York *Sun*. He had apparently put the letter aside after signing
it, come to some resolution in the meantime; and yet he
wanted Kennedy to realize that not all was perfect with him.
Kennedy replied heartily, suggesting that Edgar write some
farces "after the manner of the French Vaudevilles" to raise
some money. But when the letter arrived in Richmond, Edgar
had already left.

Poe must have been in a very bad state when he arrived at
the *Messenger* office Monday morning, September 20. The
location of the place was painfully nostalgic to him; it was on
the upper floor of a building adjacent to the store of Ellis and
Allan. His most direct route to work was one that was familiar
to him from the past, save that instead of entering the familiar
door, he went a few steps beyond it to the stairway leading to
his office. One drink that morning, apparently, had not been
enough. Moreover, his "trial" month was just up. His expectations and White's recriminations over his drinking clashed;
and Edgar left for Baltimore.

Almost immediately after his arrival there he hurried to the
courthouse and took out a license to marry Virginia. It was a
bold stroke, and although the protests against their marrying
at that time were powerful enough to make him agree to wait,
he accomplished his main purpose; rather than moving in with
Neilson, Mrs. Clemm and Virginia would accompany him back
to Richmond — if he could get his job again. He wrote humbly
to White, and got a very sympathetic letter in reply. White
advised his assistant to live with a private family "where liquor
is not used," and added, "No man is safe who drinks before
breakfast! No man can do so, and attend to business properly."

Edgar had his job again, but "it must be expressly understood by us that all engagements on my part would be dissolved, the moment you get drunk."

Immediately upon hearing of his reinstatement, Edgar packed his little family together and set out for Richmond, arriving Sunday evening, October 3, and moving into the boarding-house of Mrs. James Yarrington, on Capitol Square. They were to pay nine dollars a week for food and lodging for the three of them. The twenty-odd dollars Poe had been paid for his contributions to the September issue of the *Messenger* had been nearly exhausted by the expenses of his journey to Baltimore and back, and his salary left the slim margin of one dollar a week beyond their very basic expenses for food and shelter. He slaved to fill pages, and wrote letters to possible contributors asking for manuscripts, but White neither gave him authority to make decisions nor could bring himself to put the magazine together and get it out, so there was no issue in October, and the November one was so delayed it eventually was brought out for December. By that time the proprietor was aware that he was doing no good by holding Poe down, and announced that the "intellectual department of the paper is now under the conduct of the proprietor assisted by a gentle-man of distinguished literary talents." He did not identify Poe as the assistant, nor did he permit him to sign any of his work save that which had already been printed elsewhere, but he did mention him, in the same announcement, as a valuable contributor.

In the meantime Mrs. Clemm, freed from drudgery and well nourished at the Yarrington table, was fuming with in-activity and very concerned over the excessive proportion of Edgar's weekly pay that was going to Mrs. Yarrington. Why couldn't she open a boardinghouse? Edgar wrote to George Poe, who contributed one hundred dollars to the scheme; but even so, nothing came of it. He also wrote Kennedy, asking legal advice on Mrs. Clemm's share of a legacy, but Kennedy's investigation only showed that there was no property left in the Clemm estate. Thus they continued at Yarrington's, Mrs. Clemm working off some of her energy by helping around the house, and Virginia being tutored in French and Mathematics by Edgar whenever he could spare the time. The office was open six days a week, and Edgar would often spend Sundays there as well. Payment for the twenty reviews and an excerpt from "Politian" that he contributed to the December *Messenger* brightened their Christmas. The "Tales of the Folio Club" were finally returned from Carey and Lea, and sent on to Harper's.

Poe gradually fell into the happy routine of work that he loved, paid more in the multitudes of books that came in for review than by his marginal salary. The world began to notice the magazine and the curious discovered the name of its biting critic. He settled down to reprinting one of the Folio Club tales — carefully revised — in each issue, plus about twenty thousand words of criticism. In addition to this enormous task, he read manuscripts, handled the correspondence, checked proofs, and saw to it that the issues got out on time. He planned articles and features of his own, including a series of critical vignettes disguised as analyses of the handwriting of celebrated authors. Circulation began to go up, and White, aware of the reason through letters of praise and squeals of complaint over the sharp reviews, came to accept Poe as editor, and in February, 1836, he gave him a raise of two dollars a week.

Poe's acuteness in sensing what was good journalistic copy seems to have been almost instinctive. He had what has been called a "nose for news," a sense of what oddities would interest people and of how to present them so that their strangeness would arouse still greater interest. In his reviews he praised books of distinction soberly and thoughtfully, while he dismissed in a few lines most of those he found trivial and inferior. But if a bad book was brought out in a fanfare of publicity, he went for it hammer and tongs, displaying his spectacular wit at the same time he was gleefully pointing out the flaws of the work in question. His review of *Norman Leslie*, in the December *Messenger*, made him known all over the nation. This rather ridiculous novel, written by Theodore S. Fay, an editor of the New York *Mirror*, had been announced excitedly — primarily by the *Mirror* — in a journalistic guessing game that attributed authorship of the book to this person and that, and when Poe came across "puffery" so blatantly carried out, his greatest joy was to dash in wielding his broadaxe. His criticism of *Paul Ulric*, the following month, was not nearly so bitter, even though he wrote, "when we called Norman Leslie the silliest book in the world we had certainly never seen Paul Ulric." The author of the latter book, Morris Mattson, was not guilty of Fay's kind of puffery; and by the same token, he was less newsworthy.

He judged equally well the interest the public takes in mannerisms, and instituted a "crusade" against the practice of authors of dedicating books to their friends, a "piece of starched and antique affectation." He had himself dedicated the poem "Tamerlane" to John Neal, but only when it was reprinted in the volume *Al Aaraaf*. That book was dedicated to "Who drinks the deepest? — here's to him," and the 1831 volume to the U. S. Corps of Cadets — who, of course, paid for it. His especial *bête noire* was flattering dedications, and in his review of William Gilmore Simms's *The Partisan* he dramatized an imaginary presentation of the book by the author in person, who enters "with solemn step, downcast eyes, and impressive earnestness of manner," shakes the dedicatee by the hand, and reads the dedication with long pauses at the superfluous commas. Poe concludes that if any man with self-respect were addressed personally in the sycophantic manner of such a dedication, he would feel it "his duty to kick the author . . . down stairs."

Although he was pleased by the notoriety and even more by the subscription money flowing in, White began to get nervous over Poe's fierce criticism and the howls that were beginning to come from wounded authors and their friends. Eventually Poe asked Judge Beverley Tucker, whose opinion White respected, to intercede for him, and Tucker, who had himself been very frank in criticizing the critic, wrote to White attributing his reservations to the difference in age between Poe and himself, and adding, "Mr P.'s review of the writings of a leash of these ladies [female poets], in your last number, is a specimen of criticism, which for niceness of discrimination, delicacy of expression, and all that shows familiarity with the art, may well compare with any I have seen." One of "these ladies," Mrs. H. L. Sigourney, responded to the review a few months later. Her copy of the magazine had not reached her, but her friends told her she had been maligned, so she wrote to White with indignation, refusing to write again for the magazine (where verses of hers had already appeared), and complaining about not having received recent copies. White passed the letter on to Poe, who pleaded "guilty" to having written the review, but who sent her a copy of the magazine with the hope that she would find it not so severe as she was told it was. In her gracious reply she rejected one of his criticisms — that she was influenced by Mrs. Hemans — but referred to the *Messenger* as "my favourite periodical," and welcomed Poe's editorship, claiming that she preferred an honest and discriminating critic.

His slashing reviews began to arouse comment in the newspapers, and on the few occasions when he publicly noticed this, he replied with dignity and great cleverness. One such attack he made the leaping-off place for a judgment on American criticism and an extended discussion of the theory of poetry. In this review — of Joseph Rodman Drake's *The Culprit Fay* and Fitz-Greene Halleck's *Alnwick Castle* — he began by tracing the course of American critical opinion from its previous "servile deference to British critical dicta" to its present "gross paradox of liking a stupid book the better, because, sure enough, its stupidity is American." He then quoted the Philadelphia *Gazette's* notice of his work as "*quacky*," and entered into a masterful contrast between the two overrated poems and the ideals of poetry as he saw them. His poetic theory was, as in the "Letter to B ——," drawn from Coleridge, but his application of it made utterly clear that the poems were mechanical rather than poetical. He even rewrote a "Queen Mab" type of description of the arming of a fairy, in Drake's title poem, substituting other plants and insect parts, and commenting, "The truth is, that the only requisite for writing verses of this nature, *ad libitum*, is a tolerable acquaintance with the qualities of the objects to be detailed, and a very moderate endowment of the faculty of Comparison."

The longer Poe handled the critical notices, the greater appetite he had for writing articles of all sorts. In the very same issue as his Drake-Halleck review he published a tour de force of logical analysis on the celebrated mechanical chess player of J. N. Maelzel, exposing it as a fraud that was really operated by a man hidden in the machine. Edgar was perfectly aware of the hidden man before the apparatus was exhibited in Richmond; two boys spied the operator emerge from it when it was shown in Baltimore in 1827, and even if Poe had not seen the article "The Chess-Player Discovered" in the Baltimore *Gazette*, he would have heard about it. His cleverness lay in that he made his exposé seem to be the result of pure deduction, listing seventeen closely knit reasons why it could not be truly mechanical. This technique of starting with the answer and tracing a believable train of logic backward he would remember five years later, when, in writing "The Murders in the Rue Morgue," he created the analytical detective story.

Harper's had by now rejected the Folio Club tales, on the grounds that their publication in the *Messenger* was too recent, and that the satire in them was too subtle for the ordinary reader. J. K. Paulding, who had offered them to the publisher for Poe, wrote, "They desire me, however, to state to Mr. Poe that if he will lower himself a little to the ordinary comprehension of the generality of readers, and prepare a series of original Tales, or a single work, and send them to the Publishers, previous to their appearance in the 'Messenger,' they will make such arrangements with him as will be liberal and satisfactory." Paulding urged Poe to write "a Tale in a couple of volumes, for that is the magical number." That letter came late in March; from the May issue of the *Messenger* Poe ceased inserting his tales (nearly all had been printed anyway) and put his mind to the possibility of a novel. But with the schedule of writing and editorial labors he was engaged on, there hardly seemed any time to spare.

For the May issue Edgar eased off. Contributions were coming in as they never had before, and the spare galleys in the printshop began to fill with overset. He began to take life a little easier after five months of hard, sober work, and to enjoy the company of his little cousin. White became interested in buying a house and proposed to Edgar that if he did, Mrs. Clemm could rent it from him and open her boarding-house, with the White family as the star boarders. This seemed a marvelous scheme, and without so much as looking at the house White actually bought, Edgar borrowed $200 for furniture. The possible saving in money was important to him, but far more important was the opportunity this change in their way of living gave him to marry Virginia. Again he pestered Mrs. Clemm for her permission; the not yet fourteen-year-old girl was certainly avid. One weekend the matter came to a crisis, and eventually the mother of the girl gave in. On Monday morning Edgar and Thomas W. Clelland went to the courthouse, and, Clelland swearing that Virginia was "of the full age of twenty-one years," they were granted a license. That evening the Reverend Amasa Converse married them, at Mrs. Yarrington's. The home Edgar had sought was now the one he made.

12

Now Doubt — now Pain
Come never again,
For her soul gives me sigh for sigh,
And all day long
Shines, bright and strong,
Astarte within the sky,
"Eulalie — A Song"

A "COLLATION" was laid out in the dining room, and Virginia cut the cake that her mother and Mrs. Yarrington had spent the morning baking. There was no need for the newlyweds to steal off to change into their traveling clothes before setting out on the honeymoon; they were in their best clothes already, Virginia wearing a traveling suit for the ceremony, and Edgar in his inevitable black. There was no wine. Mrs. Clemm was beginning to realize that when Edgar was nervous or under a strain, alcohol was too welcome a relief to him. The proprietor of the friendly Petersburg *Constellation*, Hiram W. Haines, had opened his house to the young editor of the South's outstanding magazine; so when the time came, the couple bade farewell to their friends — Virginia had never been overnight away from her mother before — took a hack the short distance to the depot, and boarded the train for Petersburg, off in the hills of Virginia.

For a short time they were almost living the life Edgar had left behind him at his parting with Allan. Edward Sparhawk, who had preceded Poe on the *Messenger*, was Haines's editor;

Dr. William Robinson gave a party in honor of the young couple, where Edgar's conversation shone. In two weeks they returned to an equal display of hospitality in Richmond. This time Mrs. Clemm, tall and dignified, accompanied them, although a bit out of her depth socially. There was only one awkward moment, however; she and Edgar's sister Rosalie discovered that they disliked each other heartily. Edgar's sister was in an unfortunate position. Although, living with the Mac-Kenzies, she was never threatened with the poverty that always hung over her brother's head, she lacked the family connections and money to make a good match. If her brother had behaved himself instead of incurring John Allan's anger — Allan had even spread rumors about her birth — things might have been different, but now she was almost twenty-five, and, in that time and place, an old maid. She was to die in an old people's home in Washington at the age of sixty-three.

After the first few weeks, however, being married did not bring the change in Poe's life that he expected. The work of the magazine continued, and the review copies did not stop flowing in. He turned out his usual eight reviews, but these in June filled only half the pages that they had before, even though one was of a book of Dickens's early sketches (which Poe filled out by copying the entire essay on "Gin Shops"), and another a miscellany of Coleridge's talk and letters — either of which he might have been expected to write on at length. White promised his editor — now editor in name as well as in fact — an increase in salary to twenty dollars a week in November. But when the Poes and Mrs. Clemm went to look over White's new house, they sadly discovered that it was "barely large enough for one family," and so the plans for a boarding-house were "laid aside."

This fiasco certainly shook Edgar's faith in his employer. White was the sort of self-centered man who is thoughtless rather than malicious, and he probably really believed that he was making a good offer, oblivious of the fact that by relegating Edgar and his family to the kitchen and sleeping quarters in the top of the house he was simply hiring a staff of servants to run his house at their own financial risk. Tradition has it that Edgar moved his family into a cheap tenement. Even with the fifteen dollars a week that he was earning after his marriage, it is difficult to see how they could have afforded to stay on at Mrs. Yarrington's.

Among the June reviews, Poe "used up" a picaresque novel called *Ups and Downs in the Life of a Distressed Gentleman.* Perhaps conscious of the contrast between the gentleman and himself — his own were often "downs and ups" — he must have been struck by one episode: the protagonist, having lost his fortune as a merchant, successfully pursues a claim against the government. In 1836 the French Government began paying the spoliation claims of American citizens damaged by the Napoleonic Wars, and the American agent most active — and most successful — was Colonel John T. Pickett. James H. Causten was working with Pickett, and it was to him Edgar wrote, asking him to press for payment of the $40,000 his grandfather had contributed to supplying the Revolutionary Army. He must have been up to date on the activities of Congress, for an act of the very next day made this claim feasible — if his grandmother had not died before its passage. His cousin, Henry Herring, tried again the next year, and the claim was permanently disallowed. A few days after Poe wrote Causten, while sending out letters requesting contributions for the magazine, he added to his plea for "any thing *with your name*" to Kennedy the story of the disappointment over White's house, and the request that the Baltimore novelist lend him one hundred dollars for the period of six months, to help him pay back the amount he had borrowed for the furniture.

For the July *Messenger* Edgar's quota of eight reviews shrank to less space than he had filled since joining the staff. But he did reply again to his critics; in particular to a notice in the New Bern, North Carolina, *Spectator* that claimed he was pretentious to attempt to reach a national audience, and that it was ridiculous for a Southern journal "to assume the tone" of the critics of the established Northern and British magazines. As example, the paper quoted one of Poe's dogmatic quibbles over the grammar of a passage in Slidell's *Spain Revisited*. Poe defended his analysis, then counterattacked by finding an outrageous blunder in the notice and by quoting compliments from the victims of some of his reviews, including Slidell. He wound up with a number of favorable notices from other papers. Nearly everyone knows how to lose friends, but Edgar was already jealously insistent on keeping his enemies.

In July the Specie Circular went into effect, a Jacksonian effort against paper money that backfired into a spurt of wildcat currency issues, the flow of gold and silver westward, and inflation in the East. But this Edgar paid little attention to — the discounting of notes on out-of-state banks that were sent in to pay for subscriptions was White's job — devoting more of his thought to the subject of slavery. Abolition agitation had reached a new high, and fearing that the influx of pamphlets from the North would cause a new outbreak of the kind of slave insurrection that had terrified the state in 1831, the Virginia legislature passed an act abridging the freedom of speech and press and giving postmasters inquisitorial powers. Lucian Minor's "Liberian Literature" in the February issue had been edited "to omit all passages . . . at which offense could, by any possibility, be taken," but the Atlanta *Chronicle* still labeled it sheer abolitionism. In the April issue Poe reviewed Paulding's *Slavery in the United States* and the anonymous *South Vindicated*, expressing the views natural to a

Southerner educated at Jefferson's University by emphasizing the benevolent side of the institution, accepting it in principle as wrong but necessary and beneficial for black as well as white. Like many in his time, he accepted slavery without looking beyond his own experiences of loyalty between slave and master. Mrs. Clemm's slave Edwin was then in the seventh of the nine years of service for which Edgar had hired him out; but he might have been eating better with Henry Ridgway than his owner had been eating over that time. Edgar was still living in the Virginia of his childhood, failing to see the change that had come about in the slave economy, and probably oblivious to the arguments of his former professor George Tucker, who was opposed to slavery on economic grounds and would, in a year, publish his *Laws of Wages, Profits, and Rents,* in which he made his attitude explicit.

For the August number Poe put out his best efforts, later claiming it to be the "best number, by far, yet issued." His reviews, thirteen in number, ran to nearly the space he had habitually covered before his marriage. He instituted a new feature called "Pinakidia," consisting of aphorisms and snippets of knowledge gleaned from such works as Bielfeld's *Elements of Universal Erudition*, a work he kept permanently on his reference shelf. He published as well slightly revised versions of three of his old poems, "Israfel," "The City of Sin" (formerly "The Doomed City"), and "The Coliseum." One of the books he reviewed aroused his interest greatly. This was the report of the Committee on Naval Affairs proposing an expedition to chart the Pacific according to the suggestions of Jeremiah N. Reynolds. Reynolds was a seafarer and writer whom Poe had already made the subject of one of his autograph articles. His writings on the need for exploration of the whale fisheries would in time result in the Wilkes Expedition, one of the few scientific projects of the Jacksonians, but one from which Reynolds was excluded.

Poe's stinging reviews aroused response in the meantime closer to home. The Richmond *Courier and Daily Compiler* published a notice, in general praising the magazine, but adding, "the editors must remember that it is almost as injurious to obtain a character for regular cutting and slashing as for indiscriminate laudation." Poe had already replied twice in his own pages to such notices, once in July to the New Bern *Spectator* and once to a cheap — and untrue — slur from the New York *Mirror*, obviously in retaliation for his review of its editor's *Norman Leslie*. This time he wrote a letter to the *Courier*, claiming that "Custom debars a Magazine from answering in its own pages (except in rare cases)." First expressing outrage at their referring to "the editors," since "the Messenger has *but one* editor," he summed up his reviewing record like a critical bookkeeper: of 94 books reviewed, commendation predominated over censure for 79; praise slightly prevailed for seven; censure was predominant for five; "while the only reviews decidedly and harshly condemnatory are those of Norman Leslie, Paul Ulric, and the Ups and Downs." He pointed out that only four papers had previously condemned his criticism, two of which were edited by authors he had "used up," and another by a member of the staff of a rival magazine. The newspaper backtracked, saying it did not mean he *had* been guilty of cutting and slashing but was expressing the hope that he would not, claiming the plural of "editor" was a misprint, and misquoting itself in an effort to prove that he had misunderstood its kindly remarks. He had won another tactical victory and let the strategy go hang.

White, oblivious of the adage that bad publicity is better than none, was more nervous than ever over this fifth adverse notice. It counterbalanced the dozens of praising notices, for his mentality was that of the small-town merchant to whom local opinion is everything. Moreover, Edgar was drinking again. He had made a name for himself in the literary world, but he remained in a remote corner of it. Richmond, he knew, could not be the literary capital that New York was, and if he had to fight the Knickerbocker coterie, as he really wanted to do, it should be on equal ground. Drudgery on the magazine had kept him from original writing for a year, and the increase in his salary had, in view of the inflation, hardly made up for the loss of payments for stories. He offered the Folio Club, now with seventeen members, to Harrison Hall, pointing out hopefully that a fourth of the contents were critical remarks, *"which have never been published."* He was very proud of the "mass of eulogy" that could be used to publicize the volume.

Sometime in September, White invoked his stipulation that all engagements on his part would be dissolved the moment Edgar got drunk, and gave him a month's notice. But pleading and good resolutions caused him to change his mind. The September issue, however, was delayed — probably because White had no one to help him — but it eventually came out as usual. But both White and Poe were dissatisfied and cagy with each other; and neither forgot that Edgar's salary was due to go up five dollars a week in November. All was routine in the October issue, save that Poe showed his increasing interest in original fiction in an article on an English story, "Peter Snook." He attributed the superiority of English fiction to the low prices American writers were able to command, claiming that originality is not "a mere matter of impulse or inspiration," but "To originate, is carefully, patiently, and understandingly to combine."

In a glowing review of a new edition of Defoe's *Robinson Crusoe* the previous January, Poe deplored the knowledge that made such another book impossible to write. "Wo, henceforward," he wrote, "to the Defoe who shall prate to us of 'undiscovered new ground for any future Selkirk.'" He must have felt that lack all the more in March, when Paulding wrote him that Harper's was not interested in his tales but would certainly publish a long story. And in reading the Reynolds-inspired report of the Committee on Naval Affairs he surely began to wonder, and to look into the then popular accounts of voyages and discoveries. "MS. Found in a Bottle" had been his most praised story, even though he no longer thought much of it. Particularly fascinating to him was John Cleve Symmes's *Symzonia*, which suggested that the earth was hollow, with access to the interior through "holes at the poles."

Poe's analyses of the way a long story is written soon revealed to him that the kind of adventure he wished to describe consisted of simply one episode after another, with drama and tension built up through the impulsive curiosity — the adventurousness — of the characters. His main character would be, as always, himself, but this time not the introspective side, but the rash boy who dashed out of Allan's house without clothes or money. As a foil to this character he drew on memories of boyhood friends who were quick to accept a "dare" but not tenacious enough always to carry it out. He had great pleasure in choosing the name of his title character. Instead of *Poe*, it would be *Pym*; instead of *Edgar*, *Arthur*; but best of all was to replace *Allan* with the family name of Lord Byron. *Arthur Gordon Pym.*

The opening episode was drawn from one of the quiddities of knowledge Edgar had picked up: that at a certain stage of intoxication one can seem entirely sober, and then abruptly be dead drunk. Pym goes to a party at the home of his friend Augustus Barnard, and having drunk too much, decides to stay overnight with his friend. In the middle of the night Augustus wakes him, swearing that he is sober, and suggests they go for a sail in Pym's boat, the *Ariel*, in spite of a severe storm. Augustus, after sailing the boat out to sea, passes out, and they are run down by a whaling ship, then rescued, Pym from the copper bottom of the whaler, where he had been caught on a started bolt, and Augustus from the wreckage of the *Ariel*. Since the ship was bound for Nantucket, their home, the boys appear for breakfast the next morning with no one the wiser. This short passage, otherwise irrelevant to the plot, not only introduces two of the characters but also sets the atmosphere of a world fraught with perils where one survives by sheer chance.

But this was not very effective in filling two volumes, so Poe offered it simply as an example of the "adventures" the boys were accustomed to, and then launched into his narrative of a whaling voyage commanded by Augustus's father, on which the son was invited, and Pym, with his connivance, stowed away. As a second major episode Poe invented with excruciating detail the ordeal of the boy in the pitch-black hold for eleven days instead of the expected two or three until the ship was far enough out so that the captain would not turn back; a mutiny made it unwise for Augustus to reveal Pym's presence. For this Edgar drew on his memory of Defoe's realistic technique; in the review of *Robinson Crusoe* he had defined its fascination as "the potent magic of verisimilitude," attributing to Defoe the power of will over imagination "which enables the mind to lose its own, in a fictitious, mentality."

But Poe could devote little time to his story in view of his labors and troubles at work. Harbingers of the Panic of 1837 were more evident to White than to Edgar. The printers went out on strike, and money was very short. One day in October a letter came from Mrs. Hale, editor of *Godey's*, which she had absent-mindedly addressed to "W. G. Simms Esqr, Editor of the S. L. Messenger," and Poe's suspicions were aroused that White was actively planning to replace him. Edgar had published hardly anything of his own in the November issue, and White's troubles and the printing strike caused cancellation of that for December. Poe offered to print his long tale serially in the magazine, and that met with White's approval, even though only enough was done to make two episodes. In addition, Edgar worked hard on reviews, among them an extended and highly fascinating criticism of Washington Irving's *Astoria*. But in spite of his hard work, Christmas cheer got the best of Edgar, and White again invoked his edict. From January 3, 1837, Poe was no longer editor of the *Messenger*. White frankly admitted to Beverley Tucker that he was also "cramped by him in the exercise of my own judgment"; this is an all too frequent complaint of proprietors who are jealous of the editors they hire. Poe had brought the circulation of the magazine from five hundred up to thirty-five hundred. He had made it — and himself — known all over the nation. The dismissal was no great blow to him, for he knew he was ready to go his own way. Unfortunately, he did not see what was in store for the economic life of the nation.

The January issue, in addition to a mass of criticism by Poe, the first installment of *Pym*, and two new poems, carried Poe's "Valedictory." He was "called in another direction." The direction lay north, where he had been asked to contribute regularly to the New York *Review*, and where in time he planned to establish a magazine of his own, free from the fumbling of "businessmen." Some hotheads were trying to start a revolution in Canada, and on January 1 the Distribution Act had come into effect, scattering the funds of the United States to the state banks. But what could that have to do with literature? Edgar Poe was about to find out.

How many scenes of what departed bliss!
How many thoughts of what entombéd hopes!
"Sonnet — To Zante"

AGAIN IN MOVING from place to place Edgar Poe passed the boundary of an era without knowing it. Throughout the first months of 1837, prices rose until they were nearly double those of two years before. In early winter several British business houses failed — houses that had invested heavily in American securities, which were then thrown on the market. Business and government were at war with each other, and the public lost. According to the *New Era*, a popular newspaper run by Richard Adams Locke, the author of the "Moon Hoax" that had given notoriety to Poe's "Hans Phaall," New York flour merchants, in a conspiracy to keep prices up, had jammed their warehouses and were buying up all the grain that entered the city.

It was a chaotic, frantic city of narrow, muddy streets filled with out-of-work men to which Edgar Poe brought his wife and aunt in February, 1837. The city had more than two hundred and fifty thousand population, in comparison with Richmond's twenty thousand. A little more than a year before a vast portion of the city had burned in a fire that had raged for over twenty-four hours, and reconstruction, in spite of the bad times, was going on everywhere. More than any other place

Edgar had been in since childhood, New York had the feel of a city, and he was as fascinated by it as he had been, in spite of poverty and ill health, six years before. But Sissy was confused by it all, and Mrs. Clemm shocked at the crowded conditions and filth, so they soon moved their trunks north and rented one floor of a brick building in Greenwich Village, a more tranquil and countrified region, from which he could ride an omnibus or take a train of the Harlem line, or, in need, walk in less than an hour to the magazine offices and bookshops of lower Broadway.

With the little money they had left, it was obvious that they could not continue paying the high prices of food and fuel until Edgar could get himself established. Mrs. Clemm achieved her ambition; she took in a boarder. This was William Gowans, a bookseller of 169 Broadway, who had first been fascinated by Poe's talk, then charmed by Virginia's grace and beauty, and finally won over by Mrs. Clemm's housekeeping. He may have taken Poe to a dinner the booksellers of New York gave for some of the writers and artists of New York; there Edgar would have met for the first time some of the people with whom he had been corresponding as editor of the *Messenger* and some whose works he had reviewed, for among the guests were Bryant, Irving, Halleck (who may have remembered that after devastating Drake in his review of the two, Poe had written, "Halleck's poetical powers appear to us essentially inferior, upon the whole, to those of his friend Drake"), and J. K. Paulding, the man who had suggested that Poe write a long story.

Already he had received an inquiry from three men of Baltimore, who wanted a contribution for a new annual, the *Baltimore Book*. Poe had at least two unpublished tales on hand, so he asked them what sort of article they would like, and eventually sent them "Siope — A Fable," one of the Folio

Club tales that had been offered to Carey and Lea but had never been printed anywhere. He had also written another during his spurt of creative energy just before leaving Richmond, "Von Jung, the Mystific." This is quite typical of — but more finished than — the comic pieces he had written in Baltimore; it simply recounts a joke played on a fierce dueling enthusiast by one of his fellow students at the University of G—n, who trapped him into a challenge, then offered as the "explanation" that made combat unnecessary a Latin text on dueling that was totally unintelligible, for "Hermann would have died a thousand deaths rather than acknowledge his inability to understand any and everything in the universe that had ever been written about the duello." This story was accepted by the *American Monthly Magazine*, where it appeared in June.

Aside from these two sales, however, Poe's income ceased. He had been paid in full for the first two installments of *Pym* before he left Richmond, and, probably on the advice of Harper's, no more appeared. After he was assigned the review of J. L. Stephens's *Incidents of Travel in Egypt, Arabia, and the Holy Land*, the New York *Review* suspended publication, in view of the uncertain economic condition of the country. It looked as if Mrs. Clemm must be the mainstay of the household, and so they moved to an old house at 113½ Carmine Street, farther south in Greenwich Village. Mr. Gowans went with them, and soon there were other boarders. Merchants were failing right and left, and there were rumors that banks would stop payment of specie. On May 4, John Fleming, the president of the Mechanics Bank, was found dead in his bed, and word went around that he had committed suicide in view of possible failure. This set off a run on the bank, which soon spread to all the others. On May 10 all New York banks suspended specie payment, and the Panic of 1837 was on.

Relieved of the pressures involved in turning out a magazine, Edgar settled down to work and completely eschewed drinking. The boarders brought in enough money to put food on the table and pay the rent (although the closing of the Pennsylvania coal mines raised doubts about fuel for the following winter), and Edgar had not possessed enough paper money to feel that he had really lost anything by not being able to convert it to gold. Prices dropped. Harper's read the portions of *Pym* that he had finished and applied for copyright on the book. But before finishing the novel, Poe immersed himself in the review.

The major Sunday distraction of the time, even in New York, was churchgoing, and one of the favorite subjects for sermons was the extent to which geology and archaeology proved the literal truth of the Bible. Poe felt that that was so, making "proper allowance . . . for the usual hyperbolical tendency of the language of the East," but he insisted on making judgment from the Hebrew text of the Bible rather than from a translation. Thus when he read that Stephens had, in spite of the fate of two of his predecessors who had not returned to their homes after the journey, crossed the cursed land of Edom, he began to wonder how cursed it was.

In Isaiah one finds that the prophecy is that "none shall pass through it for ever and ever"; in Ezekiel that the Lord will "cut off from it him that passeth out and him that returneth." Poe could not read Hebrew, but he knew of the famous Charles Anthon, Professor of Classics at Columbia College, and he had reason to believe that Anthon knew of his literary work. On May 27 he wrote the language scholar, asking for the meaning of the two passages, and in a few days Anthon answered him cordially, saying, "Do not wait to pay me a formal visit, but call and introduce yourself," while enclosing a detailed explanation which Poe transplanted into his review.

It was as he thought; the prophecies did not say that no one could pass through the land, but that no one would live in it. Moreover, he discovered that Stephens had not gone through Edom at all.

Poe lost no time in making Anthon's acquaintance. Both professor in the college and rector of Columbia Grammar School, Anthon was a man in many ways like Poe, save that he was imbued with the discipline of Germanic scholarship from his father, tempered with French wit from his mother, and he was even more a self-educated man than Poe. Earlier in the year, when Columbia had held its semicentennial celebration, Anthon sulked in his room because the ceremonies were not organized to his liking; he had first proposed a play in Latin, then had written a Greek ode for the occasion; and when both were ruled out, he wrote a satiric poem, "cutting up president and professors, making them sing songs and do no pretty conduct for a professor!" It was in these words that Anthon leaked the information through his nephew to the student body. He was so irascible that the students never played the practical jokes on him that they did on the other professors, yet for all his fierceness, he spoke to them more as equals than the others did. He, and others of the New York intellectual world, provided Edgar with the literate conversation he had been starved for.

News arrived on July 25 that Victoria was now Queen of England, and at about the same time fashionable young men started wearing beards. In "Von Jung" Edgar had already poked fun at people who disguised their faces with hair. In October the New York *Review* began publishing again, printing the review of *Arabia Petraea*, as Stephens's book became known, with all its erudition from Anthon and Poe — but signed only by Poe. By this time Edgar was deep in *Pym*, and as always, he was incapable of merely imitating popular works, but made something new, even though much of the detail in his book was simply paraphrased from Benjamin Morrell's *Narrative of Four Voyages to the South Seas and Pacific, 1822-1831.* He recalled the lessons he had had in proper stowage of merchandise in a ship's hold when he was a boy returning from England, and the practical experience he had gained in his two changes of post by sea when he was in the Army, and combining this with details from other narratives of the sea, he brought his characters through the mutiny to shipwreck. A ship passes them, but it turns out to be a plague-ship reminiscent of the *Flying Dutchman,* and they are driven eventually to cannibalism.

He mixed together accounts of all sorts on sea travel, his own memories injecting them with life and continuity, but at length he moved totally into the realm of the imagination by deciding to lead his voyagers to the *Symzonia* "hole" at the South Pole, and considered using Symmes's theory that undiscovered civilizations lay in the interior of the earth's shell as he had considered describing life on the moon in "Hans Phaall." A better alternative, however, was to suggest that hints of an earlier civilization could be found *near* the Pole, and to leave a mystery at the end of the story.

Edgar surely discussed this with Anthon, for he relied on his learned friend's linguistic ability to compound the mystery. He first had Pym and his companions rescued by an English whaler, which sails into terra incognita in the Antarctic. They encounter black savages (the farther one goes into the unexplored country, the warmer the climate) in a strange land, whose treachery causes the death of all but Pym and one other. At length they come across a series of oddly shaped chasms — from above they would resemble the Ethiopian symbols for "darkness" — and on the side of the last of these, pointing south, the Arabic word for "whiteness," and the Egyptian "the region of the south." From their first encounter, the blacks

show great fear and awe of the color white. At the end the
two voyagers, with a captive native, eventually descend a cata-
ract; "But there arose in our pathway a shrouded human figure,
very far larger in its proportions than any dweller among men.
And the hue of the skin of the figure was of the perfect whiteness of the snow."

Poe realized that his story as a work of art was complete;
he had carried his protagonist through all the struggles involved
in discovery (the word formed on the sail of the mysterious
ship in "MS. Found in a Bottle," from the narrator's idle
smearing of the folded sail with tar); he had moved from the
real and familiar to the brink of the imagination. Less tangibly,
he *felt* that the work was complete; the unconscious drive
within him to create order in his being was satisfied. But as a
realistic sea narrative it was incomplete, and so he engineered
the hoax that this was the account of a real Arthur Gordon
Pym, who had died and whose remaining papers had been lost.
When the book was published in England many people accepted that as the fact, only attributing to Pym a tendency to
lard his experiences with tall tales.

But Edgar had himself traveled far in recounting the voyages
of his imaginary self. He had discovered how to develop character in fiction, and far more important, by tracing the progress of himself — as Pym — from madcap through experiences
that bring him maturity, he was able to develop a perspective
on himself that made his later work much less self-conscious.
This detachment made him a master of fiction, but it destroyed him as a lyric poet. He abandoned the Folio Club
altogether, planning to revise his tales so that they would
stand on their own, without reference to parody. He was now
completely aware of his power as a writer of fiction.

Through the summer and fall of 1837 Edgar divided his
time between work, the pleasures of conversation with his

learned and literary friends, leafing over the books in Gowans's and other bookshops, and simply enjoying the sights of the city. Fires broke out regularly and were spectacular things. It was always pleasant to stroll with Virginia around the Battery, and on September 25 there was the yacht regatta to watch. Edgar got into the habit of reading all the newspapers, the multitude of which contained marvels enough, from the many shipwrecks and collisions, fires and other catastrophes, to the demonstration of the new electric telegraph (in February, 1838) at the White House. In the election of November, 1837, the Whigs carried the state, making the first step of their ascendancy that would unseat the Jacksonians in 1840. Although he despised the narrow businessmen who supported the Whig Party, Edgar was repelled by the crude demagoguery of the Locofoco Democrats. Besides, his old friend Wirt's Anti-Masonic Party was one of the coalition that made up the Whigs.

Winter set in early, cold and severe, the muddy streets first becoming frozen in ruts and soon filling with snow. Fuel was scarce and the lodgers complained. At the end of the year excitement was aroused by the attack of Canadian forces on the American steamer *Caroline*, which had been hired to carry supplies to the Canadian rebels. The ship was sent burning over Niagara Falls. Captain Marryat spoiled the great welcome he had received in his tour of the States by drinking the health of one of the British officers. There was talk of war, but there was more activity on the part of Poe's friends in getting hold of the fourth and fifth parts of *The Pickwick Papers*, which were just arriving in the country. Business was so bad that Gowans took to running book auctions to dispose of the libraries of needy collectors. On April 23 the first steamship to cross the Atlantic, the *Sirius*, came into New York harbor, followed later in the day by the *Great Western*, the thirteen-hundred-ton marvel of the age, which had started from England three days after the *Sirius*. Spring finally came, the banks resumed payment of specie, and Edgar and Virginia celebrated their first wedding anniversary.

The Narrative of Arthur Gordon Pym was finally completed and delivered to Harper's. The book was panned for Munchausenism and did not go through one edition — Gowans later said it was the most unsuccessful of Poe's works. No further literary opportunities offered themselves in New York, and the boarders, disgruntled over the cold winter and the sparseness that was showing itself on the table, began to leave. Soon it seemed as if Edgar's challenge to New York, like his mother's, had come out in defeat for him. But unlike her, he had great artistry in reserve and knew it, so he did not retreat to the South. He had tasted the literary life of a city. Philadelphia was not much smaller than New York, and the contest between the two for dominance of enterprise in the United States was not yet over. Some of the New York literati, among them Gowans's friend James Pedder, were turning to the Pennsylvania city. So that is where Poe carried his family, after scrounging up their fares, in the summer of 1838.

14

If in many of my productions terror has been
the thesis, I maintain that terror is not of Germany but of the soul . . .

Introduction, *Tales of the
Grotesque and Arabesque*

SHORTLY AFTER HIS ARRIVAL in Philadelphia in the summer of
1838, Poe started on a piece of hack work that brought in a
small amount of money at the time, but that later caused him
great embarrassment and inconvenience. Thomas Wyatt, a
marine biologist, had written *A Manual of Conchology*, which
Harper's had published elaborately to sell at a substantial price.
The book was too expensive to be popular, and the publisher
refused to bring out a cheaper edition. Wyatt therefore approached Poe, who had a good layman's knowledge of the subject from his days of accompanying Dr. Edmund Ravenel on
shell hunts while he was at Fort Moultrie. In putting *The Conchologist's First Book* together, Poe added to Wyatt's system of
classification an explanation of the parts of shells copied from a
British book, *The Conchologist's Text Book* by Captain
Thomas Brown, and the engravers copied Brown's illustrations
as well. For the descriptions of the shellfish themselves, Poe
translated from Cuvier. Poe's name was the only one on the
title page, so it was he rather than Wyatt who was held responsible for this "plagiarism."

Even while Edgar was planning the new book with Wyatt,

however, the creative urge that had welled up in the writing of *Pym* began to express itself. He wrote a new short story, continuing the theme he first touched on in "Berenice" and developed in "Morella." Indeed, he drew details from both of them in "Ligeia," seeming, almost for the first time, to realize what he was doing. The death of someone beloved and beautiful was a painful thought to him; in "Berenice" his protagonist robbed the grave of his loved one's teeth, which had become a symbol of her beauty; this gruesome idea probably had its origin in the sentimental custom of clipping a lock of hair from the corpse as a keepsake. In "Morella," the will of the woman enabled her to possess the body of her child. In his preoccupation with death as the enemy, Poe found somewhere in his reading (he attributed it to Joseph Glanvill) a quotation that appealed to him: "Man doth not yield himself to the angels, nor unto death utterly, save only through the weakness of his feeble will."

The deaths of beloved ones spotted his life. First his mother, then Mrs. Stanard, and then Mrs. Allan had been lost to him through death. He had, through her marriage, lost Elmira, and he had nearly lost Virginia; such losses were to him very much like death. In "Morella" his protagonist was obsessed with the study of personal identity, that entity which is or is not destroyed by death. Thus, for his ultimate prose work on this theme, he created another Morella, the learned and mysterious Ligeia, using the name of the musical spirit in "Al Aaraaf" who controls sleep and waking; that is, death and reincarnation. The husband does not remember when he met Ligeia, nor does he recall ever having heard her family name. She is peculiarly beautiful, with black hair and Oriental eyes, marvelously learned, and she resents intensely the death which comes upon her.

For the first time in one of Poe's stories the protagonist —

modeled on himself — finds death something more than a stimulus to morbid introspection. His sorrow drives him from his ancestral mansion by the Rhine to a gloomy abbey in a remote corner of England, where he addicts himself to opium and marries a blue-eyed blonde woman the virtual opposite of Ligeia, but still mourns his first wife, calling out to her in anguish. The new wife goes through a succession of illnesses and eventually dies, but she revives periodically on her bier, and eventually arises, taller — like Berenice — and when she opens her eyes and unbinds her hair, both are those of Ligeia. The theme of love stronger than the grave was obviously what he was groping for in the two earlier stories, even though his concentration on the narrator — himself — obscured this fact even from him.

Poe submitted this story to the *American Museum*, which had just been started in Baltimore by two medical men he had been acquainted with there, Nathan C. Brooks and J. E. Snodgrass. It appeared in the first number. But driven by his new vein of writing, and with the chore on hand of putting together the book on conchology, he refused Brooks's offer that he review one of Irving's books, since he could not spare the time to do the thorough job he would want to. Moreover, there were nonliterary details to occupy him. On their arrival in Philadelphia, the Poes and Mrs. Clemm had stayed with Gowans's friend Pedder; then they had gone to a boardinghouse on Arch Street near Fourth. Both the expense and the lack of privacy for writing made Poe dissatisfied; when he found a small frame house for rent at a very low price in the opposite corner of the city, he took it, and they moved in early in September, setting up housekeeping on the ten dollars Brooks had paid for "Ligeia." Edgar had applied to Neilson Poe for a loan, but without success.

When Poe realized that his tales would stand on their own

and abandoned the concept of the Folio Club, he recalled a nomenclature which Walter Scott had used in an essay, "On the Supernatural in Fictitious Composition," in the *Foreign Quarterly Review* ten years before. Poe used Scott's term "arabesque" to refer to stories in which the horror was enhanced by use of the imagination; "grotesque" for those which went beyond horror to burlesque. The observation is an ancient one. A devilish figure can, in the atmosphere of a darkened temple, with appropriate sounds and smells, be a cause of terror; displayed in the open air, like the gargoyles of Gothic churches, it is simply comic. Poe discovered as early as "Metzengerstein" that if his gargoyles were too subtle to be funny, he could simply immerse them in a morbid atmosphere and make them effective in another way. He already had a reasonably balanced number of grotesques and arabesques — eight of one and ten of the other. And there were more to come.

But first he needed to clean all the parody from his mind with an out-and-out burlesque of the arrogant ignorance of female writers in general and *Blackwood's* in particular. As a gallant Southern gentleman he found it easier to make fun of bluestockings in a story than to attack them individually; in writing criticism he was always aware of the lady behind the writings, a disadvantage he never suffered in his criticism of males. This he did in a two-part narrative, "The Psyche Zenobia" and "The Scythe of Time." In the first, the Signora Psyche Zenobia (otherwise Suky Snobbs) calls upon Mr. Blackwood, who, referring to actual stories that had appeared in the magazine, gives instructions on the technique of writing: first get into "such a scrape as no one ever got into before"; then choose a style that will be sufficiently obscure; and finally, lard the composition with references to obscure bits of knowledge and quotations from foreign languages. He gives examples of all these. Thus the lady, in Part Two, climbs to the belfry of a church and studies the city through a hole in the face of the clock, oblivious of the circling minute hand until it has her caught as in a guillotine. From then until, and after, her head is wholly cut off, she records her sensations, mixed with garbled quotations from Spanish, Italian, Greek, and German; in the first, for example, intending to repeat the lines from Cervantes Blackwood had quoted to her, beginning "V*en muerte tan escondida*," she starts off, "Vanny Buren, *tan escondida.*" Any reference to that unpopular President was good for a laugh. Brooks accepted these two for the *American Museum*, where they appeared in November.

The neat regularity of the citizens of Philadelphia, who scrubbed the white steps before their prim brick houses, and whose streets were laid out in checkerboard regularity, made tremendous contrast in Poe's mind with the lively chaos of New York City, and he was amused at the broken English of the Pennsylvania German farmers who sold their produce at the municipal market that ran down the center of the High Street, then already changing its name to "Market." Moreover, the clang of bells chiming the hours, and the clatter of the watchmen banging the curb with their truncheons and calling "All's well," undoubtedly woke him up the middle of many nights. He often wished the Devil would get in their belfries and throw this redundant timekeeping askew; and therefore he imagined a regularized Dutch village, with sixty houses set in a circle, each facing a garden with twenty-four cabbages growing in it, and occupied by a housewife who holds a watch in her hand while she stirs the sauerkraut, children with watches and pipes, watches tied to the tails of the cat and the pig, and out in front the burgher, his watch in his pocket, puffing his pipe while he watches the clock in the steeple. Into this phlegmatic community he introduces the Devil, who sets the town clock to chiming thirteen, to the consternation of all the people and watches in the community.

This *jeu d'esprit* went to the Philadelphia *Saturday Chronicle*, a newspaper, since the *Museum* had ordered a critical article from him. He sent "Literary Small Talk," which appeared in two parts, the first, with linguistic paraphernalia reminiscent of the advice given the Psyche Zenobia, a commentary on Bulwer; the second on Gibbon's style. Along with these he sent a hitherto unpublished poem, "The Haunted Palace," but short of money in spite of these sales, he borrowed fifty dollars from an acquaintance named Cox, and kept on writing.

Still another matter of amusement to Poe was his fellow citizens' boasting over the frivolous gadgets which their applied science was turning out. From the telegraph to patent apple-peelers, inventions were being put on the market daily, often less convenient than the labor they were intended to save. Some Edgar welcomed — the friction match, for example, saved all kinds of discomfort on a cold morning; and rubber overshoes, although expensive (a pair cost three dollars), saved shoes in wet and snowy weather and prevented many a cold. But these were rarities among the multitude of products that clever entrepreneurs were urging on the public, and although Edgar scoffed at these latter, he could not have helped noticing the envy with which Virginia glanced at the fashionable women of the town in their hoop skirts, while she was still wearing dresses of Mrs. Clemm's manufacture. There was much talk, too, of the Seminole Wars and the atrocities the Indians committed on the invading soldiers. The result was "The Man Who Was Used Up," a satire on inventions through the secret of a military man who, in spite of his handsome appearance, turns out to consist only of a mutilated trunk and head, the rest of him filled out with artificial limbs, eyes, and so on.

But the serious artistic impulse that created "Ligeia" soon supplanted the comic vein. In his next story Poe achieved a much greater detachment, narrating as a visitor to the scene the reactions of his usual introspective protagonist to the illness, death, and emergence from the tomb of his usual beautiful woman, this time the man's sister. This third-person narration enabled a multitude of themes to fall together at once. The curse on the land of Edom, from the review of Stephens's *Arabia*, merged with the meaning of the word "house" in nearly all the arabesques after "Metzengerstein," and thus the building became symbol for the family, which decayed as it did. For the first time Poe was able to make explicit the rotting quality of pride in ancestry. The hint of incest, attractive and repulsive at once, with its mingled love and hate, was distilled in this tale from its weak infusion through the earlier tales. Poe looked clearly at the Romantic introvert he had imagined himself in the earlier tales, and saw the death wish and necrophilia in this vicarious escape from life. But most of all he analyzed deeply the extent that atmosphere made his writing effective, and brought the former "mood" under strict control.

Thus he wrote "The Fall of the House of Usher." For its setting he drew on the most striking details of places and scenes he had viewed and read about. From the first sentence the tone of his vocabulary remained gray and melancholy. Rather than display his own envy of ancient names and ancestral towers, he gave these to Roderick Usher, linking with them his degeneracy and weakness — describing himself, as Usher, with keen perception of all his weaknesses. In place of displaying his own knowledge of out-of-the-way books, he described Usher's peculiar tastes, which ranged from a comic French poem about a parrot — the "Ververt" of Gresset — through mysticism and fantasy to the *Directorium Inquisi-*

torum and a "manual of a forgotten church — the *Vigiliæ Mortuorum secundum Chorum Ecclesiæ Maguntiæ*." His usual theme of burial alive and violated tombs was made more horrible than usual, and he symbolized with great effectiveness the end of the family when the narrator, fleeing the horrible sight of the corpses of Usher and his sister Madeline, runs out of the house and across the causeway in a wild storm, then turns to see the house collapse and slide into the tarn. As evidence of Usher's madness, he attributed to him his own latest poem, "The Haunted Palace."

When he had done this, still another phase of himself emerged in the form of a story. What was the moral and artistic conscience that had forced him into so penetrating a piece of self-analysis as "The Fall of the House of Usher"? His mind went back to his bouts of conscience over his debts at the University and the perverse way that he had quelled them by compounding greater debts, and to the illness and remorse that made his drinking joyless while he was editing the *Messenger*. Usher was a character whose destiny had been ordered; but Poe had not disintegrated in the face of adversity and change as his father had. This time he called himself — and his story — "William Wilson," and he began at Bransby's school, moving its setting, however, from the plain house it had occupied in reality to the Elizabethan mansion across the street that he had used as the focus of his daydreams more than twenty years before. There Wilson first meets with his conscience and runs from it, always to find it appearing as he is about to commit evil to others, until, interrupted in his plans to seduce a beautiful woman, he kills the William Wilson who is his conscience, only to realize that by so doing he has destroyed that part of his being whereby he was not totally isolated from God and man: "*Henceforward art thou also dead — dead to the World, to Heaven and to Hope!*"

Poe carried his tale from the moral question of conscience into the realm of the philosophical and the religious by his unusual ending. Like Morella's husband, Egœus, he came finally to the question of identity; but not content, as he might have been with the earlier tales, to raise the question "What is identity?" he inquired how it might be created and destroyed. By this token, John Allan had destroyed himself by exchanging loyalty to Edgar for approval — or rather to avoid disapproval — from the society of Richmond and from his new wife's family. The narrowness of businessmen and other worldly people: was it not the result of their strangling conscience for immediate gain, and because they limited their interests and their very selves to make their wealth increase? One could be cursed by God — as were the Ushers as surely as was the land of Edom — or by oneself. By expanding his being in his work, Edgar Poe had, in his last three arabesques, "Ligeia," "The Fall of the House of Usher," and "William Wilson," come to the fullest development of the literary urge that had made more than parody of "Metzengerstein" and "Berenice."

Edgar worked long and hard, revising his earlier tales as well as working over the new ones, and experimenting with how they might be arranged in a volume if he should be able to find a publisher for one. But he did not work all the time. The Falstaff Hotel, on Sixth Street on the other side of Chestnut from Poe's small clapboard house, had become a meeting place for actors, artists, and writers; and far more than in New York, where the Knickerbockers still held sway, Edgar was recognized as a major figure and a unique one, all the more so in that he could never be persuaded to accept a drink. Here he met William E. Burton, an English comedian just two years older than himself, who had, the previous July, founded *Burton's Gentleman's Magazine*. Burton had been writing sentimental short stories, theatrical gossip, and literary criticism in order to keep the pages of his book filled without paying out much money for contributions. As competition increased he improved the appearance of the magazine with better paper, more expensive plates, and better printing, but investing in improving the contents never occurred to him. But this hack work was cutting into the time he preferred to put on the project of establishing his own theater in Philadelphia, so when he met Poe, shortly after publication of *The Conchologist's First Book*, he showed himself interested in any proposal Edgar might make in assisting him.

Poe would have taken almost any job at that time. His stories were well in hand, and although he had managed to pay a long-overdue rent bill, he still owed Cox, and very little money was in prospect. He liked the place they were living in, largely because Virginia was happy there. They had a small garden, which Sissy was contentedly tending that May, followed about by a coal-black kitten which they had named Catterina. In view of the hard times, Edgar did not dare suggest the salary he had been getting when he left the *Messenger*, in spite of his increased prestige, but compromised between that and his beginning salary in Richmond. On May 10, Burton offered ten dollars a week, promising to meet Poe's demands after the New Year. Edgar accepted, not realizing that, unlike his agreement with White, this contract was to include nearly all the writing he would do for the magazine as well as the editorial work. But a bad job was better than none, and for the July issue he turned out five pages of criticism and resurrected two poems he had excluded from previous publications, "To Ianthe in Heaven" and "Spirits of the Dead."

Thus Edgar settled down again to the routine of turning out a magazine, with its concomitant pleasure of receiving review copies of new books, but with the additional irritation that Burton was even more of a literary huckster than White. He had the actor's traditional distaste for adverse criticism. In two weeks from the time he was hired, Poe quit in a fury when Burton asked him to tone down his criticism; but Burton was a completely inperturbable man and coaxed him back with a suggestion that they start all over as if the dispute had never taken place. In addition to nine pages of criticism, Poe inserted three poems and "The Man Who Was Used Up" in the August number, and responded to a request for contributions from the Pittsburgh *Literary Examiner* with a review of Willis's play *Tortesa, the Usurer* and an article on novel writing. They were printed unsigned, as editorial matter, and extensively edited, so Poe refused to write any more for the Pittsburgh paper, saying of E. Burke Fisher, the editor, "a greater scamp never walked."

In the midst of his editorial and personal ordeals, Edgar wrote a short apocalyptic piece, "The Conversation of Eros and Charmian," in which he predicted the end of the world in a novel way: a comet flaring across the earth extracted the nitrogen from the atmosphere, leaving pure oxygen to burn up the world at the first spark. With this *The Tales of the Grotesque and Arabesque* were complete, and he sent the manuscript off to Lea and Blanchard, who agreed on September 28 to print an edition of 750 copies, Poe to receive only the copyright and a few copies (he eventually got twenty), and all profit going to the publisher. In defiance of his own strictures, he dedicated the volume to Colonel William Drayton, his old friend of Fort Moultrie days. He was aware of the success *Pym* had had in England, even though the lack of international copyright meant that he did not get any money from it, and hoping for a British reputation that might reflect materially on his career, he entered into correspondence with John Wilson, editor of *Blackwood's*. Although he came to anticipate a favorable review and some assignments from them, it is easy to see why he got neither; with his "Psyche Zenobia" and "Scythe of Time," plus "Loss of Breath, a Tale à la Blackwood," he was straining British humor to its utmost, and the dour Scots review was never very much inclined toward the comical.

Poe continued grinding out material for the "Gents' Mag," as he called it, and inserting his latest stories in hopes of favorable comment from the literary figures he had put on the free list. When he had been with the *Messenger,* he had constantly urged people to subscribe and tell their friends about the magazine, but now he always advised his correspondents not to bother to subscribe to *Burton's;* even so, the circulation kept rising under his editorship. Irving responded generously with high praise over both "The Fall of the House of Usher" and "William Wilson." Burton started a scheme of offering premiums for the best contributions in lieu of paying regular rates, then paid nothing at all, to Poe's disgust. Edgar became more determined than ever to found his own magazine, and in order to put together a backlog of funds to last while the first issue was in preparation, he began writing a column for *Alexander's Weekly Messenger,* a Philadelphia newspaper run by Charles Alexander, the printer of *Burton's.* Poe's contributions were for the most part trivial commentaries on novelties in the city, essays on various subjects — including one on "Instinct vs. Reason" in which he related how Catterina had learned to open the door when she wanted to go out — interspersed with puzzles and cryptograms. He was not the least bit abashed to advertise his work or himself, and he made a considerable splash by offering to solve any cryptogram sent him. His ability to solve these ciphers was elementary — he probably learned from an encyclopedia article — but the interest the public took in this "secret writing" made him aware of still another trick he could use, and this he remembered later when he wrote "The Gold Bug."

A month before *The Tales of the Grotesque and Arabesque* was published, Poe wrote to Lea and Blanchard, asking how much they would pay for the copyright. He needed money, and in view of the favorable comment he had received thus far, he expected a substantial sale. The publisher replied curtly that they had undertaken to publish the book solely as a favor to him, and wished that they had not. This miffed Poe considerably, especially since, in spite of excellent reviews, there was very little sale. And so his attitude, compounded with bad sales, alienated a second publisher. He felt there was reason enough that his worth was being underestimated; he had even received a request from a watchmaker in Cincinnati for an autograph of one of his poems!

As 1839 drew to a close, Edgar believed that his life's opportunity was close at hand, and he worked on, almost frantically, to grasp it. Remembering that even if *Pym* had not brought him much money, it had been reprinted in England and caused him to be known there, he started another serial story. "The Journal of Julius Rodman," an account of exploration in the Far West that had been suggested by Irving's *Astoria*. This time, however, his heart was not in it, and at no point does it become vivid or striking as *Pym*, probably because Poe knew something of seafaring, but he had never seen the American West. Installments began appearing in *Burton's* in January, and at the same time *The Conchologist's First Book* went into a second edition. Wyatt was peddling it on his lecture tours, since he could hardly expect to stir up impulse sales for his more expensive Harper edition; but that hardly endeared Poe to the publisher of *Pym*.

Poe was becoming very well known in intellectual Philadelphia. John Kearsley Mitchell, a well-known physician and lecturer on medicine, invited him to dinner, and Hiram Haines, the Virginia editor at whose home Virginia and he had spent their honeymoon, certain that they must be living in luxury, offered to send Virginia a fawn as a pet. Edgar refused on the ground that he did not know how to arrange transportation, but a fawn would probably have been as much at home in their tiny garden as an elephant. A young medical student, probably introduced by Mitchell, named Thomas Dunn English, brought his poems to Poe. Wishing to encourage a young poet, and probably feeling that however bad they were they could not be worse than the sort of thing Burton dredged up, Poe printed them in the magazine. He would come in time to regret that kindness. In May there was a Whig rally in Philadelphia, where a young delegate to the convention that nominated Harrison, Frederick W. Thomas, was pelted, during his speech, by the Locofocos. Feeling him a kindred spirit, Poe introduced himself, and they became fast friends, discovering that they had many friends in common in Baltimore, where Thomas had known Poe's brother and had even been his rival in a love affair years before.

Poe continued through the spring of 1840 doing good service for the magazine, compiling a three-part article on artistic and scientific developments, continuing the installments of "Julius Rodman," and writing criticism and general articles of a superior sort, on a salary of fifty dollars a month; but he was becoming more and more dissatisfied with the shoddy kind of journal Burton insisted on putting out, while he felt himself almost ready to found his own magazine. Burton, too, had other interests. He planned to open his own house, the National Theatre, in August, and could spare for the magazine only enough time to check over Poe's work and find fault with it. Under pressure he blew off his temper quickly, then forgot his grievance. Poe was quiet and uncomplaining up to the moment things became utterly intolerable; then he became stubborn. They existed in an armed truce until the last week in

May, when recriminations flew hard and fast on both sides. One of the matters of contention was Poe's review of John L. Carey's *Domestic Slavery*, which Burton refused out of hand to publish. He would no more think of making any comment on such a controversial subject in his magazine than he would in a farce. Furthermore, Burton had probably come across Poe's draft of the prospectus he was planning on having printed for his proposed *Penn Magazine*, and although there was no possibility of competition between this five-dollar-a-year publication of high intellectual and artistic standards, and Burton's cheap journal, Burton was too angry to take that into consideration. He told Poe he could no longer afford to pay fifty dollars a month for two or three pages of manuscript, and at this Edgar walked out.

Burton then sent his clerk to Poe's house, with a note demanding the one hundred dollars he claimed was owed him, and asked what would happen to the Rodman serial. Edgar sent the clerk back without an answer, and the next day wrote a long and careful letter to the actor, clarifying his position and claiming that his debt was not over sixty dollars. He refused to say whether he would continue "Julius Rodman" until he heard from Burton again. This brought another angry response, and Poe wrote a formal resignation, free now to get his own magazine under way. He seems to have never regretted leaving Burton, but the actor, deprived of the underpaid editor who had built up his circulation, written brilliant criticism, and inserted "The Fall of the House of Usher" and "William Wilson" in his trivial pages, kept the magazine going for only five more months, then sold it. The circulation was then thirty-five hundred.

In the greenest of our valleys
By good angels tenanted,
Once a fair and stately palace —
Radiant palace — reared its head.
"The Haunted Palace"

THROUGH THE SECOND HALF of 1840 Poe's energies were consumed in three widely different projects, none of which was of any immediate use in putting food on the table or in satisfying his growing list of creditors. His first concern was to attract subscribers, contributors, and financing for the magazine he proposed to put into circulation on the first of the year. As election drew near, however, he put more and more time into volunteer work for the Whig Party; although practical politics was a subject far from his interests, his friendship for Thomas and his distaste for mob rule (which is what he considered Locofocoism to be) aroused him to enthusiastic partisanship. And relieved of routine criticism and article writing to consume his creative energy, he launched himself once more into the writing of short stories.

Poe had completed his prospectus for the *Penn Magazine* before leaving Burton; in June he had it printed as a broadside and distributed it as widely as he could, using all the addresses of his own correspondence and all he could remember from *Burton's* and the *Messenger*. Often he would use the back of the prospectus for his correspondence, thus advertising the magazine and making personal appeals for the same cost in postage. The magazine he proposed would have the stamp of individuality he had not always been able to put on the *Messenger*, since he had in it "no proprietary right." He did not mention his experience on the *Gentleman's Magazine*, but promised to be less caustic although as severe in his criticisms as he had been in the Southern journal. The magazine would not be regional; with the world as its audience, "Its aim chiefly shall be to *please*; and this through means of versatility, originality, and pungency."

Through June and July copies of the prospectus went out. The supply was exhausted in August, so Poe had a new batch printed, revising his text to add comments on the inferior state of criticism in most magazines, and improving the style. He attracted a large number of subscribers, essays, stories, and a plethora of poems. Through his friends, announcements of the new magazine were made in newspapers throughout the country. But his labors for "Tippecanoe and Tyler too" brought him inside the Log Cabin by election time, and he surrendered to the availability of the barrel of hard cider. This, compounded with his hard work and the tensions of attempting to found a magazine without capital and to support his family without an income, caused him to be struck down with illness for the whole of December. On the day the magazine was to appear, January 1, 1841, he reluctantly announced that "Owing to the severe and continued illness of Mr Poe the issue of the first number of [the *Penn Magazine*] is postponed until the first of March next."

One of his activities showed immediate success, however, when Harrison was elected President on a count of 234 electoral votes to Van Buren's 60. In spite of Locofoco enthusiasm in Philadelphia, the Whigs carried Pennsylvania by a narrow margain. Poe's contribution had little to do with the victory;

the Whigs swayed the undecided and even some Democrats by means of two smear campaigns — Charles Ogle's speech to deny an appropriation for repair of the White House, in which he accused Van Buren of living in sybaritic luxury in a "PALACE *as splendid as that of the Caesars*," and a whispering campaign, sometimes carried out in loud shouts, over the penchant of Van Buren's running mate for Negro mistresses. Both sides unabashedly chanted scurrilous songs and slogans against the other, rather than offering any concrete program for the country; the Whigs followed Nicholas Biddle's advice to forbid Harrison's saying anything and to keep pen and ink from him "as if he were a mad poet in Bedlam."

More lasting effect on the literary history of the country than on the political was being created in the little house on Sixteenth Street that summer. Edgar's last story had been written the previous winter; it was a satire on the pretentiousness of businessmen (strange attitude for a Whig!) and appeared under the title "Peter Pendulum, the Business Man" in the February *Gentleman's Magazine*. He turned out one other grotesque while the story-writing was moving him, "Never Bet Your Head." This is the account of Toby Dammit, whose method of emphasis was to say, "I'll bet you my head." He did it once too often, for the Devil took him up on it and won; and thus Poe refuted the charge that he had never written a moral tale. This story is much more good-humored than any of his previous diableries; but the arabesques that Poe wrote the same year mark an even greater control, the result of confidence in himself and an easing of his hostility to the world.

Probably the first was "The Man of the Crowd." Poe had been fascinated by the crowds he had seen in New York; some of the people he could classify as clerks or mechanics by their appearance, but others seemed merely digits of the crowd, and he could not imagine them in any other setting. This wonder had been refreshed by his experiences with the election mobs of 1840. In his story he envisioned following a striking old man whom he could not classify, through the streets of London for an entire night. As each region became depopulated, the old man would move on to another still alive with people. " 'This old man,' I said at length, 'is the type and the genius of deep crime. He refuses to be alone. *He is the man of the crowd.*' " Edgar undoubtedly drew on his memories of London and of his walks from the school of the Misses Dubourg to Southampton Row in creating the murky atmosphere of London at night; but his choice of the British capital as setting was dictated by its greater size than any American city, making possible the existence of crowds in one section or another at any hour, and he filled out his now dim memories with a London drawn from books.

The name Dubourg, the imaginative re-creation of a city, the appearance of a mysterious genius of crime — these elements recalled to Poe's mind a series of articles he had read in the back files of *Burton's*, "Unpublished Passages in the Life of Vidocq, the French Minister of Police." He had been interested in the high passions of crime, and especially of murder, since as a boy he read of the Kentucky Tragedy, which he later adapted for *Politian*. In New York the papers had often reported sensational murder trials, and there was still talk, while he was there, of the brutal murder of Helen Jewett, for which her lover, Richard P. Robinson, was tried and acquitted — rumor had it that the jury was bribed, and a life of Robinson was hawked in the streets. The methods of the New York police were like those of Vidocq, the relentless pursuit of the obvious, with the help of informers and luck.

In his features for *Alexander's*, Poe had shown a keen ability in analysis; his review of *Arabia Petraea* was built on an acute piece of scholarly detective work, all the more difficult in that without a knowledge of Hebrew he had to guess the flaw in Stephens's reasoning first, and check it with Anthon. He had constructed an exposé of Maelzel's chess player by reasoning backwards from the facts. What about the possibility of solving crimes by sheer logic? His fictional representations of himself up to this point had almost all been in the image of a man who did not act, but who felt deeply. Yet his experience as a critic had taught him that he also was the possessor of a keen intelligence, even though he had trouble applying it to his personal gain. Using the same imaginative technique by which he had presented his emotional being in the previous tales, intensified, he would now project a character possessing his intelligence enlarged to the exclusion of emotion. This creature of pure intellect he named C. Auguste Dupin, borrowing the name Dupin from the first installment of Vidocq, since French names of one syllable, like Pym and Poe, are rare. This time "Allan" was replaced by "Auguste," in celebration of his high intelligence.

To demonstrate Dupin's powers of analysis Poe invented an ingenious incident. Recalling times, perhaps, that he and Virginia had simultaneously come out with the same idea after a period of silence — a common enough occurrence between husband and wife, at which they would link fingers and say, "Bread and butter, salt and pepper" — he had Dupin follow logically the stream of varied associations in his companion's thoughts for a period of fifteen silent minutes, from his slipping on a piece of wobbly pavement through seven different stages of reflection until he could answer his companion's unvoiced opinion of an amateur actor, startling him and bringing the awe of Dr. Watson into the world for the first time. But this only characterized the first analytical detective; to show him in action it would be necessary to invent a baffling crime for him to solve. This was suggested by a device in Scott's *Count Robert of Paris*. The chattering of an orangoutang is mistaken for the voice of someone speaking in an unknown language. Poe may also have read newspaper accounts from the country of an ape that was trained to climb in windows and steal.

From these ingredients he constructed "The Murders in the Rue Morgue." Two recluses, a mother and daughter, are murdered in their locked room. Witnesses, summoned by their shrieking, agreed to hearing two other voices, one speaking French and the other a foreign language none of them knew, although the gendarme guessed it was Spanish, another Frenchman guessed it was Italian, a Dutchman thought it was French, a Spaniard thought it was English, an Englishman thought it was German, and an Italian thought it was Russian. Both windows were nailed shut, and the door had to be forced open, so the Prefect of Police arrested a bank clerk who had delivered a large sum of money to the women the same day and who thus was the last person identified as having seen the women before their death.

Dupin reads of the mystery in the papers, visits the house, makes his analysis: the murderer entered and left by one of the windows, the nail of which had rusted through; a tuft of hair clutched in the hand of one of the victims was not human hair; the women were treated with brutal ferocity; and the marks of a hand on the throat of one are not spaced as a human hand would grip, but fit Cuvier's description of that of an orangoutang. He advertised that an animal of that description was found in the Bois; a sailor called for it; and the story of a pet escaped with a razor in its hand clears up the mystery and brings about the release of the innocent clerk, to the chagrin of the police.

In creating the analytical detective story, Poe set in train more than he thought. The brilliant amateur, the awed nar-

rator, the locked room, the misleading clue, the baffled police-
man; all these things, combined with lesser ingenious details
which later mystery writers would exploit, made a tale that
would give Poe the international reputation he so desired, and
put into being a genre of fiction that had never existed before.
There had been crime stories before 1841, but Poe was the first
to make the detection more interesting than the crime.

In the meantime events were taking place in Philadelphia
which would have their effect on the distribution of this tale
and Poe's entire future. Burton had appealed to him to return
to the magazine within a month of their dispute, but Poe
would have nothing to do with it, even though this alienated
him from Nathan C. Brooks, who was a close friend of the
actor. In November Burton disposed of the magazine, selling
it to George Rex Graham for $3500 — one dollar a subscriber.
Graham, four years younger than Poe, had worked as a cabinet-
maker while preparing himself to become a lawyer, then took
the job of assistant editor of the *Saturday Evening Post* and
bought a magazine called the *Casket* from the proprietor of
the *Post*. When he combined the *Casket* with *Burton's* to create *Graham's Magazine*, the combined circulation amounted
to about five thousand. Poe, who had withheld any contributions from Burton, immediately sent "The Man of the Crowd"
to Graham, who put it in the first number and assigned Poe a
few book reviews.

Both because he still had hopes of putting out the first issue
of the *Penn* in March, and because he still had tales to write,
Poe did not actively solicit work from Graham, and did only
routine jobs on the reviews. When they were out of the way
he continued in the rich vein of imaginative writing he had
uncovered, and wrote a tale as far in every respect from the life
he had been living in the city, mixed in politics, crowds, imagined murders, and the crass business of Philadelphia life, as

was possible. Although his theme was mystical, his illustration of it was both idyllic and fanciful. Praising nature viewed in solitude, he imagines an idyllic scene by a twining mountain river — it could have been constructed from the countryside near Charlottesville, from the nearby gorge of the Wissahickon, or it could just have been a fancy made of dreams in Virginia's garden in spring — in the midst of which is a small island, one half bright with flowers, the other shaded in gloom from the overhanging trees. In his vision a fairy in a boat encircles the island, fading and drooping more with each journey through the shade, until, as the sun sets, darkness obscures her. Although the fairy is simply a symbol of his feeling of unity with all of nature, this piece of poetic prose would have delighted Virginia or any of the children of the neighborhood who liked to visit the eighteen-year-old girl and her husband who, unlike other men, did not disappear from home at eight in the morning and not get back until seven at night, tired and disagreeable, but could always spare time to talk and hear with courtesy the most fleeting of childish concerns.

Edgar loved the country. He knew the names of wildflowers and trees, and he was fascinated by every aspect of nature. But he and Virginia had rarely been in the country and rarely were alone together. Aside from their honeymoon trip, they had lived in cities, often in the enforced conviviality of boardinghouses. But the summer after he left *Burton's*, Mrs. Clemm went to visit friends in New Jersey, staying nearly two months. He and Virginia were alone, having passed without awareness from the infatuation and impulse that had led to their marriage to the deep contentment of affectionate companions and compatible lovers. Virginia was no longer a child, but a young woman and wife of four years' maturity. Theirs was a family in more ways than by church vows; when one considers that there were not a half dozen other people he ever called by their first names, the otherwise sentimental "Eddie," and "Sissie," and "Muddie" become the daily expression of a deep attachment.

In three stories, "Berenice," "Morella," and "Ligeia," Edgar had treated the theme of the death of the beloved; but in all these the male character — himself — was always passive. The theme was death far more than it was love. But in "Eleanora" he showed the growth of love in delicately drawn symbols. The narrator tells of his lucid years: for fifteen years he and his cousin grew up together in the Valley of Many-Coloured Grass. Until she was fifteen and he twenty, the valley was sprinkled with buttercups, daisies, violets, and asphodel; but then star-shaped flowers bloomed on the trees, and the red asphodel grew in place of all the other flowers. In every way the change in the valley gently suggests her coming to puberty and the appearance of the physical in their love. But she sickens and, after he has vowed not to love anyone else, dies. He leaves the valley, from which the asphodel and the blossoms of the trees have disappeared, where dark violets grow and silence reigns; and later he marries again, hearing the voice of Eleanora absolving him of his vow, "for the spirit of Love reigneth and ruleth."

Since the story marked the change from childhood to puberty, its very logic required that it include also "the last sad change which must befall Humanity," in spite of which life and love go on. In echo of "Morella" and "Ligeia," the second wife has remarkable resemblances to Eleanora (a detail which Poe revised out of the story later, as he did reference to the girl's "aged mother"); so that whatever effect his own life had on the events of the story, Virginia was the model for both first wife and second. In this, his only effective love story, he paid his wife the highest possible tribute in a tale so exquisitely wrought that it broke through the prudery of the time in a

way that not even the early Victorians could find objection-
able.

Death was a theme he always returned to, however, usually
to present it with horror and fear. But in "The Colloquy of
Monos and Una" he conceived of a life after death that was
neither fundamentalist-orthodox nor distasteful. The two spirits
converse about their dying, and Monos describes his awareness of being mourned over and buried, until, his body disintegrated, "The sense of being had at length utterly departed,
and there reigned in its stead — instead of all things — domi-
nant and perpetual — the autocrats *Place* and *Time*. For *that*
which *was not* — for that which had no form — for that which
had no thought — for that which had no sentience — for that
which was soulless, yet of which matter formed no portion —
for all this nothingness, yet for all this immortality, the grave
was still a home, and the corrosive hours, co-mates." Poe then,
not unlike philosophers of other religions, saw death as a gradual
return to the unity — note the names "Monos" and "Una" — of
all things, seeing through the error he described in "The Island of
the Fay" "in believing man, in either his temporal or future des-
tinies, to be of more moment in the universe than that vast 'clod
of the valley' which he tills and contemns, and to which he
denies a soul for no more profound reason than that he does
not behold it in operation."

But eternal problems are easily broken in on by temporal
ones. After a month's illness he had exhausted himself of musings on death and the immortality of love and was still no
closer to launching the *Penn Magazine* than he had been at
the beginning of December. His health recovered, he called
on George Graham, probably to see if there were reviews he
could write. Graham inquired into the status of Poe's magazine project, then suggested that if he would join the staff of
his magazine as an editor, they could go into partnership at

the end of six months for the founding of the new magazine.
In January the banks had again suspended payments, and the
1841 aftermath of the Panic was making it difficult for Poe to
get financial backing. He agreed, and continuing to solicit
articles for his twice postponed *Penn Magazine*, settled down
to getting out the April issue of *Graham's Magazine*.

And round about his home the glory
That blushed and bloomed,
Is but a dim-remembered story
Of the old time entombed.
"The Haunted Palace"

GEORGE GRAHAM'S FIRST ACT on hiring Poe as editor of his magazine was to insert an announcement in the *Saturday Evening Post* that the *Penn Magazine* was "suspended." Several of Edgar's friends wrote him expressing their disappointment, but Poe replied, "The *Penn*, I hope, is only 'scotched, not killed,'" and attributed its nonappearance to the bank suspensions that again made it impossible to convert the notes with which subscriptions were paid to specie. "In the meantime," he added, "Mr. Graham has made me a liberal offer, which I had great pleasure in accepting." This offer was a salary of $800 a year, plus four dollars a page for contributions — but a page of *Graham's* ate up nearly 1300 words. Poe's duties were to write the reviews and read the last proofs; since the office was shared with the *Saturday Evening Post*, the two magazines used the same staff for routine work, headed by Charles J. Peterson, one of a family of Philadelphia literary hangers-on.

Burton, who had fitted his theater out luxuriously with the help of the $3500 he had received for his magazine, made only a brief splash with his effort to revive repertory theater. The star system was only getting into full swing. Chagrined both at his lack of success and at Graham's hiring Poe — which made it seem as if he had been the one ousted rather than his assistant — Burton began spreading rumors that Edgar was "unreliable," strongly hinting that drink was the cause. News spread quickly in the literary community of the seaboard states; Burton had heard stories of why Poe had left the *Messenger*, and decorated his story to fit. Snodgrass, hearing the gossip in Baltimore, wrote Edgar urging him to sue the actor for slander.

While he was considering this possibility, however, Poe was busy preparing the first issue of *Graham's* to go out under his editorship. He inserted "The Murders in the Rue Morgue," revising even on the proof sheets. In addition he wrote a long review of one of Bulwer's intricate novels, defining a good plot as one "in which none of the *leading* incidents can be *removed* without *detriment* to the mass." In another review, of *Sketches of Conspicuous Living Characters of France*, he made an audacious offer that was to prove remarkably good publicity for the magazine, but that would become a tedious bore to him. Scoffing at the author's amazement at the solution of a cipher without the key, he said, "any one who will take the trouble may address us a note in the same manner as here proposed, and the key-phrase may be either in French, Italian, Spanish, German, Latin, or Greek (or in any of the dialects of these languages), and we pledge ourselves for the solution of the riddle. The experiment may afford our readers some amusement — let them try it." They did, for more than two years. Confident that he was going up while Burton was going down, he decided not to sue, explaining to Snodgrass that if he sued, the actor would institute countersuit for the names Poe called him.

It was far more satisfying to work, especially since the business of the magazine was not yet using up so much of his time that none was left for his own work. Poe never could simply do his job and go home, like Peterson, but was always planning new features and attractions to increase circulation. Through the month of March he worked on a realistic adventure story, in a narrative style similar to that of *Pym*, about a fisherman whose boat was sucked into the great whirlpool called the Maelström, off the coast of Norway. There had been an account of the Drontheim whirlpool in *Alexander's Weekly Messenger* late in 1838, and recalling this, Edgar looked up more facts in the *Encyclopaedia Britannica*. The devices Poe based his story on — the thrilling quality of a narrow escape from death, avoided only through the esoteric fact that a cylinder is sucked into a whirlpool more slowly than an object of any other shape — are ordinary fiction-writers' tricks; but Poe gave the story greater power not only by his precise choice of details but also by creating a character who was a man of little thought or feeling, but of action, and by showing his complexity in the feeling of awe he felt at the grandeur of the whirlpool when he was caught in it. "A Descent into the Maelström" was finished in a hurry and placed in the May number, which went to press, like all the issues of *Graham's*, a month before publication.

One day in April a Baptist clergyman without pulpit, who had drifted into editorial work in New England and New York, came calling at the office of *Graham's Magazine*. Rufus Wilmot Griswold was then twenty-six years old, and was preparing an anthology to be called *The Poets and Poetry of America*. A subject such as that could hardly help interesting Poe, and he naturally desired to be included, so he greeted the man cordially, although there was something about his oily manner that made the usually trusting Edgar wary. He kept in touch with Griswold, later sending him a selection of his poems and a memorandum outlining his life as he wanted it presented to the public in the biographical sketch Griswold planned to head each poet's work.

His review of Dickens led him to another tour de force. *Barnaby Rudge* was then appearing serially, each installment being sold on the streets like newspaper extras, as soon as copies arrived from England and could be printed up; all American publishers were pirates in those days before international copyright. Poe decided, like his Dupin, to solve the mystery in the novel and discover what the ending would reveal. Fictional murders are easier to solve than actual ones, but Poe put another feather in his cap by correctly guessing the outcome of the story, and astonished everyone, including Dickens when, a year later, he visited Philadelphia. To get his analysis into print as quickly as possible, so he could not be accused of having received information from England, he gave it to Peterson to put in the *Saturday Evening Post*, where it appeared on May 1.

While he was busy on his reviews of Macaulay and G. P. R. James for the June issue, to which he also contributed "The Island of the Fay," Poe got a letter from his political friend Thomas, who had moved from St. Louis to Washington when the Whigs came into power, and whose friend, Jesse E. Dow, had already received political preferment. Harrison, unlike Jackson, had been reluctant to replace many previous government employees by members of his own party; but Tyler was a different sort of person altogether and was a Virginian besides. "How would you like," wrote Thomas, "to be an office holder here at $1500 per year payable monthly by Uncle Sam." The duties occupied little time, and one could "lucubrate in a literary way" to relax from "the monstrous laziness of the day."

Evidently Poe spoke to Graham of this possibility, and the publisher did not like it one bit. He brought up the subject of the *Penn*, and again promised that in a little while Edgar and he would be partners in that venture. Operating on Graham's allurements as if they were specific proposals, Poe wrote long letters to Irving, Cooper, Paulding, Kennedy, Longfellow, Bryant, Halleck, Willis — to the most famous American literary men of his time, in other words — proposing exclusive contracts for the term of one year, fees, length and type of article; illustrations would be as the author would wish. Graham thought this was going entirely too far. He was willing to pay fabulous prices to get anything from these writers for his own magazine — Longfellow had already refused — and eventually he would pay fifty dollars and more for one of the Professor's poems, and $1800 for a story from Cooper. But he held his temper and merely mildly discouraged Poe, who began to feel disgusted at his situation. Toward the end of June Poe heard that Thomas had been granted a $1000-a-year position at Washington, and listing his qualifications — he was a Virginian, had battled "with right good will" for Harrison, and he understood that the Tyler Administration had a "disposition . . . to cherish letters" — he asked if there was any chance for him; "I am *really* serious about the office."

Through the four months he had been working for Graham, Poe had been enjoying more economic security than he had known since childhood, and his greater need, to be part of a loving family, was even better satisfied. Prices were lower than they had been when he was in Richmond, and although his salary was only a trifle higher, he was getting nearly twice as much in space rates as he had from White. Moreover, he had learned to carry his month's pay directly to Mrs. Clemm, and let her manage the household. Twice he went into debt for "luxuries" for Virginia — one was probably a harp, since she was enjoying singing — and then, Graham noticed, "he was nervous to the degree of misery until he had, by extra articles,

covered what he considered an imprudent indebtedness." His
home with Virginia and Mrs. Clemm was all the luxury he
needed for himself, and there was no longer any need to go
into debt for that.

Poe sold his story "Eleanora," the great celebration of the
love between his wife and himself, to the *Gift*, Carey and
Hart's annual that had printed stories of his in 1836 and 1840.
There was no fiction of his in the July *Graham's*. Instead he
wrote a long article on "Secret Writing," to exploit further his
offer of April. This proved popular enough for him to offer
"addenda" — mainly the solutions of cryptograms submitted
by readers — through August and September. He printed "The
Colloquy of Monos and Una" in the August number as well,
and a hearty review of a satire by his Baltimore friend Wilmer,
on the literary figures of the day, again not sparing the author
of *Norman Leslie*. His editorial duties done, he wrote Thomas
to ask Kennedy, then a Congressman, to intercede for him in
the matter of a Government post, and he proposed a new collection of tales to Lea and Blanchard, adding the eight new
ones to *The Tales of the Grotesque and Arabesque*. The publisher declined, since the previous collection had not yet been
sold out.

The details of his editorial post began to pile up and hamper
his creativity. Weary of the feature on cryptography, he recalled the success of his autograph articles in the *Messenger*,
and he started writing off again for sample signatures. He had
turned the manuscripts accepted for the *Penn* over to Graham
when he joined the magazine, requesting permission of most
of the authors, but he missed some; and when one of these
turned up in the *Saturday Evening Post*, he was highly embarrassed as well as irritated with the culprit, Peterson. Thomas
sent him the manuscript of one of his songs — Virginia liked
singing the literary politician's "'Tis said that absence" even

better than she did the more popular works of T. S. Arthur, that were appearing in *Graham's* — and Poe had to see to its publication. His tale writing dragged to a new low with a story suggested by a feature in an October Philadelphia *Public Ledger*, "Three Thursdays in One Week." This was an explanation of the international date line, and Poe used the information as the means whereby two lovers, whose grumpy uncle refused to let them marry until there were "Three Sundays in One Week," were made happy. Two sailors visit them, after each had voyaged in a different direction around the world, and get into an argument over whether Sunday was yesterday or tomorrow, while to those who stayed at home, the day of the visit was obviously Sunday. Echoes of John Allan and Neilson Poe can be heard in the character and speech of the uncle. Poe slipped the story into the *Saturday Evening Post*, apparently feeling it was not the sort of thing he wanted distributed throughout the country with his name on it. The circulation of *Graham's* then was approaching the twenty-thousand mark.

A more exciting news story was making talk through that fall. In June, the body of Mary Cecilia Rogers, a New York shopgirl, was found floating in the Hudson River. She had been last seen near the river in Weehawken, New Jersey, in the company of a man in naval officer's uniform, but the police had a theory that her murder was the work of a gang. In October, the girl's fiancé was found dead near where some of her clothing had been found, either having committed suicide or dying of exposure while drunk. Poe bought all the newspapers on the case, including the New York ones, as the mystery remained unsolved. This would make a good second case for Dupin. But he had no money to spare for a trip to the scene of the crime — even a trip to Washington, to pursue a Government post, would upset their budget — and so he had to work slowly, re-creating the events from often contradictory newspaper reports and speculations. It would be a long job.

In the meantime, doubly proud of "Eleanora" for the way it expressed his happiness in his marriage, he placed reprints of it in the Boston *Notion* and the New York *Weekly Tribune*. He was examined by some practitioners of the new "science" of phrenology, "all of whom spoke of me in a species of extravaganza which I should be ashamed to repeat." He was enjoying being a part of the literary world of Philadelphia and aware of his growing fame in the country. Poe's dissatisfactions of that winter were not the aching ones of poverty or a sense of failure. He liked his work and was very proud of the fantastic rise in circulation of the magazine, even though he was rankled by Graham's extravagance over things Poe considered in bad taste — for fashion plates, sentimental pictures, and the like, Graham would pay one to two hundred dollars a plate — and he was irritated that his own contributions went in at the lowest rate for original work, while Cooper, the "hackneyed" and "awkward" writer, got many times as much, as did many others. This Poe well knew, since it was he who carried on the correspondence, offering pay "at least *as* liberal" as that of any publisher.

Occasionally Graham would protest a harsh criticism, and Poe "was weak enough" to let the proprietor modify it, or even dictate what attitude his editor should take. Poe said, "In the case of Conrad, for example; he insisted upon *praise* and worried me into speaking well of such ninnies as Holden, Peterson, Speak, &c., &c. I would not have yielded had I thought it made much difference what one said of such puppets as these, but it seems the error has been made to count against my critical impartiality. Know better next time. Let no man accuse me of leniency again." Graham was right from *his* point of view; he made a fortune from the magazine (although he later lost it on the stock market), while Poe, by Graham's testimony, was little interested in money. "Except for [his wife and aunt's] happiness, and the natural ambition of having a magazine of his own, I never heard him deplore the want of wealth. The truth is, he cared little for money, and knew less of its value, for he seemed to have no personal expenses." Poe's efforts were focused on the pages of the magazine; Graham's, for all his qualities, on the subscription list.

Edgar's days of writing poetry seemed, that year, to be far in the past; but he continued working over that which he had written, and published "To Helen," finally with the "glory that was Greece" contrasted with the "grandeur that was Rome," in the September issue, and — perhaps with some irony — "Israfel" the next month. Aside from these, his contributions fell into a routine, with the series on autographs beginning in September, and another supplement to "Secret Writing" accompanying it the next month. He was gathering strength for the next step upward in his career; with the help of Graham or without it, supported by a Government post or on his own, by hook or by crook, he *would* have his own magazine.

With the kind of success he had made for Graham, he could hardly fail. The circulation rose to twenty-five thousand by the end of 1841, and the staff was supplemented by two "lady editors," Mrs. Ann S. Stephens and Mrs. E. C. Embury. Longfellow finally acceded to Poe's request and sent a poem, "The Goblet of Life." Graham could afford to pay for it; he would take a gross sum of more than a hundred thousand dollars from the envelopes of subscribers in the year to come. Christmas on Sixteenth Street was all the merrier for the successes and pleasures the future would bring, the brightest moment in Edgar's nearly thirty-three years.

Out of debt, employed, with the determination soon to be

his own employer, contented with his home and cheerful family, Poe entered into 1842 with every confidence that his career was past the stage of desperate struggle and that his life had finally, after many turnings, entered the smooth path. In the evening, after the plentiful dinner that Mrs. Clemm now could supply without stint, the occupants of the little clapboard house were happy together. Edgar would play the flute, and Virginia would sing to her harp.

This was the kind of family party that was taking place one night in the middle of January, 1842. Suddenly Virginia's voice broke and died; blood streamed from her throat. As he ran for the doctor, Edgar could not have helped knowing what anyone of his time knew: this was the fatal stage of tuberculosis. This was not the beginning of their best days together; it was the end.

While the angels, all pallid and wan,
Uprising, unveiling, affirm
That the play is the tragedy, "Man,"
And its hero, the Conqueror Worm.
"The Conqueror Worm"

FOR TWO WEEKS POE was frantic and useless, doing nothing but watch nervously by Virginia's bedside. The first crisis past, however, he wrote Thomas, "My dear little wife has been dangerously ill. About a fortnight since, in singing, she ruptured a blood-vessel, and it was only on yesterday that the physicians gave me any hope of her recovery." By that time some healing had taken place, but the hemorrhage might occur again at any time. In order to pay the doctors and provide the diet they prescribed, Edgar went to Graham the morning after his first sleepless night by Virginia's bedside, and asked his employer to advance him two months' pay, but "he not only flatly but discourteously refused." Graham must have been in bad temper that day, and Edgar was certainly haggard and impatient. But their quarrel was of short duration, and even after he resigned from the magazine staff three months later, Poe considered the now wealthy magazine proprietor "really a very gentlemanly, although an exceedingly weak man [with whom] I had no misunderstanding."

The thirty-third year of Poe's life was the strangest he ever lived, and the most difficult to understand. Virginia's illness, which would drag on for five more years of alternate despair and hope, scarred his life so deeply that he never recovered from it. His anguish at the thought that she too, like his mother, Mrs. Allan, and Mrs. Stanard, would be taken from him, drove him to drinking again, joylessly seeking the narcosis that might make life attractive. Alcohol fired him to talk brilliantly and seek company; he never before made so many friends — and potential enemies — as he did that year. And his dream-haunted hours between night and morning — the night he feared because "I believe that demons take advantage of the night to mislead the unwary — although, you know, I don't believe in them" — gave him horrible visions that the ambition still not quenched in him translated into some of his most gripping stories.

The remainder of his time as editor of *Graham's* saw also the production of some of his most acute critical analyses. The last installments of Dickens's *Barnaby Rudge* arrived in Philadelphia and had been promptly pirated by Lea and Blanchard in the almost forgotten happy days before Virginia's hemorrhage; the great Boz was himself arriving soon, to be feted by the people who stifled their own literature because, in the absence of international copyright, they did not have to pay him royalties. Not all of Poe's *Saturday Evening Post* predictions of the outcome of the story had proved true; but boldly ignoring his bad guesses, he referred to his earlier account and elucidated the technique of the mystery story by untangling the plot and exposing Dickens's offenses against art for the sake of complexity. When the Englishman arrived in March, Edgar sent him the two articles, winning himself long interviews from the lionized author, whose later work showed that he had read them with care.

For the March number he reviewed a book of Longfellow's poems, praising them highly but commenting, "His artistical skill is great, and his ideality high. But his conception of the *aims* of poesy *is all wrong*; and this we shall prove at some future day — to our own satisfaction, at least. His didactics are all *out of place*. He has written brilliant poems — by accident; that is to say when permitting his genius to get the better of his conventional habit of thinking — a habit deduced from German study." Poe was upset enough to write "deduced" for "derived," but he had declared his war on didacticism — from which he would be turned by the side issue, part hoax and part monomania, of plagiarism in the "Longfellow war" later — but at this point he thought again, and wrote further, clarifying his distinction between truth and beauty, and defining poetry as the *"Rhythmical Creation of Beauty."* His quarrel was with the "habit of thinking" and not with the man, a distinction that Longfellow himself was one of the few to recognize.

Still another two-part review made critical history in the April and May numbers. Hawthorne's *Twice-Told Tales* had been reissued — making them, as Poe pointed out, "thrice told" — and, jubilant over their purity and originality, he defined the short story, which he called the "tale," as "affording the best prose opportunity for display of the highest talent" because of the totality of its effect, since it can be read at one sitting; and he went on to point out what he had learned from his own writing, that every word, scene, character, and incident must contribte to the total effect. "A skilful literary artist has constructed a tale. If wise, he has not fashioned his thoughts to accommodate his incidents; but having conceived, with deliberate care, a certain unique or single *effect* to be wrought out, he then invents such incidents — he then combines such events as may best aid him in establishing this preconceived effect. If his very initial sentence tend not to the outbringing of this effect, then he has failed in his first step. In the whole composition there should be no word written, of which the tendency, direct or indirect, is not to the one pre-established design. And by such means, with such care and skill, a picture is at length painted which leaves in the mind of him who contemplates it with a kindred art, a sense of the fullest satisfaction."

For these classics of literary criticism, plus general editorial duties and the reading of the last proofs, George Graham paid his editor, through the first four months of 1842, less than one day's income from subscriptions; and the circulation of the magazine continued to mount. Being so obviously underpaid rankled Poe, but neither the injustice nor his great need was as irritating to him as compromising his artistic principles with "the namby-pamby character of the Magazine," and "the contemptible pictures, fashion-plates, music and love tales" that filled its pages while he had to cut his criticisms short. He dreamed again of the *Penn Magazine*, but by now he knew that Graham would not back him, or at least, that Graham would back only the kind of magazine that was dedicated to profits rather than art. Robert Tyler, the President's son, had sent him a poem through Thomas; therefore as soon after Virginia's attack as frantic scheming replaced anxious worrying, he wrote asking if Tyler would back the magazine. But Tyler had no money besides his salary as employee of the Government, although it took Poe a long while to understand that. Thomas offered, however, to get Edgar a position in the Philadelphia customs house, and Poe chased that will-o'-the-wisp for a long time.

In the hope that country air might help Virginia recover, the family left Sixteenth Street and moved into a house in the Fairmount region, not far from the reservoir and close by the Schuylkill River. Moving and caring for his wife had kept Poe from keeping regular hours at *Graham's*, and unbeknownst to him, Graham had brought in the unctuous Griswold as substitute. Griswold had made himself a reputation that Edgar considered undeserved, with his *Poets and Poetry of America*, even though in his *Graham's* review he had not blasted it but simply implied that Griswold's literary judgment was weak and prejudiced. In the irrational state of mind brought on by his wife's illness, Poe walked into the office one day, and seeing Griswold in the editor's chair, immediately assumed that this hack had taken his position. He clapped on his hat and walked out, and all of Graham's persuasive power was insufficient to induce him to return, even though he agreed to go on contributing to the magazine. In many ways this was an improvement for him, for in addition to being freed from responsibility for the low standards of the magazine, he could devote more time to stories that would bring in at least as much as his salary. Griswold took the job — at a higher salary than Edgar had been getting — and Poe began looking forward to November, when there would be appointments to the customs service.

By the time the May number of *Graham's* was sent to press — the last one issued under Poe's direction — he was well into completing a good stock of stories of a strange, morbid sort. His reconstruction of the incidents of Mary Rogers's death, which he imagined as occurring in Paris and called "The Mystery of Marie Rogêt," was finished, the longest story he had written since *Pym*. Even before then he had completed "Life in Death" (later called "The Oval Portrait") and placed it in the April *Graham's*. This is the account of a sickly traveler who, drugged with opium, takes refuge in a chateau where he is entranced by a strangely lifelike portrait of a young woman. He looked into a catalogue of the paintings and there learned that it was a painting of the artist's wife, who had sickened and died while sitting for it, seemingly as if life had passed from her to the picture. This he wrote in expiation of the extent to which Virginia's illness had been aggravated by the poverty they had suffered through Poe's dedication to his art.

Far more gruesomely autobiographical, however, was the symbolic fantasy of color which he called "The Masque of the Red Death." The situation is like that in the framework of the *Decameron;* Prince Prospero and a thousand friends take refuge in a walled abbey to escape the "Red Death," a plague of "sharp pains, and sudden dizziness, and then profuse bleeding at the pores, with dissolution." One night they hold a masquerade through seven rooms connected at angles, each decorated in a different color — blue, purple, green, orange, white, violet, and black, in that sequence — each illuminated through two stained-glass windows of matching color, save the last, where the windows were blood red. A mysterious mummer costumed like a victim of the Red Death appears and is pursued from the blue room to the black one, where each who enters falls dead, the Prince first of all, and where an ebony clock with penetrating chime stops as well after the last of the company is dead.

This nightmare was finished for the May *Graham's,* and must have been written in the anxious weeks following Virginia's attack, when each day was passed through like one of the prince's rooms in fear of her ending by another kind of red death. Of Poe's behavior during this time, Graham observed, "His love for his wife was a sort of rapturous worship of the spirit of beauty which he felt was fading before his eyes. I have seen him hovering around her when she was ill, with all the fond fear and tender anxiety of a mother for her first-born, her slightest cough causing in him a shudder, a heart-chill that was visible. I rode out, one summer evening, with them, and the remembrance of his watchful eyes eagerly bent upon the slightest change of hue in that loved face haunts me yet as the memory of a sad strain. It was the hourly *anticipa-*

tion of her loss that made him a sad and thoughtful man, and lent a mournful melody to his undying song."

In June Poe wrote to a friend, "The renewed and hopeless illness of my wife, ill health on my own part, and pecuniary embarrassments, have nearly driven me to distraction." He wrote simultaneously to the Boston *Notion* and other publications, offering "The Mystery of Marie Rogêt," which, he said, "at the usual price, would be worth to me $100. For reasons, however, which I need not specify, I am desirous of having this tale printed in Boston, and, if you like it, I will say $50." The reasons were that he needed the money, and Graham would have found it too long and insufficiently entertaining for his magazine; he was equally desirous of having it printed in Baltimore, and wrote Snodgrass to that effect. It remained unsold for many months and ended up in *Snowden's Ladies Companion*, which he later referred to as "the *ne plus ultra* of ill-taste, impudence and vulgar humbuggery."

By the end of June Virginia, now regularly taking mead, which Poe's cousin, Elizabeth Herring, had sent, was feeling better, and Edgar had completed enough new tales to begin thinking again of offering them to a book publisher. This time they made a collection big enough to fill two volumes, for which he chose the title *Phantasy Pieces*. He revised and changed the titles of some of the early tales, apparently in memory of their original comic character; "Berenice" became "The Teeth," "A Tale of Jerusalem" was called "A Pig Tale," and "Metzengerstein" was peculiarly renamed "The Horse-Shade." He had still another nightmare story, "The Pit and the Pendulum," completed, but omitted it along with "The Mystery of Marie Rogêt" because they had not yet been placed in a magazine, and if they appeared first in a volume no editor would buy them. The Philadelphia publishers had not yet disposed of all the *Grotesque and Arabesque* volumes, so the project seemed to warrant a trip to New York. Virginia, however, "began to fret . . . because she did not hear from me twice a day," so he cut his trip short without convincing any publisher to take the book, and it was never published.

So the summer of 1842 passed in futile projects, hard work, and sinking resources. Graham was having trouble with Griswold, who was feuding with Peterson, and, indeed, with some of the contributors. Eventually Graham had to fire him, but first he made Poe a "good offer to return," but Edgar would only rejoin the magazine if permitted "to get rid of the quackery which now infects it," and so remained unemployed. Well aware of Poe's need for money, Griswold offered to pay him "whatever your charge would be" for a review of *Poets and Poetry of America*, and take care of placing it in a magazine himself. Delighted at this opportunity to reject the bribe and still pocket the money, he and his friend Hirst cooked up a devastating review, delivered it, and took his pay. "I assailed it to the extent of my powers and should like to have seen Griswold's face as he read the manuscript." Griswold never forgot.

A much more pathetic piece of cheerfulness inspired Poe that fall to write "The Landscape Garden"; it is a daydream of nightmare intensity. A young man named Ellison unexpectedly inherits a vast fortune with one hundred years' interest accumulated to it from an eccentric ancestor whose will had stipulated that his property remain invested for that time and then go to his closest living relative. After considering various ways to lead his life, Ellison decides to create a new art, landscape gardening on the grandest possible scale, to create "a Nature which is not God, nor an emanation of God, but which still is Nature." "It was in devoting his gigantic wealth to the practical embodiment of a vision such as this — in the free exercise in the open air, which resulted from personal direction of his plans — in the continuous and unceasing *object* which these plans afford — in the high spirituality of the object itself — in the contempt of ambition which it enabled him more to feel than to affect — and, lastly, it was in the companionship and sympathy of a devoted wife, that Ellison thought to find, *and found*, an exemption from the ordinary cares of Humanity, with a far greater amount of positive happiness than ever glowed in the rapt daydreams of De Staël."

This sad fantasy contrasts horribly with "The Pit and the Pendulum," in which Poe imagined himself a prisoner of the Inquisition, outwitting one sadistic attempt on his life only to be faced with another, or "The Tell-Tale Heart," in which he fancied the agony of conscience that leads a murderer to confess. In both of these he was the victim — for as murderer he is victim both of his impulse to kill and of his conscience, and his only escape is to confess and to take the consequences — not one who has the almost divine power to use the very earth as his canvas, an artist free even of ambition — and who has a healthy wife as well.

In September Thomas, in Philadelphia to speak at Independance Hall, visited Poe, assuring him that he would soon be appointed to the customs service, and adding to that the promise of Government patronage for the *Penn.* In his excitement Edgar overreached himself, and instead of hearing his friend speak spent the day in bed. But before long he was again making plans for the magazine. A Georgia physician and Shelley-mad poet, Thomas Holley Chivers, had been writing him, and on learning that Chivers's father had died, leaving him property, Poe proposed their becoming partners, estimating that he could get the magazine under way with a thousand dollars. But Chivers did not have his money yet, so Edgar went on hoping that his customs house appointment would leave him free and solvent enough "to get up such a journal as *this* country, at least, has never seen."

Another literary man, in New England, had a similar ambition. James Russell Lowell was about to join Robert Carter in publishing the *Pioneer*. Poe wrote him, suggesting that he contribute an article to each number. Lowell replied, "Had you not written you would soon have heard from me," and suggested that Poe submit stories, for which he would pay ten dollars each. "The Tell-Tale Heart" was just then in the process of being rejected by Henry T. Tuckerman of the Boston *Miscellany*, and Lowell picked up the story for his first issue. "As far as a $3 Magazine can please me at all, I am delighted with yours," Poe wrote after the book was out. His *Penn Magazine* would be of the superior five-dollar-a-year variety.

Mid-November finally arrived, the time when political spoils were to be divided. The Philadelphia papers came out with announcements of four customs house employes who had been dismissed, and among the names of Tyler men who had been appointed in their place was a certain "Pogue." Edgar assumed that the reporters had misunderstood the calling of the name "Poe," and, after awaiting for two days the summons to be sworn in, called on the Collector, Thomas S. Smith. "I asked him if he had no good news for me yet. He replied — 'No, I am instructed to make no more removals.' At this, being much astonished, I mentioned that I had heard, through a friend, from Mr. Rob. Tyler, that he was requested to appoint me. At these words he said roughly, — 'From *whom* did you say?' I replied from Mr. Robert Tyler. I wish you could have seen the scoundrel — for scoundrel . . . he *is* — 'From *Robert* Tyler!' says he — 'hem! I have received orders from *President* Tyler to make no more appts and shall make none.' " Thus ended that certain promise of a political sinecure.

There the traveller meets, aghast,
Sheeted Memories of the Past —
Shrouded forms that start and sigh
As they pass the wanderer by —
"Dream-land"

ON JANUARY 19, 1843, Edgar Poe was thirty-four years old, a
slim man a trifle over medium height, still erect in carriage and
fastidiously neat, but his complexion was pale and his dark
brown hair thinning toward the top. He was clean-shaven except for side whiskers that came down only to the point where
his cheeks curved to meet his chin, and his expressive eyes
showed their Celtic heritage in seeming sometimes gold-flecked
green, sometimes hazel. He sat at his writing table in the brick
house on Coates Street through the morning and early afternoon, nervously alert for a cough that might disturb his wife's
precarious hold on life; he could be easily startled by a slight
noise now. In the afternoons he would walk down into the
city, often ending by calling on his friends, Mayne Reid, the
Irish novelist, who was "his companion in one or two of his
wildest frolics," but who saw no harm in him; or Thomas Dunn
English, the would-be poet who gained fame, eventually, with
a sentimental song. But what brought Poe into the city — thus
into range of temptation — was arranging for the publication
of his magazine, now closer than ever to achievement. He had
a partner now, Thomas C. Clarke, an experienced publisher

who had revived the *Saturday Evening Post* twenty-odd years before, although Graham was now running this often-reincarnated journal, and was currently proprietor of the *Saturday Museum.* Poe's magazine had also suffered a change of name; it was now the *Stylus.*

On the last of January the firm of Clarke & Poe drew up a contract with the illustrator Felix O. C. Darley for pictures for "the necessary illustration of the text." No fashion plates would mar the pages of the *Stylus!* They decided that the magazine would get off to a better start if Edgar was given some publicity, so in the guise of announcing that he had joined the staff of the *Saturday Museum,* Clarke inserted a biography and portrait of Edgar in the paper on February 25, and reprinted it a week later for "those who were disappointed in obtaining copies" the first time. Edgar called the picture a "caricature," and wrote Thomas, "I am ugly enough, God knows, but not *quite* so bad as that." Henry B. Hirst was the author of the biography, although Poe of course directed how it should be written. He moved to the Spring Garden region of Philadelphia, still rural, but closer to the center of the city.

In addition, there was hope again for the customs house position. Poe had reported the behavior of the "scoundrel" Smith to Thomas, claiming that he was not a member of the Tyler political faction at all, and there was talk of his removal by Congress. Eventually the scheme was worked out that Poe's best chance of an appointment was to go to Washington and plead his own case. Early in March he somehow got hold of enough money for the trip, and set out. Being away from Virginia made him as usual nervous, and when he was greeted by Thomas and his friend Dow, he set out on a week's binge, keeping himself going by maintaining his alcohol content at a level that made him very high-spirited, and he went about the Government departments soliciting subscriptions for the *Stylus* and enjoying himself highly. "I believe that I am making a *sensation*," he wrote in a drunken letter to his partner, and if soliciting magazine subscriptions when he was presented to the President did not make a sensation, hardly anything could. On the twelfth, Dow became concerned, and wrote Clarke to come and get him. If Clarke could not, Dow said, "we will see him on board the cars bound to Phila., but we fear he might be detained in Baltimore and not be out of harm's way." They did, and Poe was met at the depot by Mrs. Clemm on the fifteenth, astonishing everyone by being sober and cheerful. He wrote his two Washington friends simultaneously, apologizing for his behavior — "Please express my regret to Mr. Fuller for making such a fool of myself in his house, and say to him (if you think it necessary) that I should not have got half so drunk on his excellent Port wine but for the rummy coffee with which I was forced to wash it down." — and asking Dow to "Call, also, at the barber's shop just above Fuller's and pay for me a levy which I believe I owe." It was not long before Poe knew that he had no further hope of preference from the Administration.

His hope, and the end of his hope, of a political job made little change in the quantity of his writing, however. In January he had published his first new poem in three years, "The Conqueror Worm." At the opposite end of the artistic scale, he was hard at work on a story that he thought might make the sensation he had mistakenly anticipated for his "solution" of the murder of Mary Rogers. All of his journalistic tricks had been popular; but the outstanding hit was his series on cryptograms. A story with a secret message in it, especially one that revealed the secret of a source of wealth, sounded like a "natural." A half dozen years before he had reviewed Robert M. Bird's *Sheppard Lee*, in which the hero's frantic quest for money includes a search for Captain Kidd's buried treasure.

The combination of ciphers and pirate gold sounded sure-fire; but Poe also recalled the comic figure of a Negro servant from the novel, and this association with the South brought back his Army days in South Carolina, and his natural-history studies with Dr. Ravenel on Sullivan's Island. He recalled the click beetle, with its death's-head spots, like a pirate flag, and the gleaming gold *Callichroma splendidum*; and putting them together he had his tale, "The Gold Bug."

Poe brought into the story all the exuberance of his remembered youth. He borrowed the idea of a Negro character from Bird's novel — not forgetting the minstrel shows that were coming into vogue — but modeled him on one of the wise but unlettered slaves of Virginia, writing field-hand dialect with the skill that he had put into the Irish of "Why the Little Frenchman." Not only was the pirate map in code; it was written in invisible ink as well, that appeared only when the paper was heated. Poe was well aware that the story was hopelessly contrived; the plot was played out halfway through, and the rest is explanation, to draw the reader's attention from the basic absurdity, that Captain Kidd had gone to ridiculously melodramatic means to make his map secret, then had dropped it on the beach where it was fortuitously found generations later. The only function of the insect which gives the story its name — and a great deal of its drama — is decoration.

In spite of its length, Graham snapped up the story for his magazine, paying, however, the usual minimum price. But Edgar learned that the *Dollar Newspaper* was offering a prize of a hundred dollars for the best story submitted, and got the story back. Unable to return Graham's money, he promised to make it up with reviews, beginning a series on "Our Amateur Poets" for the March number. "The Gold Bug" made the hit Poe expected. It won the prize and was published in two installments in the paper toward the end of June, was reprinted in the *Saturday Courier*, and reprinted again in the *Dollar Newspaper*, so great was the demand for copies. Silas S. Steele, a Philadelphia playwright, made a dramatic adaptation of it, which was given as a curtain-raiser on August 8 at the Walnut Street Theatre.

The best serious literary outlet he had, besides the embryonic *Stylus*, was Lowell's *Pioneer*. Ever since their first correspondence Edgar had sensed a kindred spirit in the New England poet. He submitted a poem, a revision of the 1831 "A Pæan," to the second number of the magazine, and a long essay on versification, "Notes on English Verse," for the third. In February, Robert Carter, Lowell's partner, wrote him that Lowell was suffering from ophthalmia. Shortly after Poe's return from the disastrous visit to Washington, Lowell himself wrote, in spite of his eye trouble, announcing the end of his magazine. His printer had caught him short of capital and had protested his note, leaving him with debts of $1800, $10 of which was due Poe. Edgar immediately wrote back, "I have just received yours of the 24th and am deeply grieved, first that you should have been so unfortunate, and, secondly, that you should have thought it necessary to offer me any apology for your misfortunes. As for the few dollars you owe me — give yourself not one moment's concern about *them*. I am poor, but must be very much poorer, indeed, when I even think of demanding them."

Poe had his own magazine to think of. He asked Lowell for a poem for the first number, and requested that he intercede with Hawthorne for a story. White, of the *Messenger*, had died, and Edgar wrote to Peter D. Bernard, his former employer's son-in-law, inquiring if he could purchase the subscription list of the Southern journal, then asked William MacKenzie, his sister's guardian, to look into the same matter. All this was taking place within two weeks of his return from

Washington. As a last effort for a Government position, he got a letter of recommendation from Robert Tyler, but as the President remained silent, it was of no use. In the middle of April Lowell reported that both he and Hawthorne would contribute to the *Stylus*, and on May 16 he sent a poem. By the time it arrived, however, that magazine was finished once for all. Poe quarreled with Clarke, and all backing was withdrawn.

Thus, while Poe's fame in Philadelphia continued to rise, his life deteriorated. John Tomlin, a poetical postmaster of Jackson, Tennessee, with whom Poe had been corresponding, fanned up his suspicions that there was a clique in Philadelphia conspiring against him. Knowing that Tomlin was also corresponding with Lambert Wilmer, an old Baltimore acquaintance whose *Quacks of Helicon* Poe had reviewed without enthusiasm the previous summer, Poe began prying and discovered that Wilmer had commented on him in a letter to Tomlin. Nothing would do but he must see the letter, and he bothered Tomlin until he got it. But the comment was mild enough, merely one item in a series of gossipy details about Philadelphia literary men, referring to "vagaries to which he has lately become subject," and regretting that "he is not a teetotaller by any means, and I fear he is going headlong to destruction, moral, physical, and intellectual." All that was true enough, save the intellectual. Poe was driven past the stage of merely thinking about asking Lowell for the ten dollars still owed him, and got it. But he was continuing to write, in a fantastic variety of manners that ranged from the nightmare to the comic, and on to the nostalgic and the bucolic.

The worst nightmare of his entire production is "The Black Cat," which was finished for the August 19 *United States Saturday Post*, as the *Saturday Evening Post* was briefly called. Poe was fearful of the fits of temper that struck him when he was drinking. Sober, he remained courteous in nearly any situation;

he was still quick to turn the other cheek. But the moment he began to be affected by alcohol, his bottled-up rage at the injustices he felt deeply was uncorked, and when he wrote Lowell that his magazine scheme had "exploded" he was probably describing exactly what had happened. The story expresses the fear that this rage might harm those he loved as it had his career, and writing it must have been torture beyond even masochism.

Poe's tenderness to the weak and his quick response to affection freely given — not the obedient adoration of a dog, but that which seems as if granted through choice — made the cat, already interesting because of its connotation of mystery, his favorite animal. In creating the main character of the story, Poe distorted all the faults of his personality in drink to mad extremes. In a rage at the cat's avoiding him when he was drunk — Edgar well knew that cats do so — the man cuts out its eye, then, when it avoided him still more, hanged it, "a sin . . . even beyond the reach of the infinite mercy of the Most Merciful and Most Terrible God." That night his house burns, and on the ruin is marked the image of a gigantic cat. Another black cat follows him home from a drinking place, and when, later, rage comes on him while his wife and he are in the cellar of their house, he attempts to attack the cat with an axe; and when his wife intervenes, he kills her and walls the body in the cellar. The police investigate but find nothing until, in bravado, he taps the wall, and a cry comes from within it; he had walled the cat up with the corpse.

In vast contrast with this story is the description of a visit to the valley of the Wissahickon (which he spelled "Wissahiccon"), a beauty spot a few miles above Philadelphia, which had been called to his attention years before in Richmond, when he reviewed Fanny Kemble's *Journal*. It is hardly more than an essay, but it has remarkable charm and tranquillity, combined with quiet humor. Two other comic pieces are more in the manner of the early grotesques, one, "Raising the Wind," and the other "The Spectacles." The first is a *jeu d'esprit* on confidence tricks, the second a too-long-drawn-out weak joke about a nearsighted young man who is tricked into going through a faked marriage ceremony with his own great-great-grandmother to teach him not to be so vain as not to wear spectacles when he needed them.

Still another story gains much of its atmosphere from Poe's memories of the mountains near the University of Virginia, "A Tale of the Ragged Mountains." The plot, weakest part of the story, is based on metempsychosis, but unlike "Metzengerstein" and "The Black Cat," the reincarnation is not for the purpose of vengeance, nor, as also in "Lygeia" and "Morella," does it follow death, but it comes as a vision. A man named Bedloe, who takes morphine for his neuralgia, walks in the hazy Indian summer into a vision in which he seems to be a defender of a besieged oriental city, where he died of a wound by a poisoned arrow. On his return he tells the story to his physician, who recalls that his friend Oldeb had died in Benares in 1780 in like fashion. Bedloe himself dies, of a poisonous leech accidentally applied to the same spot where the arrow struck Oldeb, and in his obituary the typesetter left the final "e" off his name, making Bedlo the reverse of Oldeb.

In spite of this weak and pointless piece of mystification — perhaps because of it — Edgar sold this tale to *Godey's*, where it appeared among the fashion plates in April, 1844. "Raising the Wind" had already appeared in the issue of the *Saturday Courier* for October 14, and "The Elk," the essay on the Wissahickon, was accepted for the annual the *Opal*. Before he was very far along on "A Tale of the Ragged Mountains," however, Poe tried another means of exploiting his "Gold Bug" popularity. Since no publisher would take the risk of printing his tales in regular volumes, he thought of issuing them in pamphlet form and convinced a different Graham, William H., to put out as the first of *The Prose Romances of Edgar A. Poe*, Uniform Serial Edition, a forty-page paperback containing "The Murders in the Rue Morgue" and "The Man That Was Used Up." The price was twelve and a half cents, but even "one bit" was more than people were willing to pay for short stories, and the series was discontinued.

As the year drew to an end, Poe was often sick and frequently in need, but working steadily on new stories and on the reviews with which he was paying off his debt to Graham for the money advanced on "The Gold Bug." Most of these since Griswold's anthology had come out were on poetry, and ever since his article for Lowell's magazine he had been thinking deeply about the theory of verse. His scurrilous review of Griswold had aroused considerable interest, and when, in January, 1844 an article appeared in the *London Foreign Quarterly* on American poets, attributed to Dickens, the newspapers blazed with comment. "American Notes" was still stinging the thin skins of patriots, and Poe was himself aroused at being accused by the English critic of imitating Tennyson, while "the passages quoted as imitations were written & published, in Boston, before the issue of even Tennyson's first volume."

Instead of just shouting in barrooms, Edgar found himself a platform. On January 31 he lectured on American poetry at the Odd Fellows Hall in Baltimore, and found that he not only enjoyed performing before an audience, but, at twenty-five cents admission price, he also could make a little money. On March 13 he gave the lecture in Reading, Pennsylvania, and he undoubtedly gave it many places. His voice was rich, his enunciation clear, and he read poems with a dramatic, almost histrionic power. Furthermore, his lecture necessarily included severe criticism of some of the second and third raters of

Poets and Poetry of America, and accompanying coals of fire on the head of Rufus Griswold. He tuned up his platform manner — even shaving off his side whiskers and cultivating the moustache that was to become his trademark — but did not tone down his caustic comments. Soon he had covered the local circuit, and the lecture was played out.

All this while the stories flowed out, with their themes of death and burial, of abstruse functions of the mind and madness. "The Oblong Box" tells of an artist transporting his wife's body by sea, who, when the ship sinks, goes down with the oblong box containing the body rather than abandon it. "The Premature Burial" is of a cataleptic who, coming out of a fit in a narrow ship's bunk, goes through all the terror of one who actually — as he imagines he had been — was buried alive. "The System of Doctors Tar and Fether" tells of a madhouse run on the theory that the inmates should not be locked up, until the lunatics lock up the staff. These have the confusing quality of being neither quite grotesques nor arabesques, although another, "Thou Art the Man," seems almost a parody of the analytical detective story Poe had invented.

Poe's confusion seems to have been a part of his attempts to reconcile the two divergent parts of his artistic personality, the coldly analytical and the emotionally imaginative, just as he had used "The Black Cat" as a therapeutic to the extremes of tenderness and rage in his personal behavior. Good and evil were opposites; but truth and beauty were simply separate qualities — this much he had reasoned out in his review of Longfellow's poems two years before. Both were *good* to some extent; his objection to Longfellow's poetry was its didacticism, a function of the mind that has nothing to do with art. Art is the function of taste, which is the "connecting link" between pure intellect and the moral sense. Art — the result of taste — was never perfect, just as the ultimate in intellect could never be reached, and no man was completely moral. There a thought struck Poe that made him, in time, cry "Eureka." "All things are either good or bad by comparison. . . . pleasure . . . is but the contrast of pain. *Positive* pleasure is a mere idea. To be happy at any one point we must have suffered at the same. Never to suffer would have been never to have been blessed."

Now, how to express that in a story? Poe had long been interested in hypnotism — Mesmerism, as he called it. Science was very vague about the nature of the hypnotic trance; it seemed to be a state that was neither life nor death. So he imagined a man suffering with phthisis — tuberculosis — who died under hypnotism, and who revealed the nature of God, and of life and death. God is matter unparticled — "indivisible — *one*"; things and people are the thoughts of God. Strangely enough, readers took the story as an account of an actual happening, even if they could not make much of the philosophy in it, although Poe preached his revelation in a letter to Chivers before "Mesmeric Revelation" was published, showing that *he* was convinced it was an earth-shaking discovery.

Having satisfied his moral urges, he applied this theory of relativity to a tale of ratiocination, another adventure of the detective Dupin, "The Purloined Letter." A compromising letter is stolen by a brilliant mathematician and poet. By analyzing the man's way of thinking, Dupin recovers it after the police have failed in the most minute searches, since they overlooked its being in a letter rack in plain sight, feeling that it would be concealed, exactly as the thief expected they would. But Dupin, in addition, left a letter which looked similar, turning the tables on the thief, who would compromise himself by believing that he still had it, thus proving that his certainties were as relative as those of the police.

Thus Poe reveled in high thinking at his writing table and in low abuse on the lecture platform and on the streets of

Philadelphia. "I have never yet been able to make up my mind whether I regard as the higher compliment, the approbation of a man of honor and talent, or the abuse of an ass or a black-guard. Both are excellent in their way — for a man who looks steadily up." Dreaming of his own magazine again, he wrote to Lowell, proposing that "the élite of our men of letters combine secretly" to found it, having "nothing to do with Agents or Agencies." That was sheer pipe dream, though, and Poe knew it. His situation in Philadelphia was becoming precarious, and there seemed to be no further opportunity there. He thought about New York again, and ways of breaking into its literary world. Then he remembered an incident from the time he had published "Hans Phaall" in Richmond, and he had his trick. Philadelphia was played out; on to New York!

Not the least obeisance made he; not a minute
stopped or stayed he;
But, with mien of lord or lady, perched above
my chamber door —
Perched upon a bust of Pallas just above my
chamber door —
Perched, and sat, and nothing more.

"The Raven"

ON SATURDAY MORNING, April 6, 1844, Edgar Poe loaded their trunks on a hired carriage, and he and Virginia left the Spring Garden house forever. Mrs. Clemm stayed behind to sell whatever was disposable and to close the house; there was also a volume of the *Southern Literary Messenger* to be returned to Henry Hirst for the owner, William Duane, the Secretary of the Treasury. The ride to the Walnut Street wharf was not a long one, but the driver asked a dollar, which Edgar refused to pay. Thus the expedition to conquer New York started, appropriately enough, with an argument. The New York literary scene was a battleground, where side issues simply lent piquancy to the major war, between the Knickerbocker clique — Lewis Gaylord Clark, Frederick Swartout Cozzens, Dr. John Wakefield Francis, and others — against "Young America," led by Evert Augustus Duyckinck, Cornelius Mathews, and — soon now — Edgar Allan Poe.

Poe had chosen sides in this fight long before, since he had not only offended the Knickerbockers personally with harsh criticisms but had joined with the Young Americans in favoring Hawthorne and considering Longfellow less than perfect. He made the further gesture, before leaving Philadelphia, of making peace with Mathews, whose *Wakondah* he had called "a mere jumble of incongruous nonsense," in *Graham's*, although he tried too hard to please in calling his review an "impudent and flippant critique . . . to be laughed *at*." Prudently, he burned no bridges in leaving Philadelphia; in addition to keeping up his relations with Graham and Godey, he had arranged with Eli Bowen, proprietor of the Columbia, Pennsylvania, *Spy*, to write a series of newsletters from "Gotham," and he was well prepared to burst into New York with an explosion of publicity.

The device he had thought up was suggested by the stir that had been made by Richard Adams Locke's "Moon Hoax" nine years before. A penny paper, the New York *Sun*, had published this piece of fiction about a telescope that revealed life on the moon, offering it as authentic news. The excitement was so great that other New York papers copied "Hans Pfaall" from the *Messenger* and printed the two side by side. So Poe brushed up his balloon data and the Defoe-esque narrative technique he had used in his story of a trip to the moon, but this time he left all burlesque out and narrated a balloon voyage from England that ended — conveniently for the authenticity of his local details — at Fort Moultrie. Thus he planned to so catch the progress-mad imagination of the public that he might even divert attention from the raging controversy over whether or not Texas should be admitted to the Union.

This venture had been carefully planned before Edgar and Virginia took the ferry across the Delaware, tipped a boy to put the trunks in the baggage car, and, having arrived nearly an hour too early for the train, sat in the Depot Hotel and read the papers. At seven the locomotive chugged away from the

Camden station and rushed — at twenty miles an hour — up the Delaware Valley to Trenton, and then across the neck of New Jersey to Perth Amboy. There they changed to a steamboat, and, shortly before three o'clock in the afternoon, docked in lower Manhattan, in a pouring rain. Edgar left Virginia in the ladies' cabin with the trunks, quickly encountered a man selling umbrellas, and bought one, reducing his small stock of money by sixty-two cents. He hurried up Greenwich Street to just below Cedar, and there he found a boardinghouse, made a quick bargain of seven dollars a week for the two of them, and — gone hardly more than half an hour — hired a hack and brought Virginia from the boat.

Even though "The house is old & looks buggy," the food was plentiful and good; "Last night, for supper," he wrote Mrs. Clemm the next morning, sitting in his drawers while Virginia mended his torn pants, "we had the nicest tea you ever drank, strong & hot — wheat bread & rye bread — cheese — tea-cakes (elegant) a great dish (2 dishes) of elegant ham, and 2 of cold veal, piled up like mountains and large slices — 3 dishes of the cakes, and every thing in the greatest profusion." Breakfast was equally copious, and so Poe set out well fed on his first foray in wild journalism, further armed with his transatlantic balloon story, and four dollars and fifty cents.

Just as the "Moon Hoax" had brought crowds swarming to the offices of the *Sun*, so did the "Balloon Hoax," then announced with the headline, "Astounding News." Poe said, "On the morning (Saturday) of its announcement, the whole square surrounding the 'Sun' building was literally besieged, blocked up — ingress and egress being alike impossible, from a period soon after sunrise until about two o'clock P.M. . . . As soon as the few first copies made their way into the streets, they were bought up, at almost any price, from the news-boys, who made a profitable speculation beyond doubt. I saw a half-dollar given, in one instance, for a single paper, and a shilling was a frequent price."

Early in May, Mrs. Clemm packed the Poes' black cat in her basket and took the train to Perth Amboy and on to New York — but first she took Duane's copy of the *Messenger*, along with other books, to Leary's bookshop and sold it. On May 18 Edgar's first article appeared in the Columbia *Spy*, and he set about wandering through all quarters of the city, picking up details for the column. He described the shanties of the Irish squatters and the reservoir at Forty-third Street and Fifth Avenue, and went rowing on the East River. He criticized the city government, the magazines, athletic contests, the newly returned Wilkes expedition (from which his friend Reynolds had been excluded), and the architecture of Brooklyn. He sent his story "The Oblong Box" to N. P. Willis, still editor of the New York *Mirror*, and wrote two generous columns about him when he praised it and suggested it be submitted to the *Opal*. Mrs. Hale, the editor, wanted an article rather than a tale, however, and inserted it in *Godey's*, printing Poe's "A Chapter of Suggestions" in the annual instead. This was a collection of paragraphs something like "Pinakidia."

On one of his walks around the island in the pleasant spring weather, Poe wandered up the Bloomingdale Road to what is now about Eighty-fourth Street and Broadway, and stopped at the farmhouse of Patrick Brennan, whose 186 acres stretched between the road and the Hudson. It was a charming, quiet place, and Mr. and Mrs. Brennan and their family seemed pleasant people. Virginia was beginning to suffer more frequent coughing spells, and the idea of a rural retreat appealed to him. After the first fanfare of his arrival in New York, nothing seemed to have happened, and he was more than a little reluctant to get into the free-swinging battle of New York journalism. He broached the subject of their living there with the Brennans, who after a little discussion agreed. In the early summer of 1844 they moved in. Now about five miles from the heart of the city, Edgar discontinued his *Spy* articles and began "playing the hermit in earnest." In July he wrote Lowell, "I have thus rambled and dreamed away whole months, and awake, at last, to a sort of mania for composition. Then I scribble all day, and read all night, so long as the disease endures."

While Poe was rusticating at Brennan's, the election campaign of 1844, whose main issue was over the admission of Texas into the Union, got itself under way. Sam Houston, "The Raven" of Texas, gradually maneuvered his truculent nation toward joining the United States. New England and much of the North was opposed to admitting another slave state, and put their influence behind Henry Clay, who was nominated Whig candidate for the Presidency, declaring "Annexation and war with Mexico are identical." The Democrats were deadlocked for some time, but eventually nominated the dark horse, James K. Polk, and the news was flashed by Morse's electric telegraph to Washington, where the means of transmission was considered more exciting than the news. The Tyler party withered and died as the Senate rejected the treaty that would admit Texas as a territory.

But all through the national excitement Poe lived quietly, "nor have I seen a living soul out of my family." He gradually disposed of his completed stories, scattering them through a variety of magazines and annuals. Graham suggested that Poe would be a worthy subject for one of the "Our Contributors" series in the magazine, and Lowell accepted the assignment to write it. Edgar sent him Hirst's biography that had been printed in the *Museum*, plus a list of his writings since its publication, and claimed that "The Gold Bug" had circulated more than 300,000 copies. He wrote one new poem, "Dream-

Land," which Graham published in June. Living on the farm was cheap, and the trickle of money from stories and articles just sufficed.

In September Poe came out of his lethargy and also attempted to revive his *Stylus* project. He repeated his proposal to Lowell that a group of authors band together to found a magazine, and then wrote a long and carefully revised letter to Anthon, asking him to intercede with Harper's for the publication of his works, to provide publicity for the magazine. But the publishers had lost money on *Pym*, and were still peeved over Poe's undercutting them with the conchology book. Anthon replied, "The Harpers also entertain, as I heard from their own lips, the highest opinion of your talents, but——." Another Philadelphia ghost came back to haunt him when a letter came from Duane, asking for the return of his volume of the *Messenger*. Poe took Mrs. Clemm's word that she had returned it as instructed, and suggested that it was still in Hirst's office. Hirst said that was a "damned lie."

For all the acrimony flying around (Poe also tangled with a Long Island lawyer that fall over some now forgotten point), his writings of this time show remarkable good humor. One of them, "The Angel of the Odd," recounts a drunken nightmare — verging on delirium tremens — suffered by a man who had consumed an indigestible quantity of food, drink, and literature. Among the latter, Griswold's *Curiosities of Literature* and Tuckerman's *Isabel, or Sicily, a Pilgrimage* are prominent. Although it starts well enough, the account is not fantastic enough to be really funny. Poe's own dreams, apparently, never were comic ones. Much more effective is "The Literary Life of Thingum-Bob." This is of kindred humor with "The Business Man," satirizing literary feuds and back-scratching criticism, and with many side remarks on low magazine pay.

Mrs. Clemm, at this point, decided to take things into her

own hands and called on N. P. Willis at the *Mirror*, trying to sell some of Edgar's work. She said Poe was ill, and since the paper was about to become a daily, with a weekly supplement, thus requiring a great deal more work, Willis agreed to make Poe a regular contributor. At first Edgar worked at home, but when he visited the *Mirror* office, Willis grew to like him, and described him as "invariably the same sad-mannered, winning, and refined gentleman." He lectured at Boston, at Lowell's instigation, and wrote more batches of short, esoteric paragraphs, which he contributed in two installments to the *Democratic Review* under the name "Marginalia."

But while performing these routine literary chores that fall and winter, he was completing a poem that would in a short time alter his life and even his personality. He was jealous of the time that other tasks had demanded, stifling his flow of poetry; two-thirds of all he had written dated from before 1831. Moreover, he had, he felt, brought the intellectual and the emotional into harmony in his best stories. Now he decided to write a poem that would bring to culmination — to poetic flower — the theme of his "Lygeia" series of stories. He already had his meter; Elizabeth Barrett's "Lady Geraldine's Courtship" had lines with a sinuous quality that fascinated him.

He plotted out his stanzas as he would plot a story. A bereaved lover is sitting mournfully in his room, harboring his grief. He hears a tapping, and half fearful, half hoping that it is the ghost of his sweetheart, he opens the door — but there is no one outside; it must have been the ghost. Seated again, he again hears the tapping, and again smothering his emotions with logic, he opens the window — and in walks a raven, presenting a somewhat ludicrous sight, as such birds do since, graceful enough in flight, they walk with a lurching awkwardness. The bird flutters its wings like a dowager adjusting her plumes and, ignoring him completely, flies up and perches on a bust of Pallas Athene, on the ledge of the transom over the door. The Brennans — they later claimed — had rented Poe a room with such a bust above the door.

Relieved, the lover finds this matter-of-fact intrusion very funny, and with elaborate manners asks the bird's name, to be startled by its croaking back, "Nevermore." His logic leads him to the conclusion that the raven had been somebody's pet and had been taught that one word, but obsessed with morbid superstition, he asks loaded questions, always getting the same answer: can he forget his lost love — "Nevermore"; will he meet her in heaven — "Nevermore"; and finally in nearly mad despair at having a living — and talking — reminder of his bereavement, shouts hysterically for the bird to "Take thy beak from out my heart, and take thy form from off my door!" But the same reply, as he well knew, came, "Nevermore."

As the idea for a short story, this is probably Poe's finest achievement, but he himself was torn about its quality as a poem. Sometimes he would claim, with the hysterical overdramatization of the man in the poem, that it was the greatest poem ever written; and then he could calm down and say, with a touch of modest bravado, " 'The Raven' has had a great 'run'. Thomas — but I wrote it for the express purpose of running — just as I did the 'Gold-Bug', you know. The bird beat the bug, though, all hollow." The poem fascinates readers with its hypnotic sound, that creates a uniform tone of melancholy; but this very uniformity of rhythm obscures the point; it destroys the comic climax from which the lover willfully sabotages his own mind, using his intellectual power to drive himself to an emotional frenzy. The conception is superb tragedy, with a powerful emotional purgative in the laughter of relief being forced by the effect of grief on a rational being to become the laughter of the madhouse and then worse. But without that laughter the poem depicts nothing more than a situation of sentimentality — a man trying to work up his own sorrow — and becomes an elocutionist's display piece.

About the time "The Raven" was taking its final shape, in December, Lowell wrote, introducing Charles F. Briggs to Poe. Briggs was about to start a literary weekly in New York, publishing from Number One Nassau Street, and having seen Lowell's appreciation of Poe for *Graham's* — it was to go in the February issue of the magazine, along with an engraved portrait — he was certain he wanted Edgar as a contributor. Lowell assured Poe that Briggs would "pay." The *Broadway Journal* began publishing in January, about the time Edgar moved back into the city — to Amity Street — to work in the *Mirror* office. He sold "The Raven" to the *American Whig Review* for February, and to give it a good sendoff, he had it printed in advance in the *Evening Mirror* on January 29. As expected, it made a resounding hit — he was known thereafter as "The Raven" — and Poe became immediately famous, but not rich. Some say he was paid five dollars for the poem, others insist it was ten.

To his great surprise, about two weeks before the publication of the poem, Poe was approached by his old enemy Griswold, who wanted material for another anthology. Poe responded with humility to this overture and sent him not only stories and articles, but "all my poems worth re-publishing," including "The Raven." In contrast with his willingness to consider himself in the wrong over Griswold, he again covered up for Mrs. Clemm's selling Duane's *Messenger* in a very curt letter; the volume had turned up in a Richmond bookshop and was sold to the former owner, who traced its wandering back to Leary and Mrs. Clemm. Although he never admitted that Mrs. Clemm had sold the book, he later told Hirst, "What must Mr. Duane think of me?"

Lowell's article added even more to the fame that publication and republication of "The Raven" was bringing Poe. He became known quickly from the remotest parts of the United States to England, where Elizabeth Barrett, analyzing the flaw in the poem, still wrote Horne, the British author who acted as Poe's agent, "I am of the opinion that there is an uncommon force and effect in the poem." "The Gold Bug" had recently been translated into French, and in little over a year, two translations of "Murders in the Rue Morgue" would be the occasion of a lawsuit between two French papers. On February 21, 1845, Poe signed a contract with the backer of the *Broadway Journal*, John Bisco, to be co-editor, with Briggs, supplying at least one page of "original matter" each week, for which he would be paid one-third of the profits. The very next best thing to having a magazine of his own!

Thou wouldst be loved? — then let thy heart
From its present pathway part not!
Being everything which now thou art,
Be nothing which thou art not.
"To F——s S. O——d"

THE ONLY THING THAT POE had in common with his co-editor
was friendship with Lowell; and although Lowell was one of
the very few people to whom Poe used the salutation "My Dear
Friend" in his letters, he had never met the man. Briggs was a
New Englander five years older than Poe; he was called "Harry
Franco" in recognition of a best seller, *The Adventures of
Harry Franco,* that he had published the year after *Pym* had
come out. Briggs had written for the *Knickerbocker* and was
favored by Poe's great enemy, Clark; he was an abolitionist and
a conservative Whig, and offended even Dickens with his
scissorsbill attitude toward copyright. Griswold had already been
whispering "shocking bad stories" to him about Poe, but he
reserved judgment while under the initial spell of charm at
Poe's manner — and his sudden fame.

Briggs and Poe, while their alliance lasted, made a kind of
bridge between the Knickerbockers and Young America, a precarious bridge across a chasm that was political as well as
literary. But 1845 was a year of ambiguity on both grounds,
and Poe found even the Whig *American Review* hospitable to
his writing, although it was edited by Clark's cousin, while he

continued to cleave to Clark's archenemies, Mathews and Simms. One thing everyone could agree on; Elizabeth Barrett was the gem of female poets. Edgar praised her in the *Mirror* and the *Broadway Journal*, and Duyckinck not only praised her book in the *American Review*, but gave credit to Mathews as the American editor of the volume. Everything was ripe for a snarling, screaming catfight.

Two days after his second Barrett review came out in the *Broadway Journal*, Edgar published another two-part review — of an anthology called *The Waif*, edited by Longfellow — in the *Mirror*. *The Waif* was a very unsatisfactory book, a collection of overlooked poems by second-raters, but Poe was not satisfied merely to say so; he, offended as always when art was not treated with reverence, concluded that the collection was "infected with a *moral taint.* . . . there *does* appear, in this little volume, a very careful avoidance of all American poets who may be supposed especially to interfere with the claims of Mr. Longfellow. These men Mr. Longfellow can continuously *imitate* (*is* that the word?) and yet never incidentally commend."

Poe had always praised Longfellow, while at the same time finding him a spurious poet. Five years before he had, he felt, discovered a plagiarism; Longfellow's "Midnight Mass for the Dying Year" had many similarities with Tennyson's "The Death of the Old Year." The real cause for his outrage was that Longfellow had taken an idea that Tennyson had treated well, and had made a botch of it to avoid — so Poe thought — using the same words, by which his theft might be proved. This was for *Burton's Gentleman's Magazine*. In *Graham's*, a year and a half later, he picked up Lambert Wilmer's accusations of plagiarism against Longfellow, when he reviewed *The Quacks of Helicon*, and six months after that he complained about Longfellow's didacticism and found fault with his mechanical use of meter, claiming that the English language could not be forced into the Greek hexameter. But he called him, in his review of Griswold's book, "unquestionably the best poet in America."

In addition to accusing Longfellow of literary robbery in the *Mirror* notice of *The Waif*, Poe accused James Aldrich of imitating Thomas Hood's "The Death-Bed." The accusation of plagiarism against Longfellow promised to make more of a stir than the "Balloon Hoax," even though it was anything but new. A Longfellow enthusiast, who signed himself "H," replied, and Briggs, taking advantage of the excitement to get publicity for the new paper, responded in the *Broadway Journal*, defending Aldrich by claiming that his poem was written two years before Hood's — that it was in fact written ten years after made no difference. Another journal, the *Rover*, had pointed out that a translation from the German, that Longfellow had published in *Graham's*, was really lifted from Motherwell's *Minstrelsy Ancient and Modern*. This stung Longfellow into writing Graham to proclaim his innocence, saying that he had copied the German text, "*Der Gute George Campbell*," from the *Deutscher Sänger-Saal*, which some traveler showed him on a steamboat on the Rhine, and he "could not but smile at my own ignorance," when Griswold somewhat later showed him the Scottish original, "which led me to re-translate a translation." Graham printed the letter, without commenting on how remarkable that ignorance must have been to consider "George Campbell" a German name.

Briggs and Poe carried on their profitable literary feud until Willis got sick of it and announced in the *Mirror* that he disagreed with all the "disparagement of Longfellow." It was about then that Poe left that paper to devote all his time to the *Broadway Journal*. Willis was soon leaving as well, planning to go to Europe. The whole thing seemed to have blown over when the March 8 *Weekly Mirror* came out with a reply to Poe, signed "Outis," in which the plagiarism charge was scouted on the ground that the correspondent could make a case, by the same kind of reasoning, for Poe's having stolen "The Raven" from a poem called "The Bird of the Dream." Poe, almost gratefully, leaped at this bait, and the "Little Longfellow War" was on.

For five weeks Poe continued his "Reply to Outis." His purpose was really nothing but publicity — some believe that he himself was Outis — but he soon lost track of purpose in his outrage at the Knickerbocker attitude of reverence for Longfellow. Abandoning his real complaints — that Longfellow's didacticism and his novelty-seeking attitude toward metrics were a betrayal of a real poetic gift — he concentrated on the more spectacular accusation of plagiarism, even finding imitation of "Politian" in Longfellow's "The Spanish Student." Briggs decided to "allow him to ride his hobby to death in the outset and be done with it. . . . But it will do us some good by calling public attention to our paper." So it did, but it made Poe ridiculous and wide open to attack from Clark, who put a parody of "The Raven" in the *Knickerbocker*; and the *Mirror*, now under anti-Poe management, started firing broadsides with the *Weekly News* over Poe's reputation. Longfellow wisely stayed out of the whole thing, except for his letter to Graham, and thus the attack on him ended by damaging only Poe.

That was not evident for some time, however. On February 28, "The Raven" gave his lecture on American poetry to an audience of about three hundred, most of them literary people, and won a great deal of praise. When, however, he attempted to repeat it in March, freezing rain kept all but a dozen people from coming, and they got their money back. The next morning, for the first time since he had left Philadelphia, Edgar turned up drunk, and had to be led to the *Journal* office by a friend. Disappointment over the canceled lecture was not the only cause of his slip, however. His relations with Briggs were deteriorating. Briggs considered Poe "only an assistant to me," describing him in the same terms as he did the newly employed music critic of the paper, Henry S. Watson. Moreover, the one-third interest Poe had in the *Journal* meant he was not paid for his contributions, and his share of the profits did not add up to as much as he could have earned from the voluminous mass of writing he contributed to it.

In May he wrote Thomas, "I put so many irons in the fire all at once, that I have been unable to get them out. For the last three or four months I have been working 14 or 15 hours a day. . . . I never knew what it was to be a slave before." In addition to filling a page of the *Broadway Journal* every week, he had a story or article in *Godey's*, *Graham's*, or the *American Review* nearly every issue. February's *Godey's* carried his "Thousand and Second Tale of Scheherazade," in which the storytelling queen describes nineteenth-century inventions and wonders (gleaned from the encyclopedia), but when she comes to the bustle, the king loses his last hold on his temper and has her executed. Equally at odds with the jingoism and spirit of progress of the United States in 1845 was "Some Words with a Mummy," in which Poe uses a revived ancient Egyptian to disparage modern society and the irresponsible rantings of politicians. "The Power of Words," another of his philosophical prose-poems, and "Fifty Suggestions" filled out the spring magazines.

Naturally, operating under such pressure, Poe broke loose at times. He started doing drama criticism as well as the book reviews, and on April 12 devastated a production of *Antigone*, with the result that Dinneford, manager of Palmo's Opera House, withdrew his name from the free list. Toward the end of May Lowell passed through New York, and when he called on Poe, Mrs. Clemm kept close watch over the interview, and Lowell reported, "I have the impression he was a little soggy with drink — not tipsy — but as if he had been holding his head under a pump to cool it." Lowell was already disillusioned with Poe over the Longfellow war, and this marked the end of their friendship. Poe was equally unimpressed; "I was very much disappointed in his appearance as an intellectual man. He was not half the noble-looking person that I expected to see." Chivers was in the city to publish his *The Lost Pleiad*, and one day when he was taking Poe, roaring drunk, home from the *Journal* office, they encountered Clark, whom Poe immediately wanted to knock down. Clark graciously avoided combat.

Poe's spree ended as quickly as it began, but Briggs had had enough of him, and since Bisco stuck by the poet, Briggs decided to get a new backer and get rid of the other two. Poe was looking nostalgically back on the quiet of the Brennan farm, and asked Duyckinck if he or Mathews would buy his share in the *Journal*. But at the last minute Bisco held out for more money than Briggs's backer, Mr. Homans, was willing to pay, and Edgar, still intrigued with the idea of having control of a journal, agreed to stay on. The upshot was that, after missing publication on July 5, the second volume of the paper began the next week with Poe and Watson as editors, and Briggs was out. Poe had just acquired a new enemy. On July 14, Bisco and Poe made a new contract, agreeing to share the profits fifty-fifty, and Edgar was sole editor, "uninterfered with by any party whatever."

Work then began in earnest, and to fill out the pages Poe stuck in his old stories and poems wholesale, sometimes signing them "Littleton Barry," so his name would not appear too often. He had revised them carefully, first for the unpublished "Phantasy Pieces," and then for a new edition of the tales to come out in Wiley and Putnam's *Library of American Books*. Duyckinck, who in addition to being a leading Young American was the publisher's editor, had made a selection of twelve tales for this edition, which came out on July 19. The very same day, Edgar went off to be judge at a literary contest at the Rutgers Female Institute, and was chagrined to discover that one of the other judges was the "insufferably tedious and dull" Henry Tuckerman, who had rejected "The Tell-Tale Heart." They agreed on awarding the prize, however, and Poe read the composition.

After Chivers went back to Georgia, Poe straightened himself out and went on no more sprees. He was at work at Nassau Street every morning at nine, and stayed on until three or four in the afternoon. One hot August afternoon, Crane, the office boy, fainted while he was wrapping and addressing the papers, and Poe lifted him to the table and brought him to consciousness by bathing his wrists and temples with cold water, then sent him home in a carriage. The boy adored Poe, and said he "was a quiet man about the office, and was uniformly kind and courteous to every one, and with congenial company, he would grow cheerful and even playful." A dapper young contributor named Walter Whitman also was pleased at "his looks, voice, manner and matter; very kindly and human, but subdued, perhaps a little jaded."

Things did seem to be going better for Poe. The volume of tales was selling well, bringing in a royalty of eight cents a volume. But he was not able to do more than survive economically, for he had lived so long adjusting his expenses to his meager income that he kept on spending as much as he made. He still owed money to Dow, borrowed years before, and he was even in debt to Briggs, who had advanced money for him to pay his board bill when he was in danger of being evicted. In a story called "The Imp of the Perverse," Edgar analyzed his own tendency to do impulsively what good sense told him not to do and used it to question the logic of the phrenologists. In addition he wrote a new poem, "Eulalie," and contributed a batch of "Marginalia" to *Godey's*. In September, Wiley and Putnam, pleased with the success of his *Tales*, agreed to publish a volume of poems, *The Raven and Other Poems*, and, grateful for her kind words about "The Raven," Poe dedicated it "To the Noblest of her Sex," Elizabeth Barrett. In a preface he said, "Events not to be controlled have prevented me from making, at any time, any serious effort in what, under happier circumstances, would have been the field of my choice. With me poetry has been not a purpose, but a passion; and the passions should be held in reverence; they must not — they cannot at will be excited, with an eye to the paltry compensations, or the more paltry commendations, of mankind."

In spite of this clear expression of his feelings on the matter, Poe accepted an invitation to go into Longfellow territory and read an "original" poem — that is, a new one, written for the occasion — at the Boston Lyceum on October 16. This was a last sad result of his friendship with Lowell. Since he could not write an occasional poem, he dug out "Al Aaraaf," which had not been published in the new volume, and borrowing twenty dollars against royalties, he went to Boston. The reading followed a lecture by Caleb Cushing. Poe, irritated at the "frog-pondians," prefaced his remarks by a short tirade against didacticism, and read through the long poem while the audience trickled out. Then he recited "The Raven" as an encore to the faithful who had remained in the hall — who apparently were quite responsive — then adjourned to a bar with the speaker of the evening and a few others and delivered himself of his opinion of Boston and the Bostonians by pretending that he had planned the whole thing as a hoax. Miss Walter, the editor of the *Transcript*, wrote a leading editorial in a snarling tone on the fiasco, heading it "A Failure," and this was picked up and made the occasion of an editorial prelude to the Civil War when the Southern papers came to Poe's defense.

At this point Poe's struggles had not yet brought the paper to the circulation necessary for success. Advertising was up, but printing costs and prohibitive postal rates kept the magazine from coming to even keel financially. Bisco began having financial trouble and Poe tried to borrow money for him, but without success. On October 24 Bisco had had enough and sold out to Poe for fifty dollars cash and a note for three months for the full amount of debts due the paper. Poe admitted that it had taken "a prodigious deal of maneuvering" for him to get control of the *Broadway Journal*, but only then did his maneuvers become really complicated. He wrote far and wide for money, both for the down payment and for capital to keep running, and was somewhat successful. Griswold loaned $25, and over the next months Poe got $100 from Fitz-Greene Halleck, while Horace Greeley endorsed Poe's note for $50, for the down payment.

Besides carrying on the business side of the magazine while trying to float capital, and filling its pages every week, Poe was working on a series of critical articles called "Literary America." He completed another story on mesmerism, "The Facts in the Case of M. Valdemar," about a man who dies under hypnosis and whose corpse is preserved seven months, when the hypnotist "awakened" him, causing instantaneous putrefaction. This had a very great vogue, particularly in England, and Edgar was kept busy writing to enthusiasts over mesmerism, who wondered if the story was true. "Some few persons believe it —" he wrote to a druggist in Scotland, "but *I* do not — and don't you."

It was about this time, too, that the vogue over "The Raven" made Edgar a lion in society. As author of "Lionizing," he must have been amused, but he played up to the literati who displayed him in their drawing rooms as a personification of his poem, cultivating a dramatic manner and an air of decadent melancholy. Earlier that year he made one acquaintance which meant more to him than social success. He had long been praising the poems of Mrs. Frances Sargent Osgood, and in the early spring Willis had introduced them at the Astor House. Poe warmed to her friendship, and even trotted out his old poems "To Mary" and "To Eliza" and published them in the *Broadway Journal*, each with the title "To F———." Virginia liked her and found her a good influence on Edgar, although others made gossip over Poe's obvious affection for this attractive woman of thirty-four.

But on December 26, the sixty-day note he had given Bisco as down payment for the paper, with Horace Greeley's endorsement on the back, came due, and he could not pay. He, who had made successful two other publications, and whose name had been an asset for many others, had failed with his own. He turned the paper over to Thomas H. Lane, and the last issue, put out by Lane and Thomas Dunn English, came out January 3, with Poe's "Valedictory," bidding farewell "as cordially to foes as to friends."

The skies they were ashen and sober;
  The leaves they were crispéd and sere —
  The leaves they were withering and sere:
It was night, in the lonesome October
  Of my most immemorial year . . .
              "Ulalume — A Ballad"

THE JANUARY, 1846, *Knickerbocker* struck Edgar the final blow of that year's beginning, denouncing his character, his poetry, and his criticism, and saying, "no person connected with the press in this country is entitled to less mercy or consideration." The situation was clear. Clark had become, in his own opinion, the literary dictator of America. His position was challenged by Young America, and he picked as his special opponent in that group Cornelius Mathews. Poe had offended against Clark in the past; as far back as the *Messenger* days he had said that the *Knickerbocker* "thinks it is its duty to abuse all rival magazines." Thus when Poe buzzed into the New York literary battlefield, Clark considered him just a fly to be swatted; and when he discovered that Poe had a sting like a hornet, he roared with rage. Briggs, resentful over losing the *Broadway Journal* to Poe, finally picked Clark's side, and now that Willis had left the *Mirror*, he had his fortress to fire from. Just then Poe lost his.

But not all was antagonism — yet. Relieved of the pressure of putting out his paper, Edgar swore off drinking, after a last binge as the *Journal* went down. It was then he lost his temper with Thomas Dunn English at last, but he was ashamed of it, even though he had lost all confidence in English both as a person and as a writer. Poe reveled in the attentions of literary society, usually centered at 116 Waverly Place, the house of Anne C. Lynch. There hoop-skirted ladies listened to Poe's eloquent monologues, while the men sulked by the fire. Edgar still had in mind his book on American literature, and fired by the talk at Miss Lynch's and at Dr. Francis's, he decided to write profiles of the "Literati of New York." These would be something in between his "Autography" sketches and the extended treatment he intended for "Literary America," and would be distinguished by their presentation of private opinion of the authors, rather than their "manufactured 'reputations.' " Implying that authors were praised or damned according to their allegiance in the literary war, he said, "But the very editors who hesitate at saying in print an ill word of an author personally known, are usually the most frank in speaking about him privately." Such peeks behind the scenes were perfectly suited for the ladies who sought their fashions, literary as well as sartorial, in *Godey's Lady's Book*.

The papers that Edgar wrote through the early months of the year, and that appeared in *Godey's* in six installments, beginning in May, were very uneven, and, on the most part, quite flat. Poe said, "I meant 'honest' — but my meaning is not as fully made out as I could wish. I thought too little of the series myself to guard sufficiently against haste, inaccuracy, or prejudice." In the first group he did his best analysis on the subject of Willis, and he was slyly pungent on Briggs, describing his appearance in caricature and slipping only once into invective; "Mr. Briggs has never composed in his life three consecutive sentences of grammatical English. He is grossly uneducated." That was sheer malice, stemming from Briggs's criticism of Poe's pretensions to knowledge, although as a Nantucketer, Briggs's Americanisms were in a different idiom from Poe's. He more politely found similar fault with Margaret Fuller, although he felt that the strength of her style and opinion made her usage a minor flaw. After the first batch, which Godey had to reprint to meet demand, the pieces became quite routine and generally more kind to the subjects. The series scheduled for July had more venom in them, but by the time Poe wrote those he was ill and harried.

Arthur's Ladies Magazine bought a trivial story of his, "The Sphinx," in which he took another kick at Americans' practice of overrating their own institutions. He was paid at a higher rate than usual, "but the pay is no pay for the degradation." He also wrote "The Philosophy of Composition" for *Graham's*. This work, which might better be entitled, "How I Wrote 'The Raven,' " tremendously exaggerates the extent to which his poetry was the result of conscious calculation, but he made his point all the more effectively for that exaggeration. It was necessary for him to discredit wild "inspiration" as the source of art, and by making his thinking as cool as a geometrical proof, he properly emphasized the extent to which all facets of a piece of writing must contribute to the central effect. He simply moved the logical analysis required in revision into the act of original composition.

Poe was thus working his way back to the productivity and quality of the work he had done the year before his venture with the *Broadway Journal*. Again he moved out of the city, to the farmhouse of Mrs. John C. Miller, in Turtle Bay. Virginia wrote him a Valentine poem, the first letters of the lines spelling out his name, pleading, "Give me a cottage for my home" and "Love shall heal my weakened lungs." Her wish would soon be granted. A man named John Valentine was about then considering investing in a cottage at Fordham, which he would, in a few months, rent to Poe. Edgar went on a visit to Baltimore, and after the resultant spree, was ill for some time. In the midst of his recovery, however, if not during his actual illness, troubles came again. He had written a glowing review of Mrs. Osgood's poetry for the March *Godey's*, and she had been writing him effusive letters, one of which attracted the prying eyes of Mrs. Elizabeth Ellet, one of the lesser "female poets." Gossip flowed irresponsibly, and a delegation, including the drawling Margaret Fuller, called on Poe and demanded the letters, which he instead delivered to her house. Mrs. Ellet was indignant, and her brother-in-law, somehow feeling that Mrs. Ellet was compromised, started threatening Poe, no small thing in those days of violence and prudery.

Poe, who remained ill all through the spring and summer, became upset and foolishly called on Thomas Dunn English for help, beginning his interview by apologizing for the scene of the beginning of January. English was arrogant and offensive, and soon they were at fisticuffs and had to be pulled apart by friends. The brother-in-law was calmed down, but Mrs. Ellet continued to bother the Poes, writing letters to Virginia that made her miserable; and English certainly did not forget. Briggs was now working on the *Mirror*, whose editor, Hiram Fuller, was allied with Clark, and Fuller and Briggs were ready to use any weapon that came to hand, even the vulgar English. On May 26 the *Mirror* printed an article, in the style of the "Literati," on Poe himself, and after repeating Clark's attack on him as a literary figure, added a personal description which included, "His walk is quick and jerky, sometimes waving, describing that peculiar figure in geometry denominated by Euclid, we think, but it may be Professor Farrar of Cambridge, Virginia Fence."

Poe was aware that he became too heated in thinking of these people. He certainly worked off some rage by writing a gem of a story of retribution, "The Cask of Amontillado." This account of an inebriate being lured to the cellars of his enemy — whom he considered his friend — and there walled up, is a good bit more than Poe vicariously punishing Clark and Briggs and English, however, for the two characters are two sides of the same man — Edgar Poe — as he saw himself while drinking. But he would not have been human had he not felt some emotional response to the bitter hatred English and "Harry Franco" felt for him; and either one, from their fortunate position of having powerful outlets for their opinions in the New York press while he had none, could have been the "Fortunato" who was lured to his death.

Not enough of his emotion was drained off in the story, although much of the venom had disappeared from it, when he came to the middle section of the "Literati" papers and let himself write on two "dunces" one after the other, James Aldrich and Thomas Dunn English. The profile of Aldrich simply repeated, more vehemently for its charitableness, his charges of plagiarism against the man. But next came English, and although Poe tried to be fair, he lost his temper. English was "without the commonest school education." After citing some of his grammatical errors, Poe said, "No one of any generosity would think the worse of him for getting private instruction."

That Poe thought he was writing in tongue-in-cheek manner is evident by his denying knowing English personally; he was implying that much worse could be told of the man's behavior. But when *Godey's* came out, about June 15, English went into a rage. On June 23, "Mr. English's Reply to Mr. Poe" appeared in the *Mirror* under the scare-head, "War of the Literati." English made a vicious personal attack on Poe, telling about the Boston fiasco and accusing him of getting money by false pretenses, forgery, slandering Mrs. Ellet (whom he did not name), and concluded that he could tell much worse about Poe if he had space. English's decision to attack rather than to defend himself aroused Poe's fighting spirit, and he counterattacked. Since he intended to publish it in *Godey's* — which, of course, had a much greater circulation than the *Mirror* — he took his time, writing friends in Philadelphia for details about English's escapades there. He carefully composed "Mr. Poe's Reply to Mr. English and Others," dubbing him "Thomas Done Brown," and writing in a rambunctiously comic style not to be equaled until Mark Twain. He referred as well to certain rascalities of Hiram Fuller, and consulted an attorney, E. L. Fancher, to bring suit for libel against English and the *Mirror* both.

Poe, on his part, was very careful to avoid statements that might give English grounds for countersuit, and sent his manuscript to Duyckinck and Mathews before passing it on to Godey. But Godey did not want to be drawn into the New York literary war, and besides, this was hardly the sort of thing that should be put before the eyes of his lady readers. Instead, he inserted it in the Philadelphia *Spirit of the Times*, a sportsman's magazine, as an advertisement, sending the bill to Poe. His choice of the paper was probably because its editor was J. S. DuSolle, who, Poe claimed in his piece, "bestowed" on English his "primary thrashing." "In Reply to Mr. Poe's Rejoinder," in the July 14 *Mirror*, English, commenting on how long it took Poe to respond, wrote, "it is to be inferred that Mr. Poe had some difficulty in obtaining a respectable journal to give currency to his scurrilous article." He then calmly denied the charges, making Poe's rejoinder seem not apt, but mere billingsgate. The next week Poe's lawyer instituted suit, and the following February 17, Poe was awarded $225 damages plus costs, so that the *Mirror* was out $492. English left town in fear of criminal indictment.

The younger generation, at least, felt that Poe was a figure of some interest. In April the Literary Societies of the University of Vermont invited him to read a poem, and in June a similar group at Dickinson College, in Carlisle, Pennsylvania, made the same request. Poe declined both. The little family moved to Fordham, into Mr. Valentine's cottage, in early summer. This was a truly rural setting, about thirteen miles from the city, and although the building was barely comfortable, its location was idyllic. There was a large living room downstairs, and a roomy kitchen. Upstairs were two low-ceilinged bedrooms. A large lawn surrounded the cottage, shaded by large old cherry trees. Furniture was scarce, but in the country what food they could not grow (Mrs. Clemm was an expert picker of greens) could be bought cheaply from the nearby farmers — but only, of course, through the growing season.

Poe was tired and ill, and Virginia's grip on life seemed to be slipping more every day. She rallied a bit through the summer, but as fall came on her life was clearly nearing its close. The literary ladies, now that Poe could not visit them, went to him. The tangle with Mrs. Ellet had frightened off Mrs. Osgood, but an even better friend appeared, considering their needs, Mrs. Marie Louise Shew, who had some medical training. Rosalie Poe visited, apparently forgiving Edgar for his neglect of her. Simms wrote Poe, urging him to withdraw from the literary war while there was still time: "you are now perhaps in the most perilous period of your career. . . ." Poe had nearly stopped writing altogether, but Clark was still stinging with indignation, and kept up his barrage long after Poe had withdrawn from the field, leaving, of course, a few mines to blow up in his opponents' faces.

One of these was his "Literati" sketch of Clark. He said, in the August *Godey's*, that Clark was best known for being the brother of the late Willis Gaylord Clark, that he did not write much but hired others to write what he claimed, and that he was "noticeable for nothing in the world except for the markedness by which he is noticeable for nothing." The *Knickerbocker* was praised for its contributed matter, but "As the editor has no precise character, the magazine, as a matter of course, can have none."

This was blasphemy. Clark replied in the October *Knickerbocker*, attacking, as had English, Poe's disclaimer of having met him by describing Poe's attempt to get in a fist-fight with him, but claiming that it was Mrs. Clemm — "an aged female relative" — rather than Chivers who had been with Poe. Probably expecting attack, Poe had prepared for *Godey's* of the same month a piece on Charles Fenno Hoffman, who had preceded Clark as editor of the *Knickerbocker* (and only lasted three months, against Clark's twelve years!), and deplored that the magazine had fallen to "that dreary realm of outer darkness, of utter and inconceivable dunderheadism, over which has so long ruled King Log the Second, in the august person of one Lewis Gaylord Clark." Through the same later summer and fall, the *Mirror* was running a serial called *1844; or the Power of the S. F.*, a piece of cheap Whig politics about a Democratic political plot. But the author, English, found that he was often more furious with Poe than with the Democratic Party, and inserted him into the plot as the character "Marmaduke Hammerhead." Briggs let Poe alone, for the time being, and set about satirizing the writing of Willis in a series of letters, "Ferdinand Mendez Pinto."

In the meantime Poe nursed Virginia, being in turn nursed by Mrs. Shew; read over the laudatory reviews from the English publications on the *Tales* and *The Raven and Other Poems*, now published in one binding; and found time to write long and friendly letters to George W. Eveleth, a medical student who had first communicated with him to get back his subscription money for the *Broadway Journal*. He had two big projects in mind, his "Literary America," and getting the *Stylus* under way by January, 1847. Nothing came of either one, but he made a large step forward in harnessing his rhythmic power in poetry to a truly poetic theme with the poem "Ulalume." This symbolic work, in which he — perhaps unconsciously — personified the divergent aspects of love, the spiritual and the physical, and wondered what he would do after he had lost Virginia, in whom he had been able to combine them, has the true imagery of his early lyrics developed in the richer orchestra of his later works; but the people to whom he read it, one fall day at Fordham, "could not make head nor tail of it." George Colton, editor of the *American Review*, could not resist Mrs. Clemm's pleading that he buy it so Edgar could have a new pair of shoes; but he did not publish it for more than a year.

The poem is not obscure, even though it is beyond those who in their fascination over the rhythms and romantic symbols of "The Raven" do not want anything better. Poe blended his symbols to create the limbo he was preparing himself for, the limbo of life without Virginia. A cloud-drifted night in October is made more gloomy by reference to the *Lac des Fées* of Jean François Auber, whose music was harbinger of the Impressionists, and by reference to the hazy landscapes of the Hudson Valley paintings of Robert Walter Weir. His feelings were described in terms of the antarctic volcano Erebus, or Mount Yaanek, of fiery heat in a cold world. Tempted by Venus, in spite of the fears of his soul, the poet is halted by encountering the tomb of his beloved, and wonders if the attraction of Venus was not to defer him from disintegrating in grief.

He had reason to fear. As Virginia sickened, so did he. He was voiceless in the literary world, but still attacked by Clark and his cohorts as much as before. In November, Briggs started his *The Trippings of Tom Pepper* in the *Mirror*. This was what the "Literati" might have been, if Poe had been a Briggs, a roman à clef on the literary people of New York, purely personal, and very funny. Poe is "Austin Wicks" in the story; but Briggs did not get around to satirizing him until later. Near Christmas, people began wondering what had happened to Poe, and a good thing it was, for the Poes had no money. Mrs. Clemm would not beg, but she would borrow a shilling often, "to get a letter from the post office." Mrs. Mary Hewitt tried to get up a subscription for them, and as a result, the New York *Morning Express*, on December 15, published an appeal for them that was copied in papers all over the East. Mrs. Shew sent bed clothing and other comforts for Virginia, who had been warmed heretofore only by Edgar's greatcoat and Catterina who curled up in her bed. Money and assistance came in, and Poe swallowed his pride and wrote humble thanks to those who sent it. The suit against English and the *Mirror* began, and this helped Edgar's morale tremendously.

Mrs. Shew diagnosed Poe — and took her observations to Dr. Valentine Mott, of the New York University medical school, for confirmation — as having an intermittent pulse, signifying lesion of one side of the brain; and when he was in fever he begged her to write down his ravings, for he had promised "greedy publishers" so much they would "revenge themselves by saying all sorts of evil of him if he should die." On January 29, Edgar sent urgently for Mrs. Shew, begging her to come before Virginia's death. Virginia wanted to show Mrs. Shew two letters from Mrs. Allan, that, she claimed, completely vindicated Edgar in his troubles with his foster father. Whether true or not, it shows that Virginia's last thoughts were that Edgar should not be neglected. She had no worries about her mother if Edgar could survive; but for that she felt he needed to be comforted by a different kind of affection. On January 30, 1847, she died, asking — unlike Poe's Eleanora — no more than that her husband be able to go on, and knowing that he needed a woman's love to do so.

On February 27, the *Mirror*, stung by losing the lawsuit to Poe to the extent of $492, printed an episode of *Tom Pepper* on a soirée at Miss Lynch's, at which Wicks (Poe) becomes obnoxious on one glass of wine and is left on Briggs's hands — the author put himself in Tom's place. Briggs delivers the drunken Poe to his wife, "who thanked us meekly for the care we had taken of her poor husband." After carrying Poe through a distorted version of the Ellet affair and the war of the literati, Briggs tells that he grew "too dishonest for anything respectable," and took to writing advertising for quack medicines, but swallowing some, "fell a victim to his own arts, and was buried at the expense of the public." Perhaps he did not know that Virginia was dead. But he achieved his purpose, Edgar Poe was through with literary war.

Hear the tolling of the bells —
Iron bells!
What a world of solemn thought their monody
compels!
In the silence of the night,
How we shiver with affright
At the melancholy menace of their tone!
"The Bells"

VIRGINIA WAS BURIED, not, as Mrs. Clemm feared, in the cotton sheets of her deathbed, but in fine linen supplied by Mrs. Shew. At the last moment someone remembered that there was no picture of Poe's wife, so one of the ladies who came to help with the funeral made a water-color sketch of her as she lay in her coffin. Her body was put in the burial vault of the Valentines, the owners of the cottage, in the graveyard of the Dutch Reformed Church of Fordham, and Edgar returned to the cottage in a state of collapse. He had long been prepared for Virginia's death; but his emotions had been centered on sympathy for her agony. Now he was suffering from his own shock, the reality of life without her. Unless Mrs. Clemm or Mrs. Shew watched him, he would wander off, to be found in hysterical weeping by Virginia's tomb. One or the other of them would have to sit by his bed until he fell asleep. He could not bear to be alone.

During Virginia's last winter he had been able to write a poem, an essay, and a story. Willis bought the poem, a blank-verse eulogy to Mrs. Shew, entitled "To M. L. S——," and published it in the *Home Journal* on March 13. An essay on Hawthorne, as full of praise as the two reviews of *Twice-Told Tales*, but critical of his New England parochialism, was sent to *Godey's*, but it did not appear for a long time. Godey was apparently waiting for some of the smoke to blow away from the Literati war. In addition to these Poe returned to the day-dream he had fancied five years before in "The Landscape Garden," which he had reprinted in one of the last *Broadway Journals*. This time he supplemented his dreams of creating a new art, whose materials would be nature itself (so the artist becomes creator in God's own materials) by describing some of the results Ellison had achieved with his four hundred and fifty million dollar inheritance. "The Domain of Arnheim" is approached by water, and nature is indeed tamed in it. "Not a dead branch — not a withered leaf — not a stray pebble — not a patch of the brown earth was anywhere visible." Even the water currents are organized to bring the visitor through the estate to the "semi-Gothic, semi-Saracenic" dwelling of the artist himself. This is the vision Poe fabricated through chill days and nights in his barren cottage, while the literary war thundered in the distance.

Poe's victory over the *Mirror* in court did not bring universal approbation; the very fact that he sued did not seem "playing the game." While Virginia was dying, typesetters for the *Saturday Evening Post* were setting up an editorial turning the tables on him by accusing him of plagiarism in *The Conchologist's First Book*. Horace Greeley, more put out than Poe suspected over having to pay the fifty-dollar note he had endorsed — plus seventy-five cents protest fees — commented unfavorably on Poe's suit in the *Tribune* of the 19th; two days before, the *Mirror* announced editorially, "We are undergoing the luxury today of a trial for libel on Edgar A. Poe." Poe wrote

Greeley, calling his attention to the reply to English and Fuller in the *Spirit of the Times*, which Greeley had apparently not seen, and consulted his lawyer about suing the *Post*; but Fancher had had enough and advised against it.

Chivers generously offered to provide for Poe if he would come to Georgia, saying, "New York is not the place to live in happiness. . . . Come to the South." But Poe was beginning to come out of his depression and did not even reply; since Chivers had not yet heard of Virginia's death Edgar would naturally procrastinate. He had Willis announce in the *Home Journal* his forthcoming book on American literature, and even worked on some of the sketches, most notably adding some of the billingsgate of his "Reply" to the "Literati" article on Thomas Dunn English — which he entitled "Thomas Dunn Brown," claiming that "English" was the man's *nom de plume*. With great caution he entered into correspondence with Mrs. Jane Locke, a poetess who had participated in the appeal for the Poes before Virginia's death. The Philosophian Society of Wittenberg College elected him honorary member, and Mrs. Shew gave him *carte blanche* in selecting furniture and decorations for a new house her uncle, Hiram Barney, was moving into. An elocutionist, G. P. Bronson, asked him for a poem to put in his programs. ·

But ringing more sharply through Poe's consciousness through the early spring of 1847 were the words of the burial service he had heard read over Virginia's body. He was no more capable of believing in a heaven of harps and haloes than he was of believing in the "demons" that he told Graham took "advantage of the night to mislead the unwary." Demons and angels were figures of speech to him, but he had, throughout his career, been working out a philosophy of death. In "Al Aaraaf" he had treated death as the ultimate defeat, yet man must experience death to overcome it. The concept of annihilation, nothingness, had been the theme of "Silence," one of his first stories. Since then he had from time to time written fantasies speculating on death and the end of the world, such as "The Conversation of Eros and Charmian," and "The Colloquy of Monos and Una," and in all his writing is combined a horror for dying and the grave, but an attraction to death. He spurned the rationalists for their rejection of intuition, and the traditionalists of religion for their ignorance of science. Like many of his time, he was concerned with bringing science and religion into harmony, but his attitude was that of the artist, and as artist he played God, creating his own worlds, often those of nightmare and horror, but occasionally fairylands and daydreams like those of "The Island of the Fay" and "The Domain of Arnheim."

In "Mesmeric Revelation" he rejected the concept of "spirit," instead considering that matter has two states, the "particled," which is the concrete matter that now exists, and the "unparticled," or pure mind, "the unparticled matter, in motion, is thought. . . . The universal mind is God. . . . Creatures are the thoughts of God." He argued to Lowell, who had asked for his "spiritual autobiography," that spirituality is a "*mere* word. . . . The unparticled matter, permeating & impelling, all things, is God." In sharp response to Chivers's faith in human progress, he said, "Man is now only more active, not wiser, nor more happy, than he was 6000 years ago," and then repeated the same argument, in nearly the same words. Not content now to create a world, he set about creating a universe according to his principles of beauty. Again he cried "*Eureka*," and that was the title he gave the essay that he composed in the spring sunshine, on the bench in front of the cottage, or walking up and down the garden with Mrs. Clemm.

All the curious reading he had done, and all his scouring in obscure books for "Marginalia," was brought to play in this scientific — or pseudoscientific — treatise which he considered a "Book of Truths," but "Nevertheless it is as a Poem only that I wish this work to be judged after I am dead." In nearly forty thousand words, Poe treated the creation of the universe, its nature, and its ultimate destiny to return to the prime source. In a joshing introduction, offered as the contents of a letter found in a bottle floating in the *Mare Tenebrarum* and dated in the year 2848, he traced the development of systems of logic, discarding all of them in favor of intuition. He claimed that there were two forces at work in the universe: gravitation, which is the attraction between things, and electricity, or repulsion; the interplay between them results in matter, the complexity of particled matter, which was diffused through space by the will of God. At some point the universe will have reached the point of God's ultimate design, and then the process of diffusion will reverse itself, and unity in God will again come about. "Mind is cognizant of Matter *only* through its two properties, attraction and repulsion: therefore Matter *is* only attraction & repulsion: a finally consolidated globe of globes, being but *one* particle, would be without attraction, i.e., gravitation; the existence of such a globe presupposes the expulsion of the separative ether which we know to exist between the particles as at present diffused: — thus the final globe would be matter without attraction & repulsion: — but these *are* matter: — then the final globe would be matter without matter: — i.e. no matter at all: — it must disappear. Thus Unity is *Nothingness*."

As "proofs," Poe cited Newton's law of motion (which, he claimed, was based on the intuitions of Kepler), the wave theory of light, and the nebular theory of Laplace. He dedicated the book to Alexander von Humboldt. He went deeply into astronomy and postulated a finite universe of stars, but an infinite one of space, an anticipation of non-Euclidian geometry; and he created intuitively a rudimentary theory of relativity. As "science," even in 1847, Poe's *Eureka* was an amateur work, of course; but it was a brilliant synthesis of the scientific information available to him into a work of art which is no less remarkable for its truth than its beauty. "Poe on the Creation," as Clark scoffingly called it, was the result of Poe's mind working at its brilliant best, although the body that housed that mind was racked with illness, and his spirit was severely crushed.

He was still chasing the elusive *Stylus*. But there was, as always, the fundamental problem of finding money simply to survive, and Poe was deeply conscious of being an object of charity to the literary ladies who still haunted Fordham in the hope of titillation from a little harmless flirting with "The Raven." In December he had dug out his "Notes on English Verse" from Lowell's *Pioneer* of four years ago, and he revised it extensively, using the techniques of synthesis and analysis that he was sharpening on *Eureka*. Commenting that there was no study of the rhythms of English, although much had been written on Greek, Latin, and even Hebrew, Poe set out to fill the gap. But here he was, strangely enough, too far ahead of his time to have reliable sources to work from, and he lacked the scholarship necessary to uncover new facts about linguistics. He sensed what was wrong with describing — and constructing, as Longfellow did — English verse according to the rules of Greek prosody; and although he made some effort to take into consideration the facts that English rhythms depend on stresses, and that irregularity lends it interest, he was too reluctant to give up the impressive nomenclature and rules he had learned in school, and instead of making the complex clear, as he was doing in *Eureka*, he became immersed in complications and technicalities. He was dogmatic throughout, including in his concluding passage another castigation of Longfellow's hexaʳ meters. Poe sent the essay to the *American Review*, but Colton had no taste for reviving the Longfellow war and returned it, promising to publish "Ulalume." Remembering the publicity which anonymous prepublication of "The Raven" had brought him, Edgar requested that the poem be published without his name on it.

By midsummer, Poe was feeling the anxiety all writers feel when periods of time go by without any of their works appearing in print. His last publication in *Graham's* had been the "Marginalia" of November and December; *Godey's* had had his review of Hawthorne since December without publishing it; the only work of his they had printed since the end of the "Literati" was "The Cask of Amontillado." It was time to mend fences in Philadelphia, and perhaps he could stir up some interest in the *Stylus* by visiting there. Early in August Poe set out, carrying with him a fresh batch of "Marginalia" and "The Rationale of Verse." He had been in debt to Graham since his departure from Philadelphia in 1844, for he had taken back "The Gold Bug" to enter it in the *Dollar Newspaper* contest, and he had turned the original version of "The Rationale of Verse" over to Lowell, after Graham had paid for both of them. By so doing he got more money — and prestige — for the story, but he lost on the essay. In addition, Mrs. Clemm had borrowed money from the editor to go to New York. Although Poe had, in the meantime, contributed about $150 worth of writing to *Graham's*, constant need kept him drawing not only the regular pay on that but advances on uncompleted work as well, so that his debt had increased.

When Poe arrived in the city, Graham was vacationing at Cape May, New Jersey. After waiting some time in anticipation of the editor's return, he took his manuscripts to Graham's assistant, Robert T. Conrad, and explained that he had built up a large bill for board and lodging while he was cooling his heels, and had no money to pay it. Conrad could not pay for the articles — which by Graham base rates came to about ninety dollars — out of hand, but he did settle Poe's bills up to that point, and a few days later, when Graham got back, Edgar drew ten dollars from him against the articles and went back to Fordham. There he figured up his debits and credits with Graham, finding that fifty dollars, "as nearly as I can remember," was all he owed, and asking that the balance be sent him. But Graham did not accept "The Rationale of Verse," and Poe was no better off than he had been before.

In the absence of literary income, Poe had to rely on whatever Mrs. Clemm could pick, either from the garden and grounds, or from the hearts and pocketbooks of whoever chanced to come to Fordham. This was not always given without strings attached. Mrs. Estelle Anna Lewis, a chubby poetess from Brooklyn whom Mrs. Shew despised, was generous to Mrs. Clemm, but she expected to be repaid. After several broad hints from her, Poe worked out a mock-sonnet, which he called "An Enigma" because by reading out the first letter of the first line, the second letter of the second, and so on, Mrs. Lewis's name was spelled out. This he sent to *Sartain's Union Magazine*, after it came into being at the end of the year.

But Mrs. Lewis wanted much more, and she was persistent enough to get it. When Poe saw her coming — so long as she did not see him first — he would dash for the woods, or walk over to the Catholic college in Fordham, St. John's, where he enjoyed talking to Father Doucet, or listening to him play on the college organ. What Mrs. Lewis wanted, as she eventually made clear to Mrs. Clemm, was for Poe to write favorable reviews of her work and place them in magazines, and to use his influence to bring her immortality — or, at least, better mention in Griswold's anthologies. Poe, to his abiding shame, gave in and scattered reviews of her poems to many magazines, most of which refused to print them. But it took long nagging from both Mrs. Lewis and Mrs. Clemm until Poe did so.

"Ulalume" appeared finally in the December *American Review*, and Poe set about his devious scheme for publicizing it. He sent a copy to Willis on December 8, asking him to reprint it and speculate, in the *Home Journal*, over its authorship. This Willis did, for the issue of New Year's Day, 1848. Henry B. Hirst was tipped off, and put an article in the Philadelphia *Saturday Courier* of January 22, arguing that the poem could be by no one but Poe. Other papers copied, attributing it to Willis. When the time was ripe — almost a year later — Poe acknowledged the poem, and that led to still more reprinting. He was ready to "re-establish myself in the literary world," and first considering appealing to his first favorable critic, John Neal, to help him arrange for the première performance of *Eureka* trimmed down as a lecture in Portland, Maine, he realized that his subject could hardly stir up literary animosity, and decided to give it at the New York Historical Society, where he had been successful two years before. Borrowing fifteen dollars from H. D. Chapin for the rent of the hall, he scheduled his lecture for February 3.

On the same day that he solicited help from Chapin, he offered Godey the first story he had written since Virginia's death, "Mellonta Tauta." This is the "manuscript found in a bottle," dated April 1, 2848, which he had used as the opening of *Eureka*, expanded into a satire of nineteenth-century America. Its lightheartedness is appropriate to the April Fool's Day dating. In both versions he used many plays on names as means of debunking the seriousness with which his contemporaries took themselves and their brand of knowledge: "in the night of Time, there lived a Turkish philosopher (or Hindoo possibly) called Aries Tottle. . . . His greatest disciples were one Neuclid and one Cant." As in *Eureka*, Bacon is called "Hog"; and "one Miller, or Mill . . . had a mill-horse called Bentham." He made fun of the Washington Monument Association of New York City, who laid a cornerstone before agreeing on the design of the memorial, on October 19, 1847, by having the stone discovered with still no monument above it a thousand years later; and the newspapers found in it reveal that "*the* great men in those days among the Amriccans were one John, a smith, and one Zacchary, a tailor." Although Lowell probably could not believe it, Poe was as disgusted with the jingoism of the Mexican War as he was — albeit not for the same reasons.

Poe wrote Willis, explaining that his lecture was for the purpose of raising funds to go South and drum up subscribers for the *Stylus*, and asking for notice in the paper; "that there may be no cause of *squabbling*, my subject shall *not be literary* at all. I have chosen a broad text — 'The Universe.' " He spoke for two hours, and as could be expected, the reception was mingled and confused. The *Tribune*, whose editor still held a note for fifty dollars as souvenir of confidence in Poe, praised his analysis and imagination. Although Duyckinck, probably the least biased witness of the lecture's reception, wrote his brother, "Poe succeeded only in driving people from the room," the *Literary World*, like the *Weekly Universe*, had no complaints except over the length of the lecture. The *Evening Post* and the *Express* were quite appreciative. Poe felt that the review in the latter was the only one "which approaches the truth," and he incorrectly guessed that it had been written by E. A. Hopkins, "a gentleman of much scientific acquirement." It was really written by John Henry Hopkins, a student at the General Theological Seminary and the son of a bishop.

Edgar intended to leave for Richmond on March 10, but the lecture did not return as much money as he needed to carry out his plans, and Putnam was willing to publish *Eureka* as a book, which meant an infinity of detail work with the proofs. Hopkins, the theological student, saw the manuscript of the book at the publisher's office and was outraged to discover that what he had praised was sheer pantheism. He wrote Poe, who invited him to Fordham to discuss the "new developement" he had disliked. Going away more certain than ever that Poe was a pagan, he wrote to Mrs. Shew, warning her against his madness. Upset at this, Poe asked the two of them to visit him, and they did, but for all her charity, she had a terror of unorthodoxy and was very cool. Poe was surprised at her behavior but let it pass. She had been solicitous in his moments of weakness, that he was ashamed of, so she certainly could not be put off by this piece of achievement. Not long before he had come to her house on Tenth Street, near Broadway, on a Sunday, and complained about the noise of the bells that were constantly clanging away from Grace Church, on the corner. She got a piece of paper and wrote on it, "The Bells, by E. A. Poe. The little silver bells." This was ingenious therapy for a nervous patient. Poe wrote seven short lines on silver wedding bells, then she suggested iron bells. This drew eleven lines, apparently more sincerely inspired by the racket a few houses off; then he slept for twelve hours and she took him home to Fordham. Poe much later sent this poem off to John Sartain, but submitted a considerably revised and enlarged version before Sartain could publish it in his magazine.

In contrast to the sympathy and consolation he was coming to expect from Mrs. Shew, he was being harassed by other women. One of them was Sarah Helen Whitman, a poetess of some wit and ability, but very capable of overdramatizing herself, who read a Valentine poem to Poe at one of Miss Lynch's soirées. Poe was not present, so the manuscript was passed on to him. He, somewhat weary of grinding out poems to this one and that one, tore page 91 out of *The Raven and Other Poems* and sent it to her. It was appropriate; his youthful "To

Helen" came to his mind every time he heard that name. He wrote two other poems to Mrs. Shew, "To —— —— ——" and "The Beautiful Physician"; the former went into the March *Columbian Magazine*, but the other was lost and never published. Then he began to have second thoughts about Mrs. Whitman and recalled that he had seen her once — but not met her — while he was in Providence, some years before, in pursuit of Mrs. Osgood. She had written him a poem, so Poe wrote a second "To Helen," sixty-six lines of blank verse and lush language, far beneath his usual standard. He sent her a copy, and, apparently stirred up by Miss Lynch's description of her "artistic temperament," made some inquiries of friends about her. In the meantime Mrs. Locke, to whom Poe was grateful for her assistance while Virginia was dying, kept insisting that he come to visit her in Lowell, Massachusetts, and deliver a lecture there. He was very wary of the forty-three-year-old woman's designs on him, however.

He was launched again on his literary career, but nothing seemed to be happening. It was urgent that he go South, he felt, and he tried all means of getting funds, taking an advance — of fourteen dollars — on *Eureka*, buttering up Mrs. Lewis by praising her *Child of the Sea*, and soliciting help from John Jacob Astor's grandson. Poe certainly knew that the young man — Charles Astor Bristed — was well-to-do, since Bristed had helped him once before, but he seems not to have known that old Astor left most of his money to William Backhouse Astor, making *him* the richest man in the United States, so there was little left for the Bristeds. In the hope of raising money he agreed to lecture in Lowell. Then came a great blow. Mrs. Shew had been persuaded by the "parson," as Poe called young Hopkins, that she should have nothing more to do with him. He replied in the most hysterical, misspelled letter he had written since Mrs. Clemm had threatened to take Virginia to live with Neilson Poe. He said he had "had promonitions of this for months," and complained that on her last visit she had greeted even the cat more cordially than she had him. But he accepted the rejection, out of respect for her, and they never again met. He was ripe to fall under the influence of some strong woman, but he was certain it was not going to be Mrs. Locke. Nevertheless, he went to Lowell and lectured on "The Poets and Poetry of America" — a safe enough subject out of the range of Clark and Briggs — at Wentworth Hall on July 10, 1848.

The lecture was a resounding success and brought Poe a good sum of money, but he offended his hostess utterly by the attention he paid one of her neighbors, Mrs. Nancy Richmond. Poe described "Annie" — as he came to call her — as "a young woman about twenty-eight years of age — slender, or rather slight, and somewhat above the medium height. As she approached, with a certain *modest decision* of step altogether indescribable, I said to myself, 'Surely here I have found the perfection of natural, in contradistinction from artificial *grace*. . . .' The eyes of Annie . . . were 'spiritual gray;' her hair, a light chestnut." She had about her an air of enthusiasm, of romance, of womanliness — she was interested in Edgar Poe, in other words, and not just in displaying "The Raven" for her own prestige. Poe was smitten on the spot. But there was a live and healthy Mr. Richmond.

Poe returned to Fordham on July 14, and hearing that Chivers was in New York, invited him to the cottage, "as I propose going on to Richmond on Monday." He sent gift copies of *Eureka* to some friends, packed his trunk, and set out. With him, in addition to prospectuses for the *Stylus*, he took some of his puffs of Mrs. Lewis. But in his heart was yearning for — Mrs. Osgood? She was dying of tuberculosis in Albany. Mrs. Shew? She had fallen from the bosom of Edgar Poe to that of the church. Mrs. Richmond — Annie? In the meantime, on to Richmond!

A rosemary odor,
Commingled with pansies —
With rue and the beautiful
Puritan pansies.
"For Annie"

EDGAR POE'S JOURNEY to Richmond was wholly uneventful, and his stay there unproductive. He found congenial company in a tavern close by the wharf where his boat docked, and stayed there through a long and jolly binge, reciting poems and orating in barrooms. Eventually he went to John MacKenzie's house, Duncan Lodge, where his sister lived, but before then his spree had turned bitter, and he challenged John M. Daniel, editor of the *Examiner*, to a duel. They talked it over, however, when Poe was in a less fuddled state, and instead of exchanging bullets with him, Edgar promised to send him contributions. John R. Thompson, editor of the *Southern Literary Messenger*, heard he was in the city, sought him out, and was persuaded to buy "The Rationale of Verse." Aside from that, Poe got absolutely nothing done.

In late August, Poe was aroused from his Southern idling by the promise of a Northern romance. Mrs. Sarah Helen Whitman, impressed by the poem he had written in response to her Valentine, sent him some more verses, but since they were addressed to his residence in Fordham, where there was no post office, they went instead to West Farms. Since Poe always used the post office in New York City, he left for the South without knowing that they were there, and when Mrs. Clemm heard that there was mail waiting, she sent it on to Richmond. When Poe received them he was about to embark on some enterprise, "a stern, cold and debasing, although brilliant and gigantic ambition," which he did not fancy very much, and when Mrs. Whitman seemed to be serious in her poetical flirtation, he was glad to abandon everything and rush North.

Sarah Helen Power, born in 1803 — the same day and month as Edgar Poe but six years earlier — came from an eccentric family; but in spite of all her oddities, her sister was the one pointed out as "peculiar." Her mother was as hard as the rocks of New England. Her father had gone on a voyage to the West Indies during the War of 1812, been captured, and was released in 1815, but did not go home until 1834. In 1828, Helen married John Whitman, a Massachusetts lawyer, but he died soon and she returned to Providence. She was a faddist of the worst order. Her clothing was overlaid with veils and shawls and laces and fans, which dripped from her as she animatedly talked and postured. She was a spiritualist, not out of conviction, but because it was fashionable. She was willing to be severely critical of anyone who used alcohol to excess, but she drugged herself with ether to haze the crudity of the world, and since this made her ill quite often, indulged in hypochondriac announcements of her imminent demise. She was attractive in appearance, clever and witty, but naïve to the extreme in any situation outside the little game of life she played in the dim light of her mother's heavily draped parlor.

Like a trout leaping for a luscious-looking fly, Poe shot up from the South, but when he got to Fordham he had flickering second thoughts. Trips to Providence cost money, and he had no intention of wasting what little he could scrape up in pursuit of a woman who might not even be there when he got there. He could write and ask — but how write a woman to whom he had not been introduced? He employed a ruse, one that would not fool her but that would satisfy the conventions. He wrote under an assumed name — "Edward S. T. Grey" — asking for her autograph. In the text he disguised his distinctive handwriting slightly, but on the envelope he did not. Mrs. Whitman was a better fisherman than that, however, and did not answer. As she expected, he rose to the bait, and armed with a letter of introduction from Miss Maria McIntosh, a Providence poetess, he called on her on September 21.

The second half of 1848 was a season rife with adventurousness, as if the lush rhetoric of the time had suddenly turned to deeds. The Mexican War, which Americans had let themselves be maneuvered into without reason or preparation, was won and the nation now stretched from coast to coast. It had cost nearly a hundred million dollars and thirteen thousand lives — most dead of disease — but the territorial gain was astounding, and almost as a bonus, news came that gold had been discovered in California. The nation raged over a presidential campaign without issues, for Zachary Taylor, who had been willing to run on any ticket, had not yet had time to look into them, and although the question of slavery was the most serious controversy of the time, neither of the major parties made issue of it. The magazines got into arguments over Shakespeare's education, laying the way for the controversy that would attract crackpots for generations, and Lowell supplied both sides in the New York literary war with ammunition in *A Fable for Critics*. William Alfred Jones, who had drawn Poe's ire by not including him in his study of American humorists, alienated himself from Evert Duyckinck by an affair with a seventeen-year-old girl.

Even against this background, however, what happened during Poe's four-day visit seems like the frantic pursuit of an impulse. He called on her daily, and even dared to put his arm around her waist as they sat — appropriately enough — in the cemetery. He told her, "Helen, I love now — now — for the first and only time," and insisted that the only reason he had not courted her before was that he thought she was happily married. She protested his courtship by claiming she had heart disease; and he pointed out (in a letter after he had gone back to Fordham) that nervous disorder "especially when exasperated by ether or [the next word Mrs. Whitman carefully snipped from the page] — will give rise to *all* the symptoms of heart-disease." Then he gallantly concluded, "if you *died* — then at least would I clasp your dear hand in death, and willingly — oh, *joyfully — joyfully — joyfully* — go down *with* you into the night of the Grave."

Poe was whipping himself up into emotion, but it was as real, and if anything more sincere, than her concern over her health. His first need of all was for a woman, as Mrs. Shew kept insisting, a strong and devoted woman who would take care of him. He was near the end of all of his resources, and at the end of his financial ones; she was the heir, through her mother's family, to a comfortable estate, and she had a good amount of property in her possession. All his needs would be satisfied if he married her, he thought, but how much of that thought was conscious no one can ever say.

Edgar said good-by to her on Sunday, but before leaving Providence the next day he went and sat a while in the cemetery where he had made his impassioned plea. He was clearly trying to convince himself that he loved her; the cemetery was an effective backdrop before which he could associate Mrs. Whitman with his first "Helen," Jane Stith Stanard. He had been back at Fordham only a few days when she wrote him, playing out the old dance of courtship with her reservations and reluctance. He wrote a dozen purple pages in reply — but unlike the letters he had written when really wrought up, this one is properly spelled and consciously constructed. Her answer brought up the gossip that had been spread about him by Mrs. Ellet, and referred to charges by her friends that he wanted to marry her for her money. This he denied, claiming that "long since" he had made the resolution "that, under *no* circumstances, would I marry where 'interest,' as the world terms it, could be suspected as, on my part, the object of the marriage," and that he was "relieved" to discover that she was dependent on her mother. He needn't have worked so hard; she had already wangled him an invitation to lecture in Providence in December.

At this point, Poe came to a great awakening. He wanted Mrs. Whitman, but he wanted Mrs. Richmond even more. He was to have given another lecture in Lowell in November, but his talk was canceled on account of excitement over the election, which took place that year for the first time on the same day throughout the nation, November 7. But he went to Lowell all the same, and went to Annie Richmond's house. There he pleaded with her to leave her husband and come with him; otherwise he would have to marry Mrs. Whitman. She was gentle and sympathetic in her refusal, but firm.

Annie had a deep and genuine affection for him; that he knew well. She might have married him had she not been already married, and Edgar could not see the pleasant but ineffectual Charles Richmond as a serious obstacle, nor could he understand that Annie's daughter, Carry, provided a reason that she would never run away with him. He went back to his hotel and spent a miserable night. The following morning he tried to calm himself with a walk in the brisk fall air, but depression came on worse than before, causing him to work out a fantastic scheme to resolve the situation. He bought two ounces of laudanum and, not even returning to the hotel, took a train to Boston. There he wrote a letter to Annie, reminding her of her parting promise, "that, under all circumstances, you would come to me on my bed of death." He then told her where to find him in Boston and bade her come, for he was going to commit suicide. When the letter was finished, he swallowed an ounce of the laudanum and started for the post office. Whether he intended to kill himself in any case, or if he was hoping that the fear of his death would bring out the latent love in her, and that once she had left her home to come to him she would stay, he surely did not know. Certainly if she did not come, he would have taken the rest of the laudanum, else he would not have taken the first dose, for that would have meant she thought he was bluffing and he would, out of pride, have to prove otherwise.

The only practical flaw in Poe's dramatic scheme is that he did not know anything about the use of opiates. An overdose, such as the amount of opium contained in an ounce of laudanum, is rejected by the stomach before taking effect. There could not have been a more severe chastening for him. Striding briskly to the post office, he suddenly felt nauseated, and, unable to restrain himself, went into spasms of vomiting. Passersby, surprised at seeing an erect, neat, dignified man suddenly bend over and retch into the gutter, came to his assistance; the cholera had not been bad that summer, but they had all had experience with it, and although these symptoms were different, diseases were mysterious things.

The attack ceased as quickly as it had come on, but it left Poe appallingly weak. The helpful strangers were mystified, but when Poe, fearfully embarrassed, insisted that he was all right, they let him go, and following his reluctant promise to Annie, he went on to Providence to ask Mrs. Whitman to marry him. He arrived there wretchedly ill; such shocks made havoc of his flimsy constitution. He sent Mrs. Whitman a note, saying, "I have *no* engagements, but am *very* ill — so much so that I must

go home, if possible — but if you say 'stay,' I will try & do so."
She sent a message that she would meet him at the Athenaeum
in half an hour. But when she came, instead of consolation she
brought letters that agitated friends had sent warning her
against him. He heard these, and when they had parted, he
wrote her a letter of renunciation.

The next day, however, his physical condition was worse, and
turning, as always, to a woman, he went to her house, calling
loudly for her. She and even her stalwart mother were alarmed,
and old Mrs. Powers said finally that Helen should promise "all
that he might require of me" to calm him down. Finally the
old lady let him in and talked to him for two hours while
Helen summoned up courage to flutter into the room. This
gave her mother opportunity to call a doctor, who diagnosed
that Poe was suffering from cerebral congestion. They turned
the sick man over to the care of a neighbor, William J. Pabodie, under whose care Poe came to his senses, without any
clear memory of what had happened since he took the opium.
Pabodie wanted a souvenir of his Good Samaritanship and submitted Poe to the ordeal of sitting without moving an eyelid
for two minutes while he was daguerreotyped. The picture
shows Poe bleary-eyed, the muscles on one side of his face
slumped so that his eyebrow drooped and his cheek was puffy.

Though she had bargained for a celebrity and been granted a
wreck, Mrs. Whitman by this time was sincerely moved by the
man as well as by his fame. She followed her mother's advice
and agreed to marry Poe, insisting, however, that at any sign
of the excesses she had been warned about, she would call the
wedding off. On the fourteenth he took the steamboat for New
York, writing en route to assure her that he had not broken his
promise. But on his return to Fordham he wrote Annie, telling
her all that happened, referring to Helen simply as "*her*," and
begging, "oh my *pure, virtuous, generous, beautiful, beautiful*

sister Annie! — is it not POSSIBLE for you to come [to Fordham] — if only for one little week?" Mrs. Clemm wrote her by the same mail, saying that she knew it would be inconvenient for her to travel to Fordham, but asking her to write often. She said that Edgar returned *"how changed!* I scarcely knew him." The friendship between Annie and Mrs. Clemm deepened, even though their only sympathy at first was through the affection each of them felt for Poe.

Edgar had been neglecting his career almost entirely. Just before his first visit to Mrs. Whitman, he had written Charles Fenno Hoffman, editor of the *Literary World*, complaining about misrepresentation in the review — probably by the theological student Hopkins — that journal had published of *Eureka*. The reviews of the book were in general not favorable. A week after he left Providence the last time, he remembered his renewed acquaintances in Richmond, and wrote to a young poetess he had met there on his last visit, Miss Susan Talley, enclosing a letter for her to present to the brother of the first Mrs. Allan, Edward Valentine, asking him for a loan to help establish the *Stylus*. He was obviously looking for alternatives to marriage with Mrs. Whitman. Not having heard from Annie since his letter recounting the suicide attempt, he wrote her sister, Sarah Heywood, asking her to intercede for him. Time for the lecture at Providence was approaching, and Mrs. Whitman again wrote, enclosing a poem, "Arcturus," and a new list of reports she had received about his bad character. His reply was much less impassioned than before, but he told his side of the affair of Mrs. Ellet and the letters from Frances Osgood. Even he was aware that his tone was cold, so he wrote again two days later, somewhat more feelingly, suggesting that they establish in America an "aristocracy . . . of intellect."

Good New England sense prevailed in the Power-Whitman household by the middle of December, however, and they had two legal documents drawn up, transferring the rights of Mrs. Whitman — and of her sister — under their grandfather's will to their mother. This gave Mrs. Power the authority to disinherit her daughter, and was ironclad protection against Poe's inheriting anything if Helen should die before him. They sent copies of these to Poe for his signature, gratuitously pointing out that they were taking no chances over his getting his hands on any of their money. Edgar sent them back with a note announcing his arrival in Providence four days later, concluding, "My mother sends her dearest love and says she will return good for evil & treat you *much* better than *your* mother has treated me."

On Tuesday afternoon, December 19, Poe left for Providence, calling on Mrs. Hewitt, one of the literati, on the way. "Mr. Poe," she asked, "are you going to Providence to be married?" "No, Madam," Edgar replied, "I am not going to Providence to be married, I am going to deliver a lecture on Poetry." Then he shyly added, "That marriage may never take place." He arrived on Wednesday morning, rested, and called on Mrs. Whitman in the afternoon. That night, the fifth in the Franklin Lyceum series of lecturers, Edgar Poe addressed an audience of nearly two thousand on "The Poetic Principle." It was a brilliant summary of his poetic theory, propounding that a poem must be short enough to be read in a half hour, since after that time attention flags and the effect is lost, and that it must not be didactic, but should convey its truth through the poetic experience. He defined poetry as *"The Rhythmical Creation of Beauty."* Each point he illustrated by reading, with the dramatic flair and precise attention to vowel quality he had long practiced, one or two poems, ranging from Shelley to Willis, through Longfellow, Bryant, Byron, and Tennyson. His selection was clearly to appeal to popular taste, and he catered to a New England audience by restraining his feelings about the "frog-pondians," although he left Lowell out, remembering the passage in A *Fable for Critics*, "Here comes Poe with his raven, like Barnaby Rudge,/Three fifths of him genius and two fifths sheer fudge."

The anti-Poe factions of Miss Lynch's literary circle, alarmed at the romance their hostess had abetted, were deluging their friends in Providence with letters urging them to talk Mrs. Whitman out of the marriage. But Poe and his new Helen were now committed to each other, and, having recovered from the sentimentality behind their posturing declarations of the previous months, were beginning to feel sincere affection for each other. Two days after the lecture, Pabodie witnessed Poe's signature on a document renouncing all rights in his fiancée's property, but that night some enthusiastic young men at the bar of his hotel, the Earl, insisted upon buying him drinks, and he arrived at Mrs. Whitman's feeling the effect. He was unusually quiet and put great care into every move he made, but Helen's mother and guests sniffed him out and created a scene as agitated as a revival meeting, and Poe had to testify that he would never touch another drop. He must have felt that an unwarranted intrusion upon his privacy, for the next morning he asserted his independence and called for a glass of wine with breakfast, then wrote a note to the Reverend Dr. Crocker, asking him to publish the banns the next two days, probably not knowing that state law required them to be published three days before a marriage. He entrusted the note to Pabodie, who, meaning well but really opposed to the match, did not know what to do and so did nothing.

Edgar wrote Mrs. Clemm that they would be married on Monday and arrive at Fordham on Tuesday. He and Helen went for a drive in the morning; then he helped her with some of her packing. In the afternoon they visited a circulating library, and while Poe was leafing through books, someone handed Mrs. Whitman a note tipping her off about his morning glass of wine. When they got back to her house, she broke off the engagement. Poe pleaded with her, but she sat in stony silence, somewhat relieved at "being freed from the intolerable burden of responsibility which he had sought to impose upon me, by persuading me that his fate, for good or evil, depended upon *me*."

Then Pabodie and Mrs. Power came in, and while Helen sniffed at her ether until she passed out — or could decently simulate it — the caustic old woman gave Poe a tongue-lashing while Pabodie looked on flabbergasted. At last Poe got up, said he had had enough of the "intolerable insults" of the family, and stalked out. He was back at Fordham for Christmas.

Mrs. Whitman, humiliated and probably persuaded by Mrs. Ellet and her friends that Poe would spread stories about her unless she told her version first, immediately set about writing everyone who knew either Poe or herself, including Annie's husband, that Edgar had behaved so badly *after* the first publication of the banns that she was forced to go to the minister and justify to him the reason she did not go through with the wedding. This made her a woman wronged and humiliated before the public and the church. The banns were not published, for Pabodie had not delivered Poe's note to the minister. Poe heard of this through Annie, and wrote asking Helen to retract this story, stating: "no amount of provocation on your part, or on the part of your friends, shall induce me to speak ill of you even in my own defence." She did not answer, although she told enough of the truth to Annie to exonerate Poe in her eyes. As time went on, Mrs. Whitman retained a fondness for Poe's memory, and she was his most gallant defender after his death — although she was very careful to protect her own reputation, heavily scratching out passages in his letters that were embarrassing for her, and even mutilating them by cutting words out. Her own letters she suppressed.

EDGAR POE ENTERED HIS FORTIETH YEAR in a burst of creative energy. He arranged to contribute regularly to the *Flag of Our Union*, a Boston weekly of large circulation, and to the *Metropolitan*, a new magazine. Graham had lost control of his magazine the previous August, but Poe hoped to continue writing for it, as well as *Godey's*, and he had recently mended his fences with the *Southern Literary Messenger*. The *American Review*, now the *Whig Review*, and the *Democratic Review* had both been hospitable to him, in spite of politics. Post's *Union* had failed, but it was succeeded by *Sartain's Union*, published by Poe's Philadelphia friend, John Sartain. Even an Ohio magazine called the *Gentlemen's* was soliciting contributions from him.

Chastened about love and at an impasse in scheming for his own magazine, Poe got diligently to work as soon as he had recovered from the emotional dizziness of Providence, and wrote John Thompson, proposing to contribute five pages of "Marginalia" to each issue of the *Southern Literary Messenger* for a year. Thompson agreed; readers of three other magazines had found this sort of tablet wit and knowledge, which Poe reeled off by the page, quite fascinating. It was a time-filler for the reader as much as a space-filler for the editor. He completed a short survey of the major contemporary literary critics and their methods, "About Critics and Criticism," and sent it to the *Whig Review*. He reviewed Lowell's *Fable for Critics* in time for the March *Messenger*, saying it was malevolent and objecting to the abolitionism and New England parochialism in it; but, after all, his criticism was written for a Southern journal just as ill feeling about slavery was beginning to grow into anger.

The familiar sensation of his pen scratching swiftly over sheets of his favorite blue paper brought him far back toward stability. "In fact, Annie," he wrote Mrs. Richmond, in reply to her letter recounting Mrs. Whitman's complaints against him, "I am beginning to grow wiser, and do not care so much as I did for the opinions of a world in which I see, with my own eyes, that to act generously is to be considered as design-ing, and that to be poor is to be a villain." Annie and Mrs. Clemm were the people he could count on; "from this day forth I shun the pestilential society of *literary* women."

This hard-won humility was reflected in the next phase of his thinking about landscape gardening, too. He wrote "A Pendant to 'The Domain of Arnheim,'" "Landor's Cottage," in which his taste was as fastidious as before, but the setting was com-posed of natural scenes around Fordham and the rugged topog-raphy of Manhattan Island, while the "mass of semi-Gothic, semi-Saracenic architecture . . . with a hundred oriels, min-arets, and pinnacles" was transformed into the cottage itself, a bit idealized, but life-size.

Although it is "pendant" on the earlier work in that it contains none of the theorizing that gave the former its interest, this simple narrative has much more charm. The narrator, on a walking tour, loses his way and enters a grassy road, where he is astonished to notice that every artificial touch was harmonized with nature in consummate artistry. Eventually he reaches a lovely valley containing a lake fed by a meandering brook, in one loop of which, a peninsula "which was very *nearly* an island," stands a small cottage of very pleasing design, hung with vines. He approaches, makes friends with the dog, and raps on the door. A young woman — in appearance identical to Annie Richmond — appears and invites him in, where he discovers that the furnishings are as pleasant as the building and its setting.

Significantly enough, Poe mentioned that Mr. Landor was "civil, even cordial in his manner; but just then, I was more intent on observing the arrangements of the dwelling which had so much interested me, than the personal appearance of the tenant." Not only does he thereby describe his attitude toward Charles Richmond and Mr. Richmond's manner toward him, but he implies that the artist was either not living there, or it was Annie rather than her husband. Of course *Poe* was the creator of all this, and in describing surroundings that he would consider ideal, Annie must be a part. He was tranquil, but his feelings were still stronger than his art.

In a final leg-pull of journalistic antagonisms, he also wrote a light narrative called "X-ing a Paragrab." This caricatures the rivalries of editors in terms that are exaggerated, but have the true ring of experience in a newspaper plant. One paper publishes a castigation of the other, concluding with a paragraph in which the letter "O" appears very often. The editor of the other replies, quoting his paragraph and making fun of its style; "Why the fellow is all O!" But when the printer's devil comes to set it in type, he discovers that the devil from the rival shop, probably out of sheer need, has stolen all of the lower and upper case "O's." He reports this to the foreman, who tells him to fill in with another letter; "nobody's going to read the fellow's trash, any how." Following custom, the boy uses "X's," with disastrous-looking results — "Dxn't hxllx, nxr hxwl, nxr grxwl, nxr bxw-wxw-wxw!" — and the editor had to leave town to escape indignant subscribers.

The California gold rush was causing more excitement and disrupting life to a greater extent than the country had seen before in peacetime or even during two wars. As early as December, 1848, rumors had spread that the influx of the metal would cause gold prices to be halved within a year. By ship and overland, crowds were leaving every day, and businessmen were frantic over what effect the new gold would have on commerce in general. This gave Poe the idea for a hoax. He wrote "Von Kempelen and His Discovery" as a straight account of a man in Bremen who was suspected of theft when he bought a large property and would not explain where he got the purchase money. The police shadow him to a secret laboratory where they find mysterious chemical apparatus and a large trunk full of irregularly shaped pieces of gold. Von Kempelen had not yet revealed his formula, but "it cannot be supposed that [he] can *long* retain his secret."

Charles Fenno Hoffman, who had taken over the *Literary World* from Duyckinck two years before, went mad and had to be confined to an asylum, so the Duyckinck brothers scraped enough money together to repurchase it. Poe offered his transmutation-of-gold hoax to them, but they refused it, so he sent it to the *Flag*, where it appeared on April 14. The gold hysteria grew even wilder during the delay, but the story did not have the effect Poe anticipated of "acting as a sudden, although of course a very temporary, *check* to the gold fever." He began to wonder why.

Early in February, Poe got to work again on "The Bells" and enlarged it to many times the eighteen-line version he had

sent to *Sartain's Union*. But immediately after that, he wrote
a story which transformed the personal anger of "The Cask of
Amontillado" to the more general resentment of the artist for
those in his audience who look down on him and intrude in
his private life, and for those who use their position of power to
be cruel. He had long known the chronicles of Froissart, and
he recalled the story of the masquerade in which Charles VI,
with five of his courtiers, costumed themselves as satyrs, using
pitch and flax, which caught fire. He had also read, years before, "Frogère and the Emperor Paul," the story of a practical
joke played on a jester. He created the character of a hunch-
back jester in the court of a king who loves practical jokes.
Relying on "Hop-Frog" and his compatriot, the dancer Tripetta
— who greatly resembles a slightly undersized Annie Richmond
— for the ideas for his masquerades, the crude, fun-loving king
forces a glass of wine on the jester, whom it "excited . . . almost to madness; and madness is no comfortable feeling." Tripetta tries to protect the dwarf from having to take a second
cup, but has it tossed in her face by the king for her trouble.

The jester conquers his anger and schemes out an amusing
"diversion" for the king and his ministers. They are to go to
the party as the "Eight Chained Ourang-Outangs." He dresses
them in tight-fitting shirts and drawers, then covers them with
tar, over which goes a layer of flax, as fur. He chains them together, and at the party, maneuvers them under the chandelier
chain, and as Tripetta hauls them up, sets them afire and re-
treats through the roof by climbing the chain. This was how
he vented his feelings on those who had made him miserable
because he would not fit in with their schemes, from Clark and
English to Mrs. Ellet and Mrs. Locke; but more than that, it is
a great plea of sympathy for a serious attitude toward the
artist.

Edgar had accepted the fact that Annie could not be exclusively his; yet he continued to love her and desired her love even though he must share it with Charles Richmond. He planned to visit Lowell in the late spring with Mrs. Clemm, and even told his landlord, Valentine, that he would not retain the cottage another year. He hoped that they could move to where he could be near Annie. Learning this, the Lockes started a vast whispering campaign. Their chief target was Mr. Richmond, who began to look askance on the correspondence his wife was carrying on with Poe. When he heard of this, Edgar wrote, "It had been my design to ask you & Mr R. (or perhaps your parents) to *board* my mother while I was absent at the South," but the gossip spoiled all that, and he took the cottage for another year. But he did prepare a gift for her, a poem, "For Annie." Its short cadences have a rapturous quality fitting to the theme, long in his writing, but now for the first time carried past being a mere intellectual concept, that death is the metamorphosis to a higher life; he rejoices in it, for in death his love for Annie will go through that same change, and in pure ideality he will have what he was unable to win alive. He sent her the poem on March 23, so she would have the manuscript before she saw it in print — it appeared in the *Flag* on April 28; then, thinking of the way he had called attention to "The Raven" and "Ulalume," he sent it to Willis. The *Home Journal* printed it, with very laudatory comments about Poe from Willis, in their issue for April 28, bringing down an editorial scolding from the *Flag*.

Poe's thoughts on the "gold fever" led to his writing another poem in the early spring. The hordes rushing to California were not going there for gold so much as to escape the dissatisfaction they felt in life in contemporary America. People from all walks of life, Bowery "b'hoys" planning to steal what they needed for the arduous journey, and the scions of families on Fifth Avenue and Gramercy Park, with elaborate outfits, were setting out; but a very large number of the migrants were from the educated and the middle classes. They were the ones who could afford to go and who were least contented with the petrifying societies of "Appalachia," as Poe dubbed the nation before its latest annexations. A fair number of editors left their journals to hunt for gold; to one of them, a man named De Graw, Poe had sold "A Valentine," and when he left, Poe made another copy and sent it to the *Flag*. But De Graw had in the meantime disposed of it to Sartain, and it appeared in both the *Flag* and *Sartain's Union* at the same time. Poe symbolized the gold-seekers as "a gallant knight," who searches for Eldorado until he grows old, and asks directions of a ghostly pilgrim, who replies: "Over the Mountains Of the Moon, Down the Valley of the Shadow," or in other words, your goal is really death.

As he finished each poem or story, he sent it out, endeavoring to spread his work through a variety of magazines, and if they came back, he had two certain sources of good pay, the *Metropolitan* and the less "respectable" *Flag of Our Union*. As a last resort there was the *Southern Literary Messenger*, which was not yet in good financial condition, although Thompson promised retroactive pay as soon as it was; and *Graham's*, now in the hands of Samuel D. Patterson, although Graham was trying to get it back. But the *Metropolitan* folded after two issues, and then a number of papers in succession either failed or were forced to cancel payment. He wrote Annie, "I am reduced to Sartain and Graham — both very precarious." Enough so, indeed, that he was eventually reduced to the *Flag of Our Union* and the *Southern Literary Messenger*, although Sartain paid well for "The Bells."

These reverses drove Edgar into deep depression. He was forced more and more to rely for his support on what Mrs. Clemm could beg from Mrs. Lewis, who had decided she liked the idea of having a pet critic dependent on her. He became ill, and Mrs. Clemm said to Annie, "I thought he would *die* several times. God knows I wish we were both in our graves — it would, I am sure, be far better." Poe was through with dashing off verses to women who really meant nothing to him, but he had power enough to express his emotion toward those he really loved in striking verse. After "For Annie," he wrote "To My Mother," a sonnet that transcends a hackneyed theme with its simple sincerity. He called Mrs. Clemm "more than mother unto me," because she had both acted as mother to him and been the mother of his wife, who was "dearer to my soul than its soul-life."

Time remained for Poe, in those discouraging spring days when he was "not so much *ill* . . . as depressed in spirits," to write one more poem. In "Annabel Lee" he again brought his full orchestra of words, sounds, and rhythms into play, but with less flamboyance than in "The Raven." This poem, on the death of his wife, and the love that stays heaven and hell from the power to "dissever my soul from the soul / Of the beautiful Annabel Lee," is more emotional than original, but it kept him writing, and thus probably it brought him through the month of April. Writing was the only medicine left for his melancholy.

But the West Farms post office was again holding treasure for him. Late in April he learned that there had been a letter waiting for him there since early in the year. It had been sent December 18, the day before Poe left for his lecture and marriage fiasco in Providence, from Oquawka, Illinois, a community on the Mississippi River. Edward H. N. Patterson, who wrote the letter, had come of age on January 27, at which time his father had given him a paper, the Oquawka *Spectator*, to satisfy his desire to be a publisher. In December he had wanted to establish a literary magazine with Poe as editor. The *Stylus* at last!

Poe wrote back immediately, summarizing his successes in the magazine field and suggesting further correspondence. He insisted on a five-dollar magazine. But in the meantime there was food to be got, and so he succumbed to Mrs. Lewis's insistence and recommended to Putnam a new edition of her *Child of the Sea*. Patterson replied very quickly, agreeing with Poe's concept of the magazine and proposing that if they could get a thousand subscribers in advance, he would back the magazine, for which their ultimate agreement would be for Poe to provide the contents — "you are to have the entire editorial control" — paying contributors out of his own pocket; Patterson would pay for everything else. All receipts would be shared equally. He suggested publishing from Oquawka until the circulation reached five thousand; then "it may be to our interests to publish it elsewhere — time will tell."

Poe countered with the suggestion that the title page read "Published simultaneously at New-York & *St. Louis*," but agreed to the proposal otherwise. He enclosed a title page he had designed, and announced that he was leaving for Boston and Lowell and from there would tour the South seeking subscribers, asking Patterson for an advance of fifty dollars for expenses, to be sent him at Richmond. He was expecting an equal sum for some manuscripts he had sent *Graham's*, among them "Critics and Criticism," which had come back when the *Whig Review* had had to stop paying. Cleaning out his desk, he sent a group of poems for inclusion in Griswold's tenth edition, among them the yet unpublished "Annabel Lee."

Poe's visit to New England the last week of May saw little accomplished. He was more interested in visiting Annie than in soliciting subscriptions; and not only did Mr. Richmond keep a keen eye on Poe's behavior, but Poe got himself into more hot water by running out of money. He felt that enough time had gone by since he sent his last manuscripts to *Graham's*, so he drew a draft on the magazine for fifty dollars, which, after a long struggle on Poe's part with the bankers, was refused. He was indignant and on his return wrote to the magazine, then reported to Annie, "The reason of the return of my draft on Graham's Magazine (which put me to such annoyance and mortification while I was with you) was, that the articles I sent (by mail) did not come to hand. No *insult* (as I had half-anticipated) was meant — and I am sincerely glad of this; for I did not wish to give up writing for Graham's Mag. just yet." He sent the publisher's letter to her, to prove he was telling the truth. But nothing more of his appeared in *Graham's* until the following year.

Without that money, he could not go South, so he wrote Thompson in Richmond, asking him to send on Patterson's letter, containing, he hoped, fifty dollars. He was still in Fordham three weeks later, however, and was again bullied into sponsoring Mrs. Lewis. He wrote a puff of her poems and sent it to Griswold, asking him to substitute it for the article that had appeared in the 1849 *Female Poets of America*, and adding, "I would not, of course, put you to any *expense* in this matter: — all cost shall be promptly defrayed." It was poverty that drove Poe to these ends, but he correctly summed up Griswold's character in offering him Mrs. Lewis's bribe; Griswold was not in need, but he took it.

On the same day, June 28, Edgar took Mrs. Clemm to the Lewises' house in Brooklyn, where she was to stay during his absence. He stayed overnight, and the next afternoon the Lewises and "Muddy" walked to the waterfront with him, to the pier from which the steam ferry left for Perth Amboy. As sailing time, five o'clock, approached, he said good-by to his host and hostess, then kissed the woman he now considered his mother. "God bless you, my own darling mother," he said. "Do not fear for Eddy! See how good I will be while I am away, and will come back to love and comfort you." The boat whistle blew, the roustabouts cast off, and out into the harbor, thick with ships bound for California and gold, sailed another "gallant knight . . . In search of Eldorado."

Thank Heaven! the crisis,
The danger, is past,
And the lingering illness
Is over at last —
And the fever called "Living"
Is conquered at last.

"For Annie"

THE HEAT WAVE THAT HAD STRUCK New York the middle of
June continued to oppress life in the city. The only air moving
was a light sea breeze through the day and a torpid movement
of overheated air through the night, that brought with it
hordes of New Jersey mosquitoes. After one more night in
Brooklyn, Mrs. Clemm had had enough and returned to Fordham. She waited a week for a letter from Edgar, then two days
more, when, thoroughly alarmed, she wrote to Annie, saying
she was afraid something had happened to him in Philadelphia.
In fact he had already written her, but thinking she was with
Mrs. Lewis, he had addressed it to Brooklyn, where it stayed,
in spite of Poe's enclosed note to "Give the enclosed *speedily*
to my darling mother."

Something had indeed happened to Poe. He wandered, ill,
to the house of James P. Moss, on South Fourth Street, spent
the night, and wandered away, in spite of protests, the next
morning. A week after his arrival in Philadelphia he wrote Mrs.
Clemm the letter she did not receive until much later, dating
it "New York, July 7."

My *dear, dear* Mother, —

I have been *so* ill — have had the cholera, or spasms quite as bad, and can now hardly hold the pen . . .

The very instant you get this, *come* to me. The joy of seeing you will almost compensate for our sorrows. We can but die together. It is no use to reason with me *now*; I must die. I have no desire to live since I have done "Eureka." I could accomplish nothing more. For your sake it would be sweet to live, but we must die together. You have been all in all to me, darling, ever beloved mother, and dearest, truest friend.

I was never *really* insane, except on occasions where my heart was touched. . . .

I have been taken to prison once since I came here for getting drunk; but *then* I was not. It was about Virginia.

The following Monday, the ninth, Poe, pale and haggard, burst into John Sartain's office. He begged Sartain to protect him from two men who, he said, were going to kill him. They had followed him on the train, but he had got off and returned to Philadelphia to avoid them. He insisted that Sartain cut off his moustache, so he could not be recognized. Sartain took him home with him, trimmed the moustache a bit, and served him tea. Poe made motions then to leave, and Sartain asked him where he was going. "To the Schuylkill," said Poe, so Sartain said he would go with him. Whatever Poe meant, his host took him to mean that he wanted to cool off from the heat of the city. Poe's shoes were worn down at the heels and his feet were painfully chafed, so Sartain got him a pair of slippers, and they set out.

The two men took a horse-drawn omnibus at Ninth and Chestnut Streets and rode north to the terminus, a tavern on Callowhill, then walked off in the darkness to the Fairmount reservoir. They climbed up to the landing, where there were benches, and sat down. Here Poe began talking, saying that he had been in Moyamensing Prison, where he dreamed of a radiant female figure who stood on the top of the highest tower and spoke to him across a great distance. The hallucination was very vivid, and Poe described it in powerful terms. After he was talked out, they returned to Sartain's house, where the editor made up a bed for his sick friend on the sofa. But Poe was afraid to be alone in the dark — for months after Virginia's death he had needed someone to stay beside him until he fell asleep — so Sartain placed three chairs alongside Poe's sofa and slept beside him.

The next day Poe was still agitated, but the morning after that, he was well enough to go out by himself. When he came back he had recovered some of his pride, and said the whole thing had been a delusion. Sartain asked him why he had been in prison, and Poe explained that he was suspected of trying to pass a fifty-dollar counterfeit note. But when he was brought before the magistrate, someone commented, "Why, this is Poe the poet," and he was released. But whatever money he had with him when he left New York, Poe had none now. Sartain had already paid him once for "The Bells," and had added to the price when Poe expanded and improved the poem; and besides, he was still somewhat ill at ease over buying "A Valentine" from De Graw and publishing it simultaneously with the *Flag of Our Union*, to which Poe sent the poem after De Graw left for California. He could not — or would not — help with money.

Poe got an entirely different reception from his old friend Chauncey Burr. Burr and George Lippard went about the editorial offices of the city, borrowing money for him. Godey contributed five dollars, and Patterson, the current owner of *Graham's*, another five. These they put in Poe's pocket, and then Burr bought Poe's ticket to Baltimore with his own money and saw him off in the train on Friday, July 13. Poe's valise had disappeared, but at the last minute it turned up at the railway station. The lectures with which he planned to pay his way through the South had, however, disappeared. There was a frantic search, but the manuscripts were as lost as Poe's memories of what had happened his first ten days in Philadelphia.

What had happened between Friday, June 29, and Monday, July 9? Poe was cheerful, although hiding strange forebodings of disaster, when his steamboat pulled away from the Brooklyn pier and headed through the anchored California clippers for the western end of Staten Island, Kill Van Kull and Arthur Kill and Amboy. It was not long before dusk when his train, shooting out sparks and hot cinders, started across New Jersey for the Delaware; and his journey from Bordentown to Camden was surely in the dead of night. "I believe that demons take advantage of the night to mislead the unwary — although, you know, I don't believe in them." He was too wary — and worried — by the time he took the ferry and was deposited, near midnight, on the Philadelphia waterfront. For years he had been harried by the enmity of Clark and the slanders of Mrs. Ellet and Mrs. Locke. He had been humiliated before his Annie a month before by a dishonored draft for fifty dollars. It was cholera season, worse than it had been for years, and the preventive for cholera was, by the folklore-medicine of the time, opium pills. He had had his last meal at three in the afternoon — tea — and he probably took a snack at one of the dubious eating houses along the way.

Wretchedly lonely and afraid; nervous finally to be setting out with a substantial partner on his life's ambition, his own magazine; disappointed at the difficulty he was having disposing of his latest work, which to *him* seemed good — disappointed, too, over the many copies of *Eureka* that still remained unsold in Putnam's store — ill, perhaps with food poisoning; illusions came on him. He vomited, and thought he had the cholera. As he walked the silent streets of Philadelphia, memories of Virginia came back to him, and he feared that Mrs. Clemm, too, was dead. The days and nights became a long nightmare, interrupted only by his being picked up as a drunk and thrown in prison — or at least thinking he had been. Then he turned to Moss. Another weekend, waiting for Mrs. Clemm to come and get him, his money gone, he knew not where, and he turned to Sartain. Ashamed at attempting to borrow money from Sartain to go on, he found his salvation in the good-hearted Burr. Shaken and ill, he went on with his journey.

Poe had no trouble in getting to Baltimore, and there spent seven of the ten dollars his editors had given him for a ticket on the steamboat for Richmond. On the way up the river he wrote a melancholy letter to Mrs. Clemm, and when he arrived he went to the Swan Tavern and took to his bed. He was in sadly weakened condition. Whatever illness he had, treating it with calomel — since no one thought of anything but cholera, and calomel was another disastrous specific used for that disease — had upset his whole system. Rosalie and the Mac-Kenzies tried to take care of him at the inn; then they moved him to Duncan Lodge, where he began to recover. The doctor called in, Gibbon Carter, told him he could not survive another such attack.

Still frantically worried over Mrs. Clemm, Poe wrote to her a third time, repeating his gratitude to Burr and saying, "My clothes are so *horrible*, and I am so *ill*," but sending her one of the two dollars he had left. Within two days he heard from her, and that made him feel much better. He wrote, telling more rationally of his experiences; then he replied to Patterson, acknowledging two letters and the promised fifty dollars. He also wrote Lippard, in Philadelphia, asking him to search again for the missing lectures; but they were not to be found, so he set to work rewriting "The Poetic Principle." A date was made for him to lecture in the Exchange Concert Rooms on August 17. In addition to work on the lecture, he had to write again to Patterson to talk him out of making the *Stylus* a three-dollar magazine. Patterson gave in, leaving price as well as content up to Poe, and suggesting a rendezvous in St. Louis the middle of October.

Although midsummer lectures in Richmond, particularly in so hot a summer as that of 1849, were not usually well attended, Poe's fame and his local associations brought a fashionable crowd to hear him, and he made a great success. "I *never* was received with so much enthusiasm," he wrote, and the papers reported that Richmond had never heard anything like it. From that moment on, his visit was a triumphal tour. For social as well as other reasons, he joined the Shockoe Hill Division of the Sons of Temperance, thus reassuring hostesses who might have learned of his reputation, and giving himself a valid protection against the excesses of Southern hospitality. Some invitations he had to refuse because he had no dress coat, but the others kept him busy enough. He was rarely alone, day or night, and in addition to his old friends, Robert Stanard, the Cabells and Sullys and Poitiaux, he was courted by the publishers — he gave "Annabel Lee" to Thompson, causing that man to get into a dispute with Griswold later over whose property it was — and was introduced to such families as the Talleys. The second Mrs. Allan was out of town, and that probably helped Poe's social career. So was Miss Valentine, now sixty-three years old.

Eventually Poe's reinstatement in Richmond society gave him the confidence to make a sentimental journey. It may have been the smell of Susan Talley's clothes — she kept orris root in her bureau drawers as had "Mama" Allan — or finding white violets where they used to grow in the grounds of the old Mayo house, now a deserted shell. He swept off his hat when Susan Talley led him into the ruined salon, shreds of mildewed wallpaper waving in the breeze from the rotting walls, and quoted from Moore, "I feel like one Who treads alone Some banquet hall deserted," and then was struck sadly by awareness of all that was irretrievably in the past.

One Sunday morning in August he went to the house of Sarah Elmira Shelton. A servant admitted him to the parlor and announced to Elmira that there was a gentleman who wanted to see her. She was preparing to go to church, and visibly annoyed, she walked primly down the stairs, the ribbons of her bonnet fluttering, her full skirts flicking the banisters. She crossed the hall and entered the white-curtained parlor. A slight man with a very broad forehead and piercing eyes, a dark moustache hiding the warm smile on his mouth, arose from one of the chairs by the round table in the center of the room. He stepped forward and said, "Oh, Elmira, is this you?" The moustached face seemed strange, the cheeks were sunken, but the eyes, now oddly sad, and the voice, deepened but with the undertone of familiar accents, were familiar. Memories crowded in on her of the quiet, beautiful boy, who had hated anything coarse or unrefined. Yet she had heard scandalous things of his behavior up North. "I never let anything interfere with going to church," she said, "but you must call again."

Poe did call again, and took up his courtship of Elmira where he had left it at the beginning of 1826. His life was starred with women he had lost — his mother, his foster mother, the strange, mad woman to whom he had written his finest poem, "To Helen," his Virginia, Annie — and here was one, lost to him when she had married, but who was now restored to him. The death of a beautiful woman was the most poetic of all subjects to Poe, but it was more moving, at this nostalgic moment when the peace and security of his Richmond childhood seemed closer than ever before, that one had been restored to him. She was the means by which that nostalgic happiness might be permanently recovered. Elmira Shelton was wealthy; but nostalgia meant more than money to Poe as he urged her to marry him. He mouthed courtly stereotypes for some time before she understood, and then she laughed. Poe indignantly said that he was serious. And then they fell into talk about the past, discovering for the first time the truth of what had happened twenty-two years before, of Allan's refusal to promise her father that Edgar should be his heir, and her father's shipping her off to relatives and intercepting Poe's letters.

Poe's charm was beginning to have an effect, and their mutual discovery of the trick that had been played on them was effective on them both. The coy widow said, "If you will not take a positive denial you must give me time to consider of it." He said that a love that hesitated was not a love for him, sure now of his success, and continued to bring up memories of the past. He reminded her of a sketch he had made of her long ago, and said that he had always kept it. Then he wrote Mrs. Clemm, asking her to write him that she had searched for it and not found it, and suggesting that he might have left it with the Whites. He concluded, "Do not tell me anything about Annie — I cannot bear to hear it now — unless you can tell me that Mr. R. is dead." He was not the first man who courted the second-best woman while he dreamed of the one he considered the best.

While Elmira was "considering," Poe told everyone that he was to be married. He wrote Mrs. Clemm, "Since the reports of my intended marriage, the McKenzies have overwhelmed me with attentions." He said that Elmira wanted to visit the cottage at Fordham, but he did not think it "would do." His only objection to living in Richmond was that it would mean being at a distance from the woman he really loved with an intensity that was foolhardy; "but I want to live *near Annie*." Mrs. Clemm was having her own problems. Poe had been unable to send her money since sharing his remaining two dollars with her on his arrival in Richmond, so she applied to Griswold for a loan. Eventually she was forced to fall back on Mrs. Lewis, and again pressed Edgar's puffs of the poetess on Griswold, saying that if he would publish it exactly as written, "I will promise you a favorable review of your books as they appear. You know the influence I have with Mr. Poe."

Meanwhile Poe continued to revel in Richmond society, renewing old acquaintances and being praised and asked to recite his poetry everywhere. The husband of Mrs. St. Leon Loud, a Philadelphia poetess, called and offered him a hundred dollars to edit his wife's poems, a commission which Poe immediately accepted, gloating, "The whole labor will not occupy me 3 days." Early in September he went to Norfolk and repeated his success as lecturer — although to a smaller crowd — and literary lion. On the seventeenth he returned to Richmond. But at the peak of his plans for the future, he was beginning to come apart. The day after his return to Richmond he wrote Mrs. Clemm about his plans for returning to New York, but his feeling of persecution glimmered again in his request that she sign no name to her reply and address it to E. S. T. Grey, Esq., Philadelphia, "for fear I should not get the letter."

The following Monday his "Poetic Principle" was repeated with as much success as before, although his friends noticed that a pallor was coming over his face, he seemed nervous, and his voice was exceedingly sad. The disturbance seemed to have passed the next night, however, for he went to "Talavera," the Talley home, and spoke with eager delight of the future, "like that of youth," Susan Talley observed. She said also that he passed around a letter in which Griswold expressed himself as flattered to be chosen as Poe's literary executor. Poe was the last guest to leave. He stood with his hosts on the portico chatting for a time, bade them goodnight, and walked off. "After a few steps he paused, turned, and again lifted his hat," said Susan Talley, "and at that moment a brilliant meteor appeared in the sky directly over his head, and vanished in the east." Poe laughed, the others joined in, and he marched off.

He spent the night with the MacKenzies, made his farewell calls through the day, and, in the evening, visited Elmira. He was a very confused suitor that night. He begged her to marry him, promising that he would be everything she might desire. But while he was assuring her that he was merely going to New York to wind up some last business before returning to Richmond, he said that he had a presentiment that he would never see her again. At that the practical Elmira took his pulse and felt his forehead, and, announcing that he had a fever, urged him not to leave until he felt better. Poe promised. "I felt so wretched about him all that night," she said, "that I went up early the next morning to inquire after him, when, much to my regret, he had left in the boat for Baltimore."

After leaving Mrs. Shelton's, Poe stopped in at the office of his friend Dr. John Carter and read the papers. After a time he roused himself, borrowed Dr. Carter's cane, and commented that he was going across to Sadler's restaurant for late supper. At the restaurant Poe became the center of a gay party. Even Sadler, the host, joined the group, but all remarked that Poe refused any drink. Nevertheless, the gaiety was such that it was near dawn and sailing time when Poe suddenly snatched up his palm-leaf hat and Dr. Carter's cane, and rushed for the boat. It steamed off downstream, bound for Norfolk and connections for Baltimore — and oblivion. The last nightmare, of which no memories remain, had begun. Six days later a compositor for the Baltimore *Sun* noticed a handsome malacca cane clutched in the hand of a ragged and unconscious man lying in the street. In a few days, the illness was over at last.

EPILOGUE

The spirits of the dead who stood
In life before thee are again
In death around thee — and their will
Shall overshadow thee: be still.
                "Spirits of the Dead"

THE NEWSPAPER TELEGRAPH sent the story up the eastern seaboard of Poe's death. On the day of his funeral the news appeared in the papers, one of which, at least, came to Mrs. Clemm. She wrote to Baltimore for information, and when it was certain, turned Poe's papers over to Griswold, who ill-temperedly took the job of editing the *Works*, the first two volumes of which appeared in January, 1850. Rosalie Poe retained John R. Thompson to secure her the rights (and proceeds) of Poe's work, since she claimed to be his only heir, but Griswold managed to get around that technicality. Griswold himself did not outlast Poe quite eight years, but died in the midst of literary and personal strife on August 27, 1857. In 1860 Mrs. Whitman published her *Edgar Poe and His Critics*, in which she denied most of the slurs Griswold had cast on Poe's character.

Mrs. Clemm lived for a few months with Annie and eventually went to a church home in Baltimore, where she died, a very old woman who was visited occasionally by distinguished literary people, on February 16, 1871. The Civil War disrupted Rosalie's home in Richmond, and she drifted from one institution to another until finally, at the Epiphany Church Home in Washington, she died on June 14, 1874. Lewis Gaylord Clark, against whose literary dictatorship Poe had smashed his editorial career, kept up his battles for another dozen years, but in June, 1861, he lost the *Knickerbocker*, and he died of a stroke on November 3, 1873. Annie Richmond, Sarah Helen Whitman, and Elmira Royster all lived on until the later part of the nineteenth century, sources of information — and misinformation — for Poe's later biographers. Charles Briggs helped carry Griswold to the grave, and remained a journalist until his death in 1878. As late as the nineties, Thomas Dunn English was not in hell but in Congress.

Melville, who entered the New York literary scene just about the time Poe retired to Fordham, was at the time of Poe's death occupied with his lesser, more popular works, such as *Redburn* and *White Jacket*. Poe was not long in his grave when Melville was deep in *Moby Dick*, however, and it was published in November, 1851. Less than four years later the first edition of *Leaves of Grass* was out, and the Golden Age of American literature had reached its last stage.

APPENDIX

THE POE CONTROVERSIES

RATHER THAN IRRITATE THE READER — and myself — with a complete scholarly apparatus, almost all of which is available through the *Complete Works of Edgar Allan Poe*, edited by James A. Harrison, New York, 1902; *The Letters of Edgar Allan Poe*, edited by John Ward Ostrom, Cambridge, Mass., 1948; *The Poems of Edgar Allan Poe*, edited by Killis Campbell, Boston, 1917; and *Edgar Allan Poe: A Critical Biography*, by Arthur Hobson Quinn, New York, 1942; and which is superfluous to the whole purpose of this book, I offer, in these short essays, a summary of the basic points of scholarly controversy over the life of Edgar Allan Poe, and the reasons that I have chosen one side or another — or my own, independent of that of others — in each of those questions which might interest the reader. Quibbling such as that over what Poe meant by "Nicéan" barks in "To Helen," the subject of a great many articles, seems to me fruitless; Poe was dreaming of an ideal, not a historical, Greece, and his poem is not one whit changed whether the word refers to ships from Nicaea or Nice, or if Poe made his word out of the Greek *Nike* or was simply referring to Ulysses' ship and forgot that the ship should be Phaeacian. Literary detective work is interesting only if the scholar some day finds the murderer rather than just arguing over the clues.

Probably the most important problem in the study of Poe's life is the one that has received the least careful attention — the character and motivation of the people involved, and most of all, that of the main character. Psychoanalysis beyond the grave cannot harm the patient, but only by making the most tenuous of assumptions — in this case that Poe was impotent, or a dipsomaniac, or a drug addict — can enough evidence be built up for diagnosis. In place of these techniques, I have tried to let the

[272]

actors in Poe's life speak and move for themselves, in the context of their own lives, and by so doing I hope I have made them human, or at least, less like figures out of a morality play.

John Allan, then, becomes neither the honest and thrifty merchant out of *Poor Richard* nor an unreformed Scrooge, but a man whose personality, even whose sentimentality, was exactly opposite to Poe's. He was an immigrant boy with a rich uncle, through whose aid he established a business that was successful until he overexpanded it at the wrong time, but who had no ultimate financial worries, because that uncle would eventually die and leave him a fortune. He and Poe grew up in anticipation of inherited wealth, but Allan took good care not to offend his benefactor, to whom he was tied by blood relationship, while Poe, although probably more loving and beloved, was less certain of his position, and fluctuated between defying Allan and kowtowing to him.

Poe's prime motivation was to make his mark on the world through literature, and for that obsession I think we should be profoundly grateful. As a Virginia gentleman he would have been merely another of the nearly forgotten list of faceless dilettantes like Thomas Holley Chivers. Had he gone through West Point and taken a commission, the Confederacy would have gained another brilliant tactician, which would have done neither it nor us any good; they had a surplus of tacticians but lacked strategists. Had he been able to keep an editorial job, much of his best work would have been lost, for he wasted a great deal of time on trivial reviews as it was.

The drive for literary fame in Poe was complicated by his major emotional need; he had a double-barreled, chronic case of galloping homesickness. Home meant refuge to him, and he never was able to get family life and security lined up together. After John Allan's troubles started, Poe was never again certain of his place in the family. At every separation from Mrs. Clemm, after she became the mother-figure in his life, he became nearly hysterical, even if he was to be away only a day or two. He complained all his life over the lack of a father.

Since home was the maternal womb to him, what was the marriage bed? This is the most debated question of all. The many stories of his affairs with women in his youth can be, as Professor Quinn pointed out [Quinn, 196-97; for the "Baltimore Mary" gossip see Hervey Allen, *Israfel*, 267-72], largely discounted; not only are they based on reminiscences drawn from imaginative old women by even more imaginative interviewers to suit a preconceived image of the man most of them remembered only vaguely — Edgar Poe was *not* a good match, so their interest in him could have been at most simply flirtatious — but their descriptions of his flights of passion are patently absurd. Poe was an unmitigated prude as is clearly shown in his letters and works.

The great love affair with Elmira Royster has, I am certain, been exaggerated [for a good arguing of the opposite view see David M. Rein, *Edgar A. Poe: The Inner Pattern*, New York, 1960], and the first such exaggerator was Poe himself. Except for its importance in giving him what should, in recognition of a brilliant analysis of American peculiarities, be called the Lolita complex, it probably served only as a focus for Poe's nostalgia. To have married Elmira in 1827 or thereabouts, Poe would have had to be Allan's heir; she was therefore only a part of the great might-have-been. His hasty (and almost absent-minded) courtship of her just before his death was an attempt to do what Thomas Wolfe knew one cannot do, go home again.

His entanglements with the flock of other women who were around during Virginia's last illness and death clearly resulted from the anticipated and then actual disruption in his life by her dying. He was like the man who, weeping uncontrollably at his wife's funeral, was consoled by a friend with the thought that in a few months he might marry again, and replied, weeping more deeply, "Yes, but what shall I do *tonight?*" He very nearly did marry Mrs. Sarah Helen Whitman, for she was the most genuine of the biddies who clustered around the literary lion. Moreover, she bore the magic name "Helen." But at the same time it was she who first wooed him, and at the same time she was second choice to Mrs. Annie Richmond, who unfortunately already had a husband.

Much mystery has been made of Poe's relationship with his wife, but it seems evident that the closest we can come to the truth is his story "Eleanora," written in 1841, when he was thirty-two and she was midway between eighteen and nineteen. In this story the narrator lives with his cousin and (in the original version only) her mother in the "valley of many-colored grass" until she is fifteen and he twenty; then, Poe delicately reveals, their love became physical. Virginia virtually grew up with Poe. She was seven when he came to Baltimore for the first time, and she was halfway to her ninth birthday when he made his home permanently in the same house with her. From then until she was almost thirteen, during which time, considering her physical condition, she probably came into puberty, they lived virtually as brother and sister — his nickname for her was "Sissy," and for Mrs. Clemm, "Muddy."

When he left for Richmond, to edit the *Messenger*, he wanted to send for the Clemms as soon as arrangements could be made, and when Mrs. Clemm considered accepting an offer for the two of them to move in with Neilson Poe (who was married to Mrs. Clemm's stepdaughter), Edgar wrote a pathetic letter begging them to come to him, saying "I love, *you know* I love Virginia passionately devotedly," threatening suicide if they did not come to him, and in a postscript to Virginia, addressed her as "darling little wifey" [Ostrom, 69-71]; he was so upset he took to drinking and disgraced himself with alcohol for the first time in his life. Four weeks later he left his job (probably quitting before he was fired), dashed back to Baltimore, and took out a marriage license; then, talked out of his impulsiveness, probably by Mrs. Clemm and J. P. Kennedy, he made peace with his employer and took the Clemms to Richmond.

In spite of efforts to raise money so that Mrs. Clemm could open a boardinghouse, they lived in that of Mrs. Yarrington, and from there on May 16, 1836, Poe and Virginia were married, he twenty-seven years old and she thirteen years and nine months, although affidavit was made, in the marriage bond, that she was "of the full age" of twenty-one years. Since they were living in a boardinghouse, there was no question of propriety in Edgar's supporting a nubile cousin and her mother, and in that day and place of "kissing cousins," the exchange of platonic affection would have seemed perfectly natural. The only reason they could have had for getting married was that they wanted to go to bed together. (For the opposite view see Rein, who argues Poe's "hostility" to Virginia with a different kind of reasoning than that by which he analyzes Poe's feelings for Elmira. His evidence, besides psychoanalysis through the "Lygeia" type of story, is Poe's reported confidence that for the first two years of his marriage he had been "husband in name only," and a love-letter to Mrs. Whitman [Ostrom, 393]. In the latter he was arguing that he "loved now for the *first* time" to a woman he was wooing but did not marry because of the "suspicious & grossly insulting parsimony of the arrangements into which you suffered yourself to be forced by your Mother" [Ostrom, 421] — she would not give him control of her money. Although no husband of my acquaintance does not feel on occasion that marriage is a trap he was lured into, the evidence of Mrs. Phelps [*Israfel*, 458], and of John MacKenzie [Susan Archer Weiss, *The Home Life of Poe*, New York, 1907] has the ring of gossip; and although Heywood [Frederick W. Coburn, "Poe as Seen by the Brother of 'Annie,'" *New England Quarterly* XVI (Sept., 1943), 471] is more reliable, I cannot see Poe discussing the secrets of his marriage bed with anyone.)

Mrs. Clemm, too, has been the subject of a great deal of speculation from those who would gag at a gnat but swallow a fly. Hervey Allen and Mary Phillips make her into a mixture of Mrs. Wiggs of the Cabbage Patch and Whistler's mother. Montagu Slater, in *The Centenary Poe* [London, 1949] calls her "Maria" (which Poe never did) and says, "Her possessiveness had an animal ferocity." She was an unintellectual woman, but the only practical member of the family; she not only managed the household, but also took over some aspects of marketing Poe's work. Her preoccupation with the family's survival was the only reason it did survive, and in putting that first she frequently operated in conflict with Poe's sense of personal honor and professional integrity. At her worst she could nag Edgar into reviewing the poems of Mrs. Sarah Anna Lewis — for a price — and write Griswold to publish one such in his anthology; "If you will do so I promise you a favorable review of your books as they appear" [Harrison XVII, 395]. She bullied the editor of the *American Review* into accepting a poem he did not want because Edgar needed new shoes to replace those he had split in a jumping match with the editor.

When he and Virginia went to New York from Philadelphia, leaving her to close up their home, she sold a volume of the *Southern Literary Messenger*, borrowed from the Secretary of the Treasury, and Poe had another smudge added to his reputation by belligerently sticking to her story that she had returned it to the law office of Henry Hirst. After his manner he supported her, and after hers, she supported him. She was the aboriginal literary agent, as well as the mother without whom he was always despondent, and "Sissy had a hearty cry last night because you and Catterina [the black cat that could open the door for herself] weren't here" [Ostrom, 407].

About Poe's own character I shall let my text speak for itself save brief mention of his drug-taking, drinking, and lying. Poe's worst — or at least noisiest — enemy, Dr. Thomas Dunn English, testified that in his opinion Poe was not a drug addict [Quinn, 350]. Quinn correctly reasons that if he had been accustomed to opium, he would not have overdosed himself with laudanum in his suicide attempt in Boston [Ostrom, 402]. For what is to me the definitive argument against Poe's being addicted, see Quinn, 693-94.

Modern usage of the expressions "he drinks" and "he doesn't drink" creates the absolute that there is no middle ground between a total abstainer and an utter sot, even though a large proportion of humanity consume some alcohol during their lifetime, and yet remain sober most of the time. It has been said that "all writers are drunks," and although that is obviously not true, there must be some reason it was said. My guess is as follows: a man like Poe works fiercely hard or not at all; the very excellence of his work shows that. Moreover, there is a kind of intoxication, a heightened urgency, in his hours of work that comes but rarely to the man who works from nine to five and thus paces himself to fill time instead of pages. When he stops work he is exhausted, but the momentum of his emotional surge goes on, so that he needs the effect of more alcohol to relax himself than does the office worker, and thus he can easily pass from the intoxication of creative work to the intoxication of alcohol before he accomplishes his purpose — simply relaxation — in taking the first drink. Poe knew very well he should not take the first one, and he rarely did. The number of times documented in the forty years of Poe's life that he drank any alcohol are few and separated by long periods of time, usually years.

Although he was probably normal enough to begin with, Poe gradually developed a great intolerance for alcohol. He never did like it, moreover. At the University he would, according to the reminiscences of his classmates, usually toss off one glass and be satisfied. His company commander for nearly two years in the Army said that he was "intirely free from drinking." Lambert Wilmer [see Thomas O. Mabbott, ed., *Merlin*, New York, 1941] said that save for one or two "incidents" during the time he knew Poe in Baltimore, Poe did not drink at all. Poe's reputation as a drunk began while he was working on the *Messenger* in Richmond. Then, he said [Ostrom, 156] "I certainly did give way, at long intervals, to the temptation held out on all sides by the spirit of Southern conviviality." From then to the end of his life, he could go long periods, years even, without drinking; but when things got too much for him, or he fell into too convivial company, he took refuge in alcohol, almost invariably influenced by very little, and invariably with severe illness the next day or even longer. Moreover, he was not an amiable drunk; he had a perfectly valid grudge against the world for heaping fame and fortune on people who were decidedly inferior to him while he struggled simply to survive, and when drink unlocked the restraints of rigid courtesy and painful dignity from him, he wanted to seek out his enemies and knock them down — and, let it not be forgotten, he tried to seek out those he had wronged and apologize. Although he presents it in different light, English told of one such occasion in his reply to the "Literati" [Harrison XVII, 236]. Poe's contemporaries did not criticize him for drinking, not in that hard-drinking time, but for being influenced by it.

Poe's lies were of two kinds, the public and the private, and in them he was, again, not much different from anybody else. Like most of us, he shaped his manner of speaking or writing letters to the person of his hearer. To John Allan he offered affection shyly, since Allan was always reserved, and presented his situation either too optimistically or, when he was in trouble, too pessimistically. Writing to Kennedy he was much warmer and completely accurate.

His various reporting of his salary at the *Messenger* is typical of his slanting information: White paid him ten dollars a week plus standard rates for original contributions. Figuring that he could earn half again his salary by his writings, he told Mrs. Clemm [Ostrom, 70] that his salary was $60 a month. To Kennedy it was $520 a year (no undignified wage, but an annual salary!), and when White gave him a two-dollar raise, he told Kennedy, "Mr. W. has increased my salary, since I wrote, 104$. for the present year." [Ostrom, 73 and 84] To George Poe, to whom he wanted to appear a man of substance, it was "about $800 per ann:."

His public lies were akin to those perpetuated every day in job résumés and application forms, and that are not totally unknown in the pages of *Who's Who*, save that in addition to omitting some facts and putting others in a light very favorable to himself, he juggled dates, as I shall point out in a later essay on Poe's "Legendary Years." There is some truth in all lies, and certainly his most revealing prevarications are his works.

The best summary of the fable and fact of Poe's life is Haldeen Braddy, *Glorious Incense*, Washington, 1953.

THE DEATH OF POE

What happened to Edgar Poe between his departure from Richmond, probably early in the morning of September 27, 1849, and the time Walker found him, was a mystery even to him, it seems certain, in his dazed condition. He would have arrived in Baltimore either Friday the 28th or Saturday the 29th. Tradition has it that he called on friends who were not at home. Whether he was "cooped" or not, it was a lost weekend for him, for no record has been discovered of his whereabouts until the following Wednesday.

Walker's note was copied from the original in the possession of Mrs. Snodgrass by William Hand Browne, and can be found in Harrison I, 328. Dr. Snodgrass's accounts of the poet's death are the result of years of temperance lecturing in which he used Poe as a horrible example of the evils of drink, making the example more horrible at every telling. Equally unreliable is Dr. Moran's *A Defence of Edgar Allan Poe* [Washington, 1885]. The only details we can count on at all are Moran's and Neilson Poe's letters to Mrs. Clemm written shortly after the events. For the record, here they are.

Baltimore, Oct. 11, 1849

My Dear Madam, — I would to God I could console you with the information that your dear son Edgar A. Poe is still among the living. The newspapers, in announcing his death, have only told a truth, which we may weep over & deplore, but cannot change. He died on Sunday morning, about 5 o'clock, at the Washington Medical College, where he had been since the Wednesday preceding. At what time he arrived in this city, where he spent the time he was here, or under what circumstances, I have been unable to ascertain.

It appears that, on Wednesday, he was seen & recognized at one of the places of election in old town, and that his condition was such as to render it necessary to send him to the College, where he was tenderly nursed until the time of his death. As soon as I heard that he was at the College, I went over, but his physicians did not think it advisable that I should see him, as he was very excitable. The next day I called & sent him changes of linen, &c. And was gratified to learn that he was much better, & I was never so much shocked, in my life, as when, on Sunday morning, notice was sent to me that he was dead. Mr. Herring & myself immediately took the necessary steps for his funeral, which took place on Monday afternoon at four o'clock. He lies alongside his ancestors in the Presbyterian burying ground on Green Street.

I assure you, my dear madam, that, if I had known where a letter would reach you, I would have communicated the melancholy tidings in time to enable you to attend his funeral — but I was wholly [illegible] how to address you. The body was followed to the grave by Mr. Herring, Dr. Snodgrass, Mr. Z. Collins Lee (an old classmate), and myself. The service was performed by the Rev. Wm. T. D. Clemm, a son of James T. Clemm. Mr. Herring & myself have sought, in vain, for the trunk & clothes of Edgar. There is reason to believe that he was robbed of them, whilst in such a condition as to render him insensible of his loss.

I shall not attempt the useless task of consoling you under such a bereavement. Edgar has seen so much of sorrow — had so little reason to be satisfied with life — that, to him, the change can scarcely be said to be a misfortune. If it leaves you lonely in this world of trouble, may I be allowed the friendly privilege of expressing the hope that, in the contemplation of the world to which he has gone & to which we are all hastening, you will find consolations enduring & all sufficient. I shall be glad, at all times, to hear from you, & to alleviate, in every way in my power, the sorrows which this dispensation may expose you. I only wish my ability was equal to my disposition.

My wife unites with me in expressions of sympathy.

Truly your friend & servant
Neilson Poe

Mrs. Maria Clemm

This letter can be found in Harrison, XVII, 400-401.
Moran's letter appears in Harrison I, 335-66, as follows:

Baltimore City Marine Hospital
November 15, '49

Mrs. Clemm:

My dear Madam, — I take the earliest opportunity of responding to yours of the 9th inst., which came to hand by yesterday's mail. . . .

But now for the required intelligence. Presuming you are already aware of the malady of which Mr. Poe died, I need only state concisely the particulars of his circumstances from his entrance until his decease.

When brought to the hospital he was unconscious of his condition — who brought him or with whom he had been associating. He remained in this condition from five o'clock in the afternoon — the hour of his admission — until three next morning. This was on the 3d October.

To this state succeeded tremor of the limbs, and at first a

busy but not violent or active delirium — constant talking — and vacant converse with spectral and imaginary objects on the walls. His face was pale and his whole person drenched in perspiration. We were unable to induce tranquillity before the second day after his admission.

Having left orders with the nurses to that effect, I was summoned to his bedside so soon as consciousness supervened, and questioned him in reference to his family, place of residence, relatives, etc. But his answers were incoherent and unsatisfactory. He told me, however, he had a wife in Richmond (which I have since learned was not the fact), that he did not know when he left that city, or what had become of his trunk of clothing. Wishing to rally and sustain his now fast sinking hopes, I told him I hoped that in a few days he would be able to enjoy the society of his friends here, and I would be most happy to contribute in every possible way to his ease and comfort. At this he broke out with much energy, and said the best thing his best friend could do would be to blow out his brains with a pistol — that when he beheld his degradation, he was ready to sink into the earth, etc. Shortly after giving expression to these words, Mr. Poe seemed to doze, and I left him for a short time. When I returned I found him in a violent delirium, resisting the efforts of two nurses to keep him in bed. This state continued until Saturday evening (he was admitted on Wednesday), when he commenced calling for one "Reynolds," which he did through the night until *three* on Sunday morning. At this time a very decided change began to affect him. Having become enfeebled from exertion, he became quiet, and seemed to rest for a short time; then gently moving his head, he said, *"Lord help my poor soul!"* and expired.

This, Madam, is as faithful an account as I am able to furnish from the Record of his case.

. . . His remains were visited by some of the first individuals of the city, many of them anxious to have a lock of his hair. . . .

Respectfully yours,
J. J. Moran, *Res. Phys.*

Moran's second paragraph implies that Poe died of alcoholism (something the doctor utterly denied in his book about Poe's death), or that he did not know what his patient was suffering from. Cold perspiration is not a sign of alcoholism — the opposite indeed — but it could be a sign that Poe was drugged. If Moran is to be relied on in his account of Poe's mild delirium, when he spoke to figures on the walls, his conversation with the poet was also carried out in Poe's delirium, and the "wife in Richmond" was Virginia, the despair over his depravity from perhaps fifteen years before. Poe almost certainly died of an organic illness; probably one that he had been suffering from for a long time. It may have been diabetes or a brain tumor.

The lucid last moment, and pious last words, were so much a convention of "consolation" at the time, and so unlikely considering Poe's condition, that I rule them out; notice Neilson Poe's suggestion that Mrs. Clemm console herself by thinking of her own end. He was so reluctant to give her what she really needed, some money, that he virtually says, "Drop dead!" He, Moran, and Snodgrass were obviously people more concerned with themselves and their flimsy reputations than they were with the truth. Snodgrass, for all his lecturing thereafter, did not even bother to investigate Poe's illness, or even to visit him. He knew which side his bread was buttered on — something that Poe, bless his soul, never did.

For Griswold's slanders and forgeries, see Quinn, especially 444-50, 669-71, 279-82.

THE EARLY YEARS

There is little to argue about in Poe's childhood and youth. Quinn [697-724] has traced through advertisements and playbills the theatrical careers of David Poe and Elizabeth Arnold, but who her father was is still unproved. I believe that Quinn [727-29] properly identifies Edgar Poe's birthplace as 62 Carver Street in Boston. Through the kindness of the Real Estate Division of the Boston Edison Company, I was able to track that property back to the Henry Haviland who can be identified by the Ward 12 Street Book as owner of the house David Poe was living in in 1808 and probably through the spring of the following year. Mr. Abbott Lowell Cummings, Assistant Director of the Society for the Preservation of New England Antiquities, was kind enough to inspect the house now standing on that lot, property of the Boston Edison Company; but he finds that it could not have been built before 1830, although the mantels in the upper rooms might have been salvaged from an earlier building, conceivably one that had occupied the same spot.

The fascinating information that Mary Phillips collected from a local historian about Poe's schooldays in Scotland must be abandoned in view of the simple fact that Poe did not stay in Scotland long enough to go to school; in like manner she reports a totally imagined journey into Pennsylvania at some undetermined time, that Henry W. Shoemaker, a Pennsylvania local historian, invented all by himself. The house described in "William Wilson" is obviously not the austere building that housed the Manor House School, but was probably based on "The Laurels" opposite.

The firm of Ellis and Allan was the victim of the slump of 1819 and never recovered. It officially "failed" in 1824 — in the same year Allan was not given a part of his uncle's business because of the number of legal claims on him — but as late as the end of 1833, Allan wrote to his partner that it was time to "obtain a final settlement of Business of our old firm of Ellis & Allan," because "My Health is perhaps as good as it ever will be." Since the nadir of his fortune was at a time of glory for Poe — Lafayette's visit to Richmond — his letter to Henry Poe complaining of Edgar's behavior is understandable, but Poe himself never seems to have understood why Allan's generosity to him was never revived. This I believe explains Poe's writing Allan that he had paid his debt to Sergeant Graves on June 25, 1829, when on May 3, 1830 he still owed him money; this worried Professor Quinn so much that he wrote [168] "The only explanation which would save Poe's reputation for honesty is that he paid Graves for acting as his substitute, but that he still owed him money borrowed for other reasons." I am afraid in this case nothing can save Poe's reputation for honesty. He always juggled figures in his letters to Allan because the older man was fierce about "extravagance." By so doing he hoped to regain his old position with Allan, and then paying Graves would have been no trouble at all. An insight into his probable attitude toward his rearing can be found in Mrs. Clemm's letter to Neilson Poe, August 19, 1860 [Harrison I, 430], in which she says, "I attended to his literary business, for he, poor fellow, knew nothing about money transactions. How should he, brought up in luxury and extravagance?"

THE ''LEGENDARY YEARS''

In 1841 Poe wrote a memorandum from which Rufus Griswold constructed the biographical sketch that he used in his anthologies. Included in it was the following account: "I ran away from home without a dollar on a quixotic expedition to join the Greeks, then struggling for liberty. Failed in reaching Greece, but made my way to St. Petersburg, in Russia. Got into many difficulties, but was extricated by the kindness of Mr. H. Middleton, the American consul at St. P. Came home safe in 1829, found Mrs. A. dead, and immediately went to West Point as a Cadet." In the same document he claimed he was born in 1811, instead of 1809; he moved his 1815 voyage to England to 1816, and his return in 1820 to 1822. He claimed three years' attendance at the University of Virginia, from 1825 to 1827, while he really spent only the latter year there. He implied that he spent eighteen months at West Point before Allan remarried, and added fifteen years to Allan's age. He mentioned two British journals he had lately been writing articles "continuously" for, but claimed he could not name them. None has been found, but he wrote Snodgrass in 1839 [Ostrom, 116], "I have made a profitable engagement with Blackwoods' Mag: and my forthcoming Tales are promised a very commendatory Review in that journal from the pen of Prof. Wilson. Keep this a secret, if you please, for the present." He may have had the vague promise that so dogs a writer's efforts to break into a new market.

Nevertheless, in view of the fabricated dates, Poe's second trip to Europe began to be doubted as soon as it was discovered that he had enlisted in the Army in Boston, May 26, 1827, under the name Edgar A. Perry, and served until April 15, 1829; it seemed obvious that he had invented the trip to cover up the fact that he had been a common soldier. There was not time between his departure from Richmond, which had to be after March 20, 1827, and his enlistment two months later, for such a journey, even though we do not know what Poe did during that time except get himself to Boston and his book to a publisher. Moreover, sympathetic critics were delighted at that discovery, for Griswold had implied that Poe's "many difficulties" at St. Petersburg were the result of a drunken binge. In Lowell's article in *Graham's*, however, the difficulties were over a passport.

Since discovery of Poe's Army record, biographers — save the romantic Mary Phillips, who put an ocean voyage into nearly every gap in the Poe chronology, to justify the reams of folklore Scottish local historians had sent her — have simply accepted that Poe was a liar, and it is to their credit as scholars, who must never be liars, that they know nothing of the psychology of altering the truth. Poe always took liberties with dates in his own life. When he enlisted in the Army he added four years to his age, but gave the correct day and month of his birth. Not only in the Griswold memorandum, but also in the story "William Wilson," he deducted two years. In the first version of the story he gave the narrator his own birthday, but made the year 1811. Later he changed that to the correct 1809, but in 1845 he moved the date up to 1813, and in 1849 he wrote Griswold [Ostrom, 445], "It is a point of no great importance — but, in one of your editions, you have given my sister's age instead of mine. I was born Dec. 1813 — my sister Jan 1811."

The other dates he shifted around to lend verisimilitude to his story, but the only thing he invented was the trip to Russia, and he omitted not only the Army experience but also the entirety of his career as a poet, his marriage, and most of his journalistic career. Now we are back where we were: there is no evidence that Poe did or did not make a second trip to Europe; we know only that he did not do it before he entered the Army. The only time in that general period unaccounted for is from the end of January, 1830, to the beginning of May the same year — a period of three months during which he bought nothing at the Ellis-Allan store, did not write Allan, and at the end of which Allan scolded him severely, then forgave him enough to equip him for West

Point. Furthermore, he offers one concrete detail of his trip: he was rescued from his difficulties by Henry Middleton. Now Poe was full of quaint and curious knowledge, but I wonder how many of the readers of Poe could name the American consul at Leningrad at this moment? Henry Middleton was American Minister to the Russian court from 1819 until August, 1830. He should have been replaced after the Federalists went down in defeat before the Democrats, but Andrew Jackson took more than a year to name his own candidate for this obscure post, and when he did, the successor, John Randolph of Roanoke, considered the job a long time and took even longer to get there. Randolph was appointed to the post well before he actually relieved Middleton, and it is difficult to see how Poe would have known who was in St. Petersburg unless he had been there. Moreover, when Poe first wrote his memorandum, in 1841, Middleton was still alive to read it. There are no documents remaining, and as the Wife of Bath tells us, experience is no authority. Middleton would have considered helping an American boy a personal, not an official, duty, and at any rate he did not correspond directly with the State Department, but his Secretary, Beaufort T. Watts, wrote to Henry Cruger in Charleston, and Cruger passed information on to Van Buren. My last effort, in Europe and America, to settle this problem was aided by Mr. James W. Patton, Director of the Southern Historical Collection of the University of North Carolina Library, to whom I am deeply grateful. Ingram's report that the consul at St. Petersburg knew nothing of Poe's story is meaningless, since he could never have consulted Middleton, who died in 1846.

Without evidence no case can be made. But if Poe was in Europe as a young man, some of his familiarity with French customs not listed in encyclopedias or other books might be explained, as well as why he would have encountered Béranger's *Le Réfus* so soon after its publication as to use it in "Israfel" and recall it for the motto of "The Fall of the House of Usher." I like to think, also, that he made a side journey to the childhood home of one of his favorite French writers, then still living, Chateaubriand. The Château of Combourg is reached by crossing the northern plateau of Haute Bretagne, "a singularly dreary tract of country," with a blue-green tinge from the low foliage, up to the *étang* — or tarn

— that lies in "unruffled lustre by the dwelling." The Michelin Guide *Bretagne* says of it, "*Le vieux château, presque désert, est lugubre; l'étang, les bois, la lande qui l'environnent portent à la tristesse.*" It might be the house of Usher — but without the crack.

THE POEMS OF 1831

My interpretation of "To Helen" and the details which inspired it are stolen, lock, stock, and barrel, from Professor E. Sculley Bradley. The sources of "Israfel" are drawn from Killis Campbell's excellent *The Poems of Edgar Allan Poe* [Boston, 1917], which will remain the definitive edition of Poe's poems until Thomas Ollive Mabbott gives us his new edition of Poe's works. Considering Poe's knowledge of French literature, however, I cannot agree with Campbell's source-hunting for "The City in the Sea" (first called "The Doomed City," then "The City of Sin"). Sunken cities are common enough in folklore, but the most obvious origin is the Breton Ville d'Is, which tradition says was so beautiful that the Lutetians, seeking a name for their city, called it "Paris" to indicate that it was "*pareille à Is.*" The king's daughter, Dahut, gave the key to the gate in the dike to the Devil, who let the water in, and Dahut became a siren, living at the bottom of the sea.

I call the poems new in the 1831 edition a result of the highest lyric impulse of Poe's youth, and "To Helen" his ultimate masterpiece. This I stand by. "The Raven," "Annabel Lee," and "The Bells" are flamboyant, but they are mechanical; as Professor Gay Wilson Allan says, "the critic ruined the poet." The failure of "The Raven" is discussed in the text, but it is perhaps interesting to note at this point that translations of this and some of Poe's other late poetry are often better than the original. "*Jamais plus*" is more colloquial than "Nevermore," but in Czech the refrain sounds very much like the croak of a raven!

THE TALES OF THE FOLIO CLUB

There has been much controversy about the "Tales of the Folio Club," the best accounts being Thomas O. Mabbott's "On Poe's

'Tales of the Folio Club,' " *Sewanee Review* XXXVI [1928], 171-76; and James S. Wilson's "The Devil Was in It," *American Mercury* XXIV [1931], 219. Poe's manuscript (printed in Harrison II, xxxvi-xxxix) is a small quarto from which all but four pages have been torn, leaving the introduction and a fragment of "Siope" ("Silence: A Fable"). This is probably a fragment of the manuscript that went the rounds of the publishers in 1835 and 1836.

Scholars are agreed that "Metzengerstein," "The Duke de l'Omelette," "A Tale of Jerusalem," "A Decided Loss" ("Loss of Breath"), and "A Bargain Lost" ("Bon-Bon"), the five stories published in the Philadelphia *Saturday Courier,* are among the missing ones. "Siope" is part of the manuscript. "MS. Found in a Bottle" was in a similarly titled volume when it was submitted to the Baltimore *Saturday Visiter.* "Epimanes" was submitted as a Folio Club tale to the *New England Magazine* in 1833. Poe mentioned "Lionizing" in a letter to Thomas W. White on July 20, 1835. That leaves two unaccounted for, if we discount the memory of John H. B. Latrobe, one of the *Visiter* judges, who said, in his address at the Poe Memorial Exercises in Baltimore in 1877, that "A Descent into the Maelström" was one of the volume.

My purpose is to show how Poe developed his technique of the short story rather than to add my guesses to those of my betters, but I had to make some judgment of which were the missing tales in order to carry out this purpose, which I believe to be valid whether I chose the right ones or not. We may never know. This was my method: Following Professor Wilson's lead, I tried to assign the tales to their Folio Club members. His article, mentioned above, clearly identifies "The Duke de l'Omelette" as Poe's "quiz on Willis," as J. K. Paulding called it, and it seems likely that this is the tale read by Mr. Snap, who is the only editor present. Poe himself, in a letter to John P. Kennedy, February 11, 1836, refers to "Loss of Breath" as on the "extravagancies of Blackwood"; thus it can be assigned to Mr. Blackwood Blackwood. It is easy to couple Mr. Solomon Seadrift with "MS. Found in a Bottle," and Chronologus Chronology, "who admired Horace Smith," with the parody of Smith's *Zillah,* "A Tale of Jerusalem." From here on the guesses get wilder. "Metzengerstein" must have been among the tales, and the member most appropriate for that story would be Mr. Horribile Dictu, who "graduated at Göttingen." The style of "Epimanes" suggests that it was by the member "who admired Sir Walter Scott." In the letter to Kennedy mentioned above, Poe said that "Lionizing" was intended to satirize "the rage for Lions," and therefore is the story most appropriate for himself, in view of the exposé intended.

Remaining are four members, Convulvulus Gondola, De Rerum Naturâ, a very little man in a black coat with very black eyes, and the host (and therefore author of the worst tale the previous meeting), Mr Rouge-et-Noir, "who admired Lady Morgan"; and two tales, "A Bargain Lost" and "Siope." It is more than likely that "The Visionary," published in *Godey's Lady's Book* in January, 1834, was also one of the Folio Club tales, and since the narrator in that story is a widely traveled man who is, at the beginning, afloat in a gondola, it could be assigned to Mr. Convulvulus Gondola, "a young man who had travelled a good deal." Neither of the remaining tales can by any stretch of my imagination be assigned the host; they must belong to the little man in black and De Rerum Naturâ — and the only hint is that the latter "wore a very singular pair of green spectacles," and in a revision of "A Bargain Lost" for the *Southern Literary Messenger* — one so extensive that the setting is changed to France and the philosopher renamed "Bon-Bon" — the Devil wears green spectacles with side-glasses. Was the Devil a member of the club?

Which is the missing Folio Club tale? In my opinion, there is only one of Poe's stories which could be by the man "who admired Lady Morgan" — "Why the Little Frenchman Wears His Hand in a Sling." No publication of this story has been discovered prior to the volume *Tales of the Grotesque and Arabesque*, in 1839, but neither was "Siope" published until 1838; and since the former is the only story in that volume not previously published in a magazine, that may simply mean that Poe, who was always in need of money, had not been able to sell it. If so, it surely had undergone considerable revision, but it is still nearly weak enough to be attributed to the member who had, the month before, written the worst story, even though the Irish dialect in which it is told is fairly well handled.

Another equally weak "grotesque" purported to be an earlier

draft of "The Spectacles," which Poe published in the *Dollar Newspaper* March 27, 1844, was published in pamphlet form by Richard Gimbel in July, 1938 (for sale in the Poe House in Philadelphia) as the missing Folio Club tale, but Heartman and Canny, *A Bibliography of First Printings of the Writings of Edgar Allan Poe* [Hattiesburg, Miss., 1943] identifies the document from which this was printed as an ingenious forgery which Mr. Gimbel unwittingly purchased. The forging of Poe documents has proved to be so profitable that ingenuity has been expended on it that might better have been put to legitimate Poe research, perhaps with a little counterfeiting on the side to finance the long work required.

In tracing the evolution of Poe's short stories I have followed each through its various revisions, referring to the Philadelphia *Saturday Courier* versions (reprinted in J. G. Varner, *Edgar Allan Poe and the Philadelphia Saturday Courier* [Charlottesville, 1933]) for their status in 1831-32, and summarizing and quoting from the various later drafts as I cover the stages of Poe's career when revision was made. Poe's awareness of what he was doing is revealed in his letters. He wrote White on April 30, 1835, that "Berenice" was "by far too horrible," but similar in nature to stories which gained celebrity. "You ask me in what does this nature consist? In the ludicrous heightened into the grotesque: the fearful coloured into the horrible: the witty exaggerated into the burlesque: the singular wrought out into the strange and mystical." He told Kennedy, nearly a year later, "Most of them were *intended* for half banter, half satire — although I might not have fully acknowledged this to be their aim even to myself."

Moreover, his revisions show that he kept reducing the parody elements in the stories that were not understood by others as having anything funny about them, and he took some of the non-comic elements out of the others. In the second version of "Loss of Breath," he took the main character through additional, more ridiculous experiences, then restored his breath to him rather than have him die of electric shock. By 1840 Berenice no longer grows to monstrous size, and her hair more conventionally lightens in color as a result of her illness. In "A Tale of Jerusalem," "Abel Shittim" is changed to "Abel Phittim," and his comment at the end that he should now be called "Boanerges, 'the Son of Thunder,'" was excised. He knew what he was doing — after he had done it.

POE AND DR. GRISWOLD

It is very difficult to refer to Poe's relations with Rufus Wilmot Griswold without showering abusive adjectives on one or the other. Griswold's effect on Poe's reputation was more damaging than that of John Allan on Poe's life. George E. Woodberry, whose biography of Poe is understanding but unsympathetic, whispered to Thomas O. Mabbott at the opening of the Poe shrine in Richmond, "John Allan is damned," but John Allan can be understood, while Griswold, who carried a grudge for seven years and took his vengeance only after his victim was dead, has been exposed as sinning against Poe on every count but the Sixth Commandment, but not officially damned. Dante, I think, would know exactly where to put him.

Poe first met Griswold in the early spring of 1841, when the anthologist visited Philadelphia collecting material for his *Poets and Poetry of America*. Poe by that time was nostalgic about his early lyric impulse and wanted to be included in the anthology. When invited, he sent "The Haunted Palace," "The Coliseum," and "The Sleeper," plus the autobiographical note referred to in the essay on the "Legendary Years." Poe also acted as intermediary between some poets and Griswold, and at least two of these were not included in the book even though they submitted work: Henry Hirst and Frederick Thomas.

Poe reviewed the book cordially in the June *Graham's*. (Professor Quinn is of the opinion that that review is not Poe's work, but it is clearly an early draft of the review Poe signed in the Boston *Miscellany* for November, 1842.) In addition, Poe spoke well of Griswold in "Autography," in the December, 1841, *Graham's*, and probably was responsible for a brief notice in the May number. The story of Poe's resigning from the magazine because he found Griswold in his chair is from Gill's 1873 conversation with Graham, and rings true. Poe wanted to leave the magazine, primarily because he was not able there to exercise his talents fully, and he was feeling his pride. When Griswold made his offer of a bribe for a good review [Ostrom, 211-12], Poe inflicted a punishment to fit the crime, in spite of the supercilious attitude of English and others [Harrison XVII, 438] about it.

What happened to that review is another question. The review published with Poe's name, that was sent by Griswold to Bradbury and Soden for the *Miscellany*, was generally favorable. Another, very severe one appeared anonymously in the Philadelphia *Saturday Museum* on January 28, 1843, and was, in Dr. Mabbott's opinion, a collaboration by Poe and Hirst. I agree, but put forth another hypothesis. Poe, by everyone's acount, was fierce if offended but very quick to forgive. His next contact with Griswold was on January 14, 1845, when the anthologist wrote him, asking for information for a new book. (There is a completely spurious exchange of letters that Griswold forged to make it seem as if Poe approached him. See Quinn, 443-50 and Ostrom, 508-509.) Poe replied with humility, saying, "I have been aware, for several weeks, that my reasons for speaking of your book as I did (of *yourself* I have always spoken kindly) were based in the malignant slanders of a mischief-maker by profession." Poe was at that exact time in an imbroglio over Mrs. Clemm's not having returned a volume of the *Messenger* to Hirst; thus Hirst was obviously the mischief-maker referred to.

My theory is that Poe, under the influence of Hirst, whose work was not included in the anthology, had written the fierce review he referred to, and that when Griswold read it he took it back to Poe crying "fraud." Poe then wrote the review that appeared in the *Miscellany*, but, again prodded by Hirst, put the original in the *Museum*, where Griswold certainly recognized it as Poe's work.

Still another piece of pettiness comes from this time. The following letter, which has disappeared if it ever existed, can be found reprinted from the Griswold Memoir in Harrison XVII, 145 (treated as spurious by Ostrom, and doubted by Quinn):

Philadelphia, June 11, 1843

Dear Griswold, — Can you not send me $5. I am sick, and Virginia is almost gone. Come and see me. Peterson says you suspect me of a curious anonymous letter. I did not write it, but bring it along with you when you make the visit you promised to Mrs. Clemm. I will try to fix that matter soon. Could you do anything with my *note?*

Yours truly,

E. A. P.

On several points, aside from there being no manuscript, this smells fishy. Poe, fastidious about salutations, would not have addressed Griswold by his last name alone while there was any ill feeling between them. There is good reason to believe that Graham fired Griswold for an anonymous attack *he* made on Peterson. Poe was not in the habit of using the word "fix" in the American sense. But more significantly, Poe had too many alternatives to humiliating himself before Griswold, and in April he wrote William MacKenzie, "Virginia is nearly recovered" [Ostrom, 233]. The date is approximately the time that the partnership with Clarke was "exploded" [see letter to Lowell, June 20, 1843, Ostrom, 234], but he did not until September feel pressed enough to ask Lowell for the ten dollars still owing him. Furthermore, in his January 16, 1845, letter to Griswold there is no mention of any reconciliation since the review.

Poe did attempt to borrow money from Griswold on October 26, 1845, as he did also from Chivers, Kennedy, Duyckinck, his cousin Neilson Poe, and Halleck, in order to keep the *Broadway Journal* going. He almost certainly did not get it, although Griswold forged a letter from Poe, thanking him for the loan of twenty-five dollars. Poe next wrote Griswold in May of 1849, over the tenth edition of the anthology. Except for a letter offering a puff of Mrs. Lewis's poetry for *Female Poets of America*, implying that Griswold would be paid for publishing it, there was no further correspondence between them, unless Poe really did ask Griswold to be his literary executor at the time he was going to visit Richmond for the last time. While Poe was away, Mrs. Clemm begged Griswold for a loan, then later she urged the article on Mrs. Lewis on him, offering good reviews of his work as a bribe for publishing it. After Poe's death, Griswold wrote to Mrs. Whitman [Harrison XVII, 405-406] "*I was not his friend, nor was he mine,* as I remember to have told you. I undertook to edit his writings to oblige Mrs. Clemm. . . . I cannot refrain from begging you to be very careful what you say or write to Mrs. Clemm, who is not your friend or anybody's friend, but whose heart and understanding are full of malice and wickedness." Mrs. Whitman did not follow his advice.

In his excellent study of the literary war between the Knicker-bocker clique and the "Young Americans" (which shows Poe at his very worst), *The Raven and the Whale* [New York, 1956], Perry Miller says of Griswold, "did not ample documentation prove that he actually existed, we might suppose him, along with Dodson and Fogg, one of the less plausible inventions of Charles Dickens." Lowell, in *A Fable for Critics*, said he "leads on/The flocks whom he first plucks alive, and then feeds on." In smearing Poe's reputation he was catering to the massive enmity that Clark and others felt for their late antagonist. If Poe wrote the *Saturday Museum* review, his comment, "if he is spoken of hereafter, he will be quoted as the *unfaithful servant who abused his trust*," is true, certainly, for in forging Poe's letters he gave himself a place in literary history he would not otherwise have had. Those curious about his peculiar career may consult Jacob L. Neu, *Rufus Wilmot Griswold*, Studies in English No. 5, University of Texas, 1925.

POE'S ATTEMPTED SUICIDE

In my account I disagree with the only two major commentators who were neither too prudish to discuss the facts nor too busy licking their chops over them to try to understand what really happened, Quinn and Ostrom. Poe first met Mrs. Whitman about September 21 [Quinn, 575]. He may have seen her, as he claimed, two years before, but in 1848 he responded to her ardent literary courtship and actually got an introduction, visiting her, putting his arm around her (daring, then!) in a cemetery, and leaving September 25, having said good-by the day before.

According to Mrs. Whitman, Poe was to have lectured in Lowell early in November, but the date was canceled on account of excitement over the election. He went to Lowell anyway, stopping off, Quinn claims, at Providence on the way. From Lowell, Ostrom [403] believes that Poe's letter to Annie on November 16 "shows Poe setting out for Providence on November 4, buying laudanum there and returning to Boston on November 5, writing the unsent letter to Mrs. Richmond and swallowing the laudanum on November 5, recuperating and proceeding to Providence sometime before the morning of November 7, when he wrote his note of Tuesday, November 7, to Mrs. Whitman."

I believe Ostrom correctly assumes that "Poe was in Lowell probably to see Mrs. Richmond before going to Providence." Now this means that Poe went to Providence (the standard route to Boston was steamship to Providence, then railway to Boston, to avoid the trip around Cape Cod), on to Boston, then to Lowell, and from Lowell back to Providence (through Boston), between November 2 (or 3) and 5. What Poe wrote, that leads to such a conclusion, is "I remember nothing distinctly, from that moment [when he last saw Annie] until I found myself in Providence — I went to bed & wept through a long, long, hideous night of despair — When the day broke, I arose & endeavored to quiet my mind by a rapid walk in the cold, keen air — but all *would* not do — the demon tormented me still. Finally I procured two ounces of laudanum & without returning to my Hotel, took the cars back to Boston." Then he tells of writing her and taking the drug, only to be caught by the heaves on his way to the post office.

The crucial thing here is Poe's punctuation. Once in the first sentence quoted he uses a dash as a full stop, once as a comma, and once as a semicolon. When he used it as a full stop, he followed it with a capital letter; the other two times he did not. But at the point in doubt, he started his clause with "I," which would be capitalized in any case. Out of a sense of geography, then, I feel that he was saying that his memory remained vague until he arrived in Providence, but that on leaving Annie (he had apparently been begging her to run away with him, or divorce her husband, so he would not have to marry Mrs. Whitman) at her home in Lowell, he went to his hotel, and after a miserable night got up, and, still depressed, bought laudanum. It would have done no good for him to take it in Lowell, for coming to his "death bed" there would involve no commitment, so he went to Boston, which she could reach quickly. But throwing up brought him to awareness of how dangerous and melodramatic were his plans, and he went on to Providence.

SELECT
BIBLIOGRAPHY

This is not a complete bibliography or even a list of all the works consulted in the preparation of this book. It is instead a list of readings that might be interesting to anyone desirous of investigating the subject further, and its most practical characteristic is that none but the most useful and most reliable sources are included.

BIBLIOGRAPHIES

Heartman, C. F., and J. R. Canny. *A Bibliography of First Printings of the Writings of Edgar Allan Poe*. Hattiesburg, Miss., 1940.
Literary History of the United States. Edited by Robert E. Spiller, Willard Thorpe, *et al*. Volume 3. New York, 1946, Supplement, 1959.
Publications of the Modern Language Association. Annual Bibliography.

WORKS

The Complete Works of Edgar Allan Poe. Edited by James A. Harrison. 17 vols. New York, 1902. Supplemented by:
The Poems of Edgar Allan Poe. Edited by Killis Campbell. Boston, 1917.
Doings of Gotham. Collected by Jacob E. Spannuth. Preface, Introduction and Comments by Thomas O. Mabbott. Pottsville, Pa., 1929.
Edgar Allan Poe and the Philadelphia Saturday Courier, Introduction by John Grier Varner. Charlottesville, Va., 1933.
Politian. Edited by Thomas O. Mabbott. Richmond, 1923.
Brigham, Clarence S. "Edgar Allan Poe's Contributions to *Alex-*

ander's Weekly Messenger." Proceedings of the American Antiquarian Society LII (April, 1942), 45-125.

LETTERS

The Letters of Edgar Allan Poe. Edited by John Ward Ostrom. Cambridge, Mass., 1948.

Edgar Allan Poe Letters Till Now Unpublished. Introduction and Commentary by Mary Newton Stanard. Philadelphia, 1925. (Illustrated by photographs of the Poe-Allan correspondence; the handwriting and Allan's notes are interesting.)

Ostrom, John Ward. "Supplement to *The Letters of Poe.*" *American Literature* XXIV (1952), 358-366.

———— "Second Supplement to *The Letters of Poe.*" *American Literature* XXIX (1957), 79-86.

Hagemann, E. R., ed. "Two 'Lost' Letters by Poe, with Notes and Commentary." *American Literature* XXVIII (1957), 507-510.

SECONDARY MATERIALS

Alterton, Margaret B. *Origins of Poe's Critical Theory.* Iowa City, 1925.

Campbell, Killis. *The Mind of Poe, and Other Studies.* Cambridge, Mass., 1932.

Davidson, Edward H. *Poe: A Critical Study.* Cambridge, Mass., 1957.

Facts About Poe. Portraits and Daguerreotypes of Edgar Allan Poe. By Amanda P. Schulte, *with a sketch of the Life of Poe, by James S. Wilson.* University of Virginia Extension Series, X, No. 8, April, 1926.

Fagin, N. Bryllion. *The Histrionic Mr. Poe.* Baltimore, 1949.

Mabbott, Thomas O. *Merlin, Baltimore, 1827, Together with Recollections of Edgar A. Poe, by Lambert A. Wilmer.* New York, 1941.

———— (with Hervey Allen), *Poe's Brother.* New York, 1926.

Miller, Perry. *The Raven and the Whale.* New York, 1956.

Quinn, Arthur H. *Edgar Allan Poe: A Critical Biography.* New York, 1941.

Wilson, James Southall. "The Devil Was In It." *American Mercury* XXIV (Oct., 1931), 214-220.

Wimsatt, W. K., Jr. "Poe and the Mystery of Mary Rogers." *PMLA* LVI (March, 1941), 230-248.

——— "What Poe Knew About Cryptography." *PMLA* LVIII (Sept., 1943), 754-779.

Wyllie, John C. "A List of the Texts of Poe's Tales," *Humanistic Studies in Honor of John Calvin Metcalf* (Charlottesville, Va., 1941), 322-338.

INDEX

INDEX

INDEX

INDEX